用老外的方法学英语

林雨薇 —— 著

北京理工大学出版社
BEIJING INSTITUTE OF TECHNOLOGY PRESS

使用说明 User's Guide

1 全彩图片解说，脑中快速联结英语单词

● 看的说的都是英语

本书以老外的方法，从生活周围的各种场景切入，让读者看到每张图片，都可以从中发现英语单词，一旦养成以图记词的习惯，就连走在路上都可以记单词。记住单词后再通过不断的练习，大声说出口，以后只要一出门，看的说的都变成英语了！

● 除了图中的单词以外，图中场景还可以用到的单词通通帮读者搜集好了！一张图，即可记忆至少 10 个单词，让读者的单词量就是比别人多！

● 单词分类记忆最快速

本书将单词按照情境主题分类，看到标题即可迅速联结同性质的单词，条理分明，让读者记起单词来事半功倍！

2 图说文字融合会话，说话也可图解

每单元的会话皆搭配该单元的情境图，让读者一看就能够明白，在哪些场合、哪些人可以用上这些句子。

3 情境分类会话，书到用时好方便

本书精选15大主题，各主题中涵盖多个情境小单元，针对每种不同的情况，将老外绝对会用到的会话分类排列，让读者需要时随手一翻，就能翻到该说的那句话！

使用说明 User's Guide

 4 重点处小笔记，学语法和句型

句子之间的小标示仿照学生上课笔记制作，让读者对本书产生熟悉感外，又能便利且快速地检索句子中的生词、短语、语法，既可记住会话应用，又同时练习了其他部分的英语技巧！

This armchair is on sale on Father's Day to attract more buyers.
这款扶手椅在父亲节特价吸引了更多的买家。

"be on sale" 为 "特价，减价" 的意思，要特别注意，和 "be for sale" (出售中) 的意思有所区别。

Body lotions and hand creams are hot deals in winter season.
身体乳和护手霜是冬季的热销产品。

buyer 当名词时为 "买家；顾客" 的意思，其用法和 "customer" 相当。

Rita always follows the fashion trend.
瑞塔总是跟随时尚潮流。

"follow the trend" 为 "随随潮流" 的意思，也有较负面的意思，为 "随波逐流"。

During the Christmas season, there are many parents bringing their children to toy departments.
在圣诞季时，有很多父母会带着小孩到玩具部。

department store 百货公司　　sale [seɪl] 特卖会
bargain ['bɑːrɡən] 便宜货；物超所值的商品
armchair ['ɑːrmtʃer] 扶手椅
lotion ['loʊʃn] 乳液　　hot deal 热销商品

You can buy clothes in the shopping mall.
你可以到购物中心买衣服。

Some big department stores only sell their own brand goods.
有些大型的百货公司只会卖它们自有品牌的商品。

"goods" 当名词时，为 "商品；货物" 的意思；也可以换成 "products（产品）" 或是 "commodity（商品；日用品）" 等词。

My dad likes to shop at a warehouse; my mom prefers to go to a retail store even though it is a bit more expensive. But for a good bargain, they both enjoy going to a thrift store.
我爸爸喜欢去批发店购物，我妈妈比较偏好去零售店购物，即便是有点贵。但为了买到好价位的商品，他们两个都喜欢到慈善商店里买东西。

The special exhibition in the museum usually requires a separate ticket.
博物馆里的特展通常需要另购门票。

v-ing 的形式单取。

Elaine likes to shop till she drops.
伊莱恩喜欢疯狂采购，买到手软为止。

"to shop till sb. drops" 为 "买到手软" 的意思。

1. The bakery sells chocolate cakes on Valentine's Day.
   = The bakery _____ chocolate cakes on Valentine's Day.
2. If you buy something at that antique shop, it will cost you an _____ and a _____.
3. I help my sister _____ her homework.
4. This brand of pens is out of stock.
   = This brand of pens is _____.

老外不会教你的小秘密

★ 在中国有 Chinese Valentine's Day（农历七夕），在西方有 Valentine's Day（西方情人节），在这么重要的日子，男男女女都会向自己心仪的对象告白，但这是需要勇气的。因此，为了鼓励他人追求自己喜欢的男生或女生，我们可以说：

♦ You should get up the nerve to woo my best friend, Yvonne.
你应该鼓起勇气向我最好的朋友——伊冯求婚才是。

♦ Why don't you have the nerve to go after that pretty girl?
你为何不鼓起勇气来追求那位漂亮的女生呢？

5 随时有练习、随时有新知

● 轻松地看完一个单元后，赶紧来小复习，这样不仅能够加深该单元的学习印象，也能让读者学会更多句子！

● 还有老外都不会教你的小秘密，包含各种万能短句或国外生活的点点滴滴。

6 各章节的 EASY 小游戏，等你来挑战

每个章节附有作者精心设计的小游戏，不管是看图配对、连连看，还是猜谜，都让学英语变得轻松，让你可以边学边玩。

7 老外亲录英语 MP3，边听边学超简单

本书邀请外籍老师录制英语 MP3，下载到手机直接听，不仅方便省时，又能够随时随地学习。

★ 本书附赠音频为MP3格式。

目录

Contents

Chapter 1
肚子饿了怎么办
When you are hungry…

Unit 1 ❀ 准备大吃一顿！Grab a bite! ……… 002

Unit 2 ❀ 今天想点什么？Are you ready to order? ……… 007

Unit 3 ❀ 麻烦制造者 Troublemaker ……… 012

Unit 4 ❀ 吃饱后该做的事 Check, please! ……… 017

Chapter 2
购物去
Go shopping

Unit 1 ❀ 货比三家不吃亏 Shopping around ……… 024

Unit 2 ❀ 万能店员 We can do everything ……… 029

Unit 3 ❀ 最聪明的消费者 The smartest consumers ……… 034

Unit 4 ❀ 售后心得 After you bought… ……… 039

Chapter 3
庆祝时间
Let's celebrate

Unit 1 ❀ 东方佳节 Eastern festivals ……… 046

Unit 2 ❀ 西方庆典 Western holidays ……… 051

Unit 3 ❀ 欢庆时光 Party time ……… 056

Chapter 4
哥哥姐姐动起来
Get started

- **Unit 1** 来场刺激的 Exciting games ········· 062
- **Unit 2** 球来就打 Get the ball rolling ········· 067
- **Unit 3** 地上跑 & 水里游 Land or Water ········· 072
- **Unit 4** 全民疯奥运 Olympics ········· 077

Chapter 5
健康很重要
The most important thing

- **Unit 1** 到处都在痛 Get hurt ········· 084
- **Unit 2** 心痛的感觉 See the doctor ········· 089
- **Unit 3** 用药须注意 Medicine & Prescription ········· 094
- **Unit 4** 关注健康 Last but not least ········· 099

Chapter 6
快乐去上学
Go to school

- **Unit 1** 我要考第一名 First place in my class ········· 106
- **Unit 2** 校园风云榜 Classmates ········· 111
- **Unit 3** 学校这个地方 The place called school ········· 116
- **Unit 4** 各种重大日子 Calendar ········· 121

目录 Contents

Chapter 7
马路如虎口
Terrible traffic

- Unit 1 ● 行人要注意 Watch out ········ 128
- Unit 2 ● 驾驶要小心 Be careful ········ 133
- Unit 3 ● 上班族们 The commuters ········ 138
- Unit 4 ● 特殊交通方式 Special means of transportation ········ 143

Chapter 8
让你财源滚滚
Make lots of money

- Unit 1 ● 先找个工作吧 Find a job ········ 150
- Unit 2 ● 工作上的大小事 Lots of work ········ 155
- Unit 3 ● 行行出状元 Master it ········ 160

Chapter 9
科技，始终来自人性
Technology comes from humanity

- Unit 1 ● 光速的时代 Internet generation ········ 166
- Unit 2 ● 生活中无所不在 Everywhere in our lives ········ 171
- Unit 3 ● 现代人的生命线 Modern people's lifeblood ········ 176

Chapter 10
环游世界8分钟
Travel around the world

- Unit 1 ● 起飞！请系好安全带 Fasten your seatbelt ········ 182
- Unit 2 ● 出门逛逛 Fooling around ········ 187

Unit 3 ● 需要休息一下 Take a rest ······ 192
Unit 4 ● 平平安安回家 Come back safe and sound ······ 197

Chapter 11
生活中的必要之美
No music no life

Unit 1 ● 进入音符的世界 Enter the world of music ······ 204
Unit 2 ● 聚光灯下 Under the spotlight ······ 209
Unit 3 ● 倾听最美的声音 The sound of music ······ 214
Unit 4 ● 跟我一起大声唱 Sing out Loud ······ 219

Chapter 12
一场视听享受
What a movie!

Unit 1 ● 看电影去 Go to See a Movie ······ 226
Unit 2 ● 开拍啦！Action! ······ 231
Unit 3 ● 你也可以是电影名嘴 Be a movie critic ······ 236

Chapter 13
爱与和平救地球
Love & Peace

Unit 1 ● 关于爱 About love ······ 242
Unit 2 ● 关于家庭 About family ······ 247
Unit 3 ● 关于差异 About the difference ······ 252
Unit 4 ● 关于恨 About hatred ······ 257

目录 Contents

Chapter 14
喜怒哀乐爱恶欲
Mood swings

- Unit 1 ❀ 天天都有好心情 Happy every day ········· 264
- Unit 2 ❀ 天空蓝蓝的 The sky is blue ············· 269
- Unit 3 ❀ 午后雷阵雨 Thunderstorms ············· 274
- Unit 4 ❀ 复杂的心情天气图 So complicated ······· 279

Chapter 15
我看见了……
I can tell…

- Unit 1 ❀ 星座真好玩 Star signs ················· 286
- Unit 2 ❀ 东方主义 The mysterious East ·········· 291
- Unit 3 ❀ 别再相信没有根据的说法了 Superstitious ··· 296
- Unit 4 ❀ 科学也无法解释 Unknown ··············· 301

Chapter 1 肚子饿了怎么办

When you are hungry…

牛排、薯条、冰激凌、炸鸡、可乐……刚到国外,首先要做的当然就是大吃美食了,快来学学该怎么和这些美食变朋友!

Unit 1
准备大吃一顿!

Unit 2
今天想点什么?

Unit 3
麻烦制造者

Unit 4
吃饱后该做的事

Unit 1 准备大吃一顿！
Grab a bite!

原来老外这样记单词 / 老外从小到大学习单词的方法，就是看到什么就学什么！

cheesecake [ˈtʃiːzkeɪk]
n 奶酪蛋糕

strawberry tart
phr 草莓挞

cupcake [ˈkʌpkeɪk]
n 杯子蛋糕

pastry [ˈpeɪstri]
n 糕点

macaron
n 马卡龙

bun [bʌn]
n 小圆面包

其他衍生单词：

sundae [ˈsʌndeɪ] n 圣代冰激凌　　**cafeteria** [ˌkæfəˈtɪriə] n 自助餐　　**egg roll** phr 蛋卷

doughnut [ˈdəʊnʌt] n 甜甜圈　　**egg tart** phr 蛋挞　　**French cookie** phr 法式曲奇

Unit 1 准备大吃一顿！ Chapter **1** 肚子饿了怎么办

老外最常用的单词 / 连这些单词都不会，你还敢说你学过英语吗？

老外主食都吃这些

croissant [krəˈsɑːnt] n 羊角面包
toast [təʊst] n 吐司 v 敬酒
bagel [ˈbeɪɡl] n 百吉饼
spaghetti [spəˈɡeti] n 意大利面
wheat [wiːt] n 小麦
pizza [ˈpiːtsə] n 比萨
hamburger [ˈhæmbɜːrɡər] n 汉堡

向老外介绍东方主食

sushi [ˈsuːʃi] n 寿司

dumpling [ˈdʌmplɪŋ] n 饺子
fried noodles phr 炒面
fried rice phr 炒饭
steamed bun phr 馒头
rice dumpling phr 粽子
rice porridge phr 粥
turnip cake phr 萝卜糕

其实吃这些才会饱

oyster [ˈɔɪstər] n 生蚝
tuna [ˈtuːnə] n 金枪鱼
steak [steɪk] n 牛排
barbecue [ˈbɑːrbɪkjuː] n 烤肉
lobster [ˈlɑːbstər] n 龙虾
crabmeat [ˈkræbˌmiːt] n 蟹肉
shrimp roll phr 虾卷

用英语聊天，原来这么简单 / 老外每天说的英语，其实就是这几句。

约翰：今天想吃点什么？　梅丽莎：嗯……让我想想。

Situation 1
向朋友推荐店家

This place is noted for local specialties.
这个地方以当地的特产闻名。

Grammar-1
"be noted for"为短语用法，解释为"以……而闻名"，与此相似的用法还有"be famous for"、"be well-known for"和"be famed for"等。

There is a new Chinese restaurant at the city center.
市中心开了一家新的中餐厅。

Grammar-2
"sample"当名词时，解释为"样本；试用品"之意；当动词时，则有"抽样调查；浏览"的意思。

There are always some free samples of hand-made cookies in that bakery.
那家面包店总会有很多手工饼干的试吃品。

local ['ləʊkl] a 当地的；地方的

specialty ['speʃəlti] n 名产；特产；特制品

hand-made ['hænd'meɪd] a 手工的　　bakery ['beɪkəri] n 面包店

Situation 2
询问服务生关于菜品

Your pizza looks good. Do you recommend this?
你们的比萨看起来不错。你推荐这个吗？

What is today's special?
今日的特色菜是什么呢？

What do you recommend?
你推荐什么呢？

Unit 1 准备大吃一顿！

Chapter 1 肚子饿了怎么办

Grammar-3
"come with" 为短语用法，解释为"搭配；附带着"的意思。

What **comes with** the spaghetti?
意大利面的附餐是什么呢？

special ['speʃl] n （菜单上的）特色菜

recommend [ˌrekə'mend] v 推荐；介绍 反 deter [dɪ'tɜːr] v 威慑住；吓住

Situation 3
向餐厅订位

I **have a reservation under** Hanks.
我用汉克斯的名字订位。

Grammar-4
"have a reservation" 为 "预约" 的意思，其用法也可以使用动词形式的 "book（预订）" 或 "reserve（预约）" 或是短语 "make a reservation" 来代换。"under + 姓氏" 的用法，解释为 "以……的名义来……"。

I would like to reserve a table at 6:00.
我想预约 6 点的位子。

Situation 4
要向服务生点餐

We still need a few minutes to decide.
我们还需要一点时间来决定。

I'll **go with** that!
我就点那道菜！

Grammar-5
"go with" 解释为 "同意或接受某样事物" 的意思。

Grammar-6
点菜时可以说，"I'll have the…" 或是 "I'd like the…" 来做开头，千万不要一开口就说 "I want…"，这样会让点餐的服务人员觉得无礼！

I'll **have** a set meal, please.
我要一份套餐，谢谢。

Grammar-7
"a set meal" 解释为 "套餐"，主要是因为 set 当作形容词时，有 "【英】定菜定价的；客饭的" 意思。

I'll have what he's having.
我点跟他一样的。

I'd like the dressing **as well**!
我也想要沙拉酱！

Grammar-8
"as well" 解释为 "也"，是副词短语用法，但其位置永远在句尾。和其相同用法的副词还有 "also"，放置句中；"too" 则置于句尾，其前必须加上 "逗号"。

I'd like my mashed potatoes with gravy.
我想要土豆泥配肉汁。

I want a tuna **sandwich** with ketchup.
我要一个金枪鱼三明治加番茄酱。

Grammar-9
"sandwich" 当名词时，解释为 "三明治"；当动词时，则有 "夹在中间" 之意。

Hot coffee would be great.
热咖啡很好。

I don't feel very hungry; just give me **a glass of** orange juice.
我不是很饿，给我一杯橙汁就好。

Grammar-10
"a glass of" 是固定短语，即 "一杯" 的意思，通常是指果汁类的饮料。

have [hæv] v 有；吃；要

dressing ['dresɪŋ] n 沙拉酱；拌沙拉等的调料 同 sauce [sɔːs] n 调味酱；酱汁

Situation 5
餐桌上该注意的事

Grammar-11
"pass sb. sth." 是"把某物递给某人"的意思，其中"pass"为及物动词，我们也可以将其改为"pass sth. to sb."。

- Could you **pass me the pepper**❶?
  你可以把胡椒粉递给我吗？

- Could I have some sugar, please?
  能给我一些糖吗？

- Different cultures have different table manners. You have to **adjust to**❷ them.
  不同的文化有不同的餐桌礼仪，你必须适应它们。

Grammar-12
"adjust to" 是"适应"的意思，和其相同用法的短语为"adapt to（适应于）"。

pepper ['pepər] n 胡椒粉　　culture ['kʌltʃər] n 文化
table manners phr 餐桌礼仪

不怕你学不会

1. This place is famous for local specialties. Let's try something special!
   = This place is _____ local specialties. Let's try something special!

2. I have a reservation under Whites.
   = I _____ a table under Whites.

3. I'd like ice-cream as well!
   = I'd like ice-cream, _____ !

4. Do you want some spaghetti?
   = Do you want some _____ ?

5. You need to adjust to the culture or you would get hungry here every day.
   = You need to _____ the culture, or you would get hungry here every day.

解答：1. well-known for/noted for　2. booked　3. too　4. pasta　5. adapt to

Unit 2 今天想点什么？
Are you ready to order?

原来老外这样记单词 / 老外从小到大学习单词的方法，就是看到什么就学什么！

grape [greɪp]
n 葡萄

blueberry [ˈbluːberi]
n 蓝莓

kiwi [ˈkiːwiː]
n 猕猴桃

orange [ˈɔːrɪndʒ]
n 橙子；橘子

strawberry [ˈstrɔːberi]
n 草莓

grapefruit [ˈgreɪpfruːt]
n 西柚

其他衍生单词：

raspberry [ˈræzberi] n 覆盆子
watermelon [ˈwɔːtərmelən] n 西瓜
pineapple [ˈpaɪnæpl] n 菠萝
mango [ˈmæŋɡəʊ] n 芒果
guava [ˈɡwɑːvə] n 番石榴
papaya [pəˈpaɪə] n 木瓜

老外最常用的单词 连这些单词都不会，你还敢说你学过英语吗？

 老外饮料都喝这些

milkshake ['mɪlkʃeɪk] n 奶昔

lemonade [ˌlemə'neɪd] n 柠檬水
soda ['səʊdə] n 苏打水
orange juice phr 橙汁
mineral water phr 矿泉水
soft drink phr 无酒精饮料
cola ['kəʊlə] n 可乐
beverage ['bevərɪdʒ] n 饮料

 老外在酒吧都喝这些

champagne [ʃæm'peɪn] n 香槟

liquor ['lɪkər] n 含酒精饮料
brandy ['brændi] n 白兰地
vodka ['vɑːdkə] n 伏特加
beer [bɪr] n 啤酒
cocktail ['kɑːkteɪl] n 鸡尾酒
tequila [tə'kiːlə] n 龙舌兰酒
alcoholic [ˌælkə'hɔːlɪk] a 含酒精的
wine [waɪn] n 葡萄酒
mixed drink phr 混合鸡尾酒

 再忙，也要和你喝杯咖啡

coffee machine phr 咖啡机

espresso [e'spresəʊ] n 特浓咖啡
caffeine ['kæfiːn] n 咖啡因
mocha ['məʊkə] n 摩卡咖啡
creamer ['kriːmər] n 奶精
froth [frɔːθ] n 奶泡
latte art phr 咖啡拉花艺术

用英语聊天，原来这么简单
老外每天说的英语，其实就是这几句。

Unit 2 今天想点什么？

Chapter 1 肚子饿了怎么办

Waitress: May I take your order?
Josh: Sure, please give us six packs of beer first.

服务生：可以帮你们点餐了吗？ 乔希：当然，先来6瓶啤酒吧！

Situation 1
如果你在国外打工，要帮客人点餐

- Could I **order** ❶ now, ma'am?
  小姐，可以点餐了吗？

  > **Grammar-1**
  > "order" 当动词时，意为"订购；点菜/饮料"。但在句子中，我们也可以替换成短语模式，也就是将"order"当名词使用，即"place an order"的用法。

- Are there **any** ❷ foods you don't like to eat?
  你有什么不吃的食物吗？

  > **Grammar-2**
  > "any" 常用于疑问句或否定句中，意思为"任何"，可用于修饰可数与不可数名词。

- What do you want for **dessert** ❸ ?
  你想要吃什么甜点呢？

  > **Grammar-3**
  > "dessert" 为名词"甜点"之意，容易混淆的单词为"desert"，为"沙漠"之意，要稍加注意两者的差别才行！

- Would you like cream and sugar in your coffee?
  你的咖啡要加奶和糖吗？

- You have ordered a pizza. **For here or to go** ❹ ?
  你点了一个比萨。要在这里吃还是外带呢？

  > **Grammar-4**
  > "For here or to go?" 为一短语用法，即"在店里吃还是外带？"的意思。这时你只要回答"For here, please.（店里吃，谢谢。）"或是"To go, please.（外带，谢谢。）"就可以了。若是透过电话点餐，客服人员一定会说"For delivery or takeout?"，这是在询问你"要外送还是外带？"

- Would you like noodles or rice?
  你吃面条还是米饭呢？

- Would you like some whipped cream on your latte?
  你的拿铁上要加鲜奶油吗？

Grammar-5
"flavor"当名词时，为"口味；调味料"之意；当动词时，为"给……调味"的意思。

Grammar-6
"Which do you prefer…?"为一个句型，即"两者间你比较喜欢哪一个？"的意思。

Which flavor of ice cream do you prefer, maple walnut or vanilla?
你喜欢什么口味的冰激凌，枫香核桃还是香草呢？

ma'am [mæm] n 夫人；太太；小姐

want [wɑ:nt] v 想要 同 wish for phr 希望；愿望

flavor [ˈfleɪvə] n 味道；香料   walnut [ˈwɔːlnʌt] n 核桃；胡桃

vanilla [vəˈnɪlə] n 香草

Situation 2
如果你要为客人推荐餐点

Is there anything you'd particularly like to try?
你有没有特别想要品尝些什么呢？

You can order some cookies or waffles.
你可以点饼干或松饼。

Grammar-7
通常要用较委婉的方式询问他人的时候，可以用"Would you like…"的句型来表达，不仅可以传达自己的想法，也不失礼。

Would you like some appetizers?
你要不要来点开胃菜呢？

Grammar-8
礼貌上，会询问他人是否"要来一点……"的说法，可以使用"How about…"置于句首的句型。要注意的是，其后需接名词或动名词（V-ing）的形式。

How about having some crème brûlée?
要不要来点焦糖布丁呢？

particularly [pərˈtɪkjələrli] ad 特别；尤其 同 especially [ɪˈspeʃəli] ad 尤其；格外

appetizer [ˈæpɪtaɪzər] n 开胃菜；开胃的食物

crème brûlée phr 焦糖布丁

Situation 3
如果你点餐时，有特殊要求

I'd like a Caesar salad, but could I get the dressing on the side?
我想要吃恺撒沙拉，但沙拉酱另外放可以吗？

Could I have extra cream for my bread?
可以帮我的面包多加一份奶油吗？

Grammar-9
"be allergic to"是"对……过敏"的意思，需注意的是，其后接介词"to"，且须衔接名词。

I'm allergic to MSG.
我对味精过敏。

Grammar-10
要向他人请求，可以使用较委婉的语气来表达，即"May I…"的句型最为合适。

Grammar-11
在点餐时，如果不喜欢吃有些食材或是酱料，可以用"hold"来告诉服务员，解释为"不要加……"的意思。

May I have some more crisps?
我可以再多要一点薯片吗？

Please hold the onions and mayonnaise.
请不要加洋葱和蛋黄酱。

I have difficulty using chopsticks, could you give me a spoon and fork?

我不会使用筷子，可以给我勺子和叉子吗？

Caesar [ˌsiːzər] n. 恺撒，恺撒沙拉

on the side phr 另外放；放旁边

allergic [əˈlɜːrdʒɪk] a. 过敏的；对……极讨厌的 allergy [ˈælərdʒi] n. 过敏

MSG abbr 味精　　crisp [krɪsp] n.【英】薯片

have difficulty doing sth. phr 对于做某事感到困难

老外不会教你的小秘密

★ 英语菜单通常会以上菜的先后，分为餐前的开胃菜 *appetizer*，主菜 *entrée*，最后才会上甜点 *dessert*，可是通常在用餐前会请客人先点饮料 *drink* 或是 *beverage*。

不怕你学不会

1. I'm allergic to shrimp.

   = I have _____ to shrimp.

2. I want to try all of the food here, particularly seafood.

   = I want to try all of the food here, _____ seafood.

3. May I place an order for you?

   = May I _____ for you?

答案：1. an allergy　2. especially　3. order

Unit 3 麻烦制造者 Troublemaker

原来老外这样记单词 / 老外从小到大学习单词的方法，就是看到什么就学什么！

spoon [spuːn]
n 汤匙

tray [treɪ]
n 托盘

teapot [ˈtiːpɑːt]
n 茶壶

fork [fɔːrk]
n 叉子

plate [pleɪt]
n 盘子

mug [mʌɡ]
n 马克杯

其他衍生单词：

cooker [ˈkʊkər] n 厨具
napkin [ˈnæpkɪn] n 餐巾纸
toothpick [ˈtuːθpɪk] n 牙签

chopsticks [ˈtʃɑːpstɪks] n 筷子
disposal chopsticks phr 免洗筷
butter knife phr 奶油刀

老外最常用的单词 / 连这些单词都不会,你还敢说你学过英语吗?

Unit 3 麻烦制造者

肚子饿了怎么办

可以形容食物口味的单词 ★★★

sunny-side up phr 太阳蛋(只煎一面)

crisply ['krɪspli] ad 酥脆
salty ['sɔːlti] a 咸的
greasy ['griːsi] a 油腻的;多脂的
undercooked [ˌʌndər'kʊkt] a 不熟的;煮得不够的
tasteless ['teɪstləs] a 无味的;乏味的;没有味道的
delicious [dɪ'lɪʃəs] a 美味的
hard-boiled ['hard'bɔɪld] ad 全熟的

老外都用这些东西做菜

cinnamon ['sɪnəmən] n 肉桂

mint [mɪnt] n 薄荷
basil ['bæzl] n 罗勒
mayonnaise ['meɪəneɪz] n 美乃滋
ketchup ['ketʃəp] n 番茄酱
yeast [jiːst] n 酵母
cocoa powder phr 可可粉
almond oil phr 杏仁油
olive oil phr 橄榄油
exotic cuisine phr 异国美食
canned food phr 罐头食品

我们都用这些东西做菜

mustard ['mʌstərd] n 芥末

vinegar ['vɪnɪɡər] n 醋
ginger ['dʒɪndʒər] n 姜
pickle ['pɪkl] n 腌菜;泡菜
garlic ['ɡɑːrlɪk] n 蒜
soy sauce phr 酱油

chili sauce phr 辣椒酱
sesame oil phr 芝麻油

用英语聊天，原来这么简单
老外每天说的英语，其实就是这几句。

Hey! This salad was very unfresh!

Gordon

戈登：嘿！这盘沙拉很不新鲜！

Situation 1
如果你要和店家提出抱怨

- The steak was cooked way too long.
  这块牛排煎得太久了。

  Grammar-1 "too" 为副词，解释为 "太……；非常"，其后通常会接形容词。

- The fried noodles are too❶ salty and greasy.
  这炒面太咸太油了。

- Excuse me.❷ The steak is almost undercooked.
  不好意思，我的牛排几乎没熟。

  Grammar-3 "dish" 为名词时，解释为 "碗盘；菜肴" 等意思，若为动词时，则解释为 "盛……于盘中"。

- The dish❸ is too tasteless.
  这道菜太没有味道了。

Grammar-2 当麻烦别人或打扰别人、表示不赞成或不同意时，可以用 "Excuse me.（不好意思；抱歉）" 来表达。

- This coffee is a little bit bland.
  这杯咖啡有点淡而无味。

way too phr 太过于……　　almost ['ɔːlməust] ad 几乎；差不多

Situation 2
对食物有特别的喜好

- I prefer exotic food.
  我比较喜欢异国风味的食物。

- Frog legs taste like chicken.
  青蛙腿吃起来像鸡肉。

014

Unit 3 麻烦制造者

Chapter 1 肚子饿了怎么办

My family usually <mark>eat</mark> cereals and French toast <mark>for breakfast</mark>.
我家通常吃麦片和法式吐司当早餐。

> Grammar-4
> "eat...for breakfast" 为 "早餐吃……" 的意思。

I love eating Thai food, which tastes sour and spicy.
我喜欢吃泰式料理，吃起来又酸又辣。

My father loves to have a cup of latte <mark>while</mark> he is reading newspapers.
我爸爸喜欢在看报纸的时候喝一杯拿铁。

> Grammar-5
> "while" 当连词时，解释为 "当……的时候；然而"。需要注意的是，其后所接的时态为进行式。当动词时，则有 "消磨时间；蹉跎" 的意思。

I like mixed drinks a lot.
我非常喜欢喝调酒。

Cathy is a big eater. She can eat <mark>a loaf of bread</mark> for a single meal.
凯西是个大胃王。她可以一餐吃一条面包。

> Grammar-6
> "a loaf of bread" 是 "一条面包" 的意思，且因为 "bread" 为不可数名词，需要以单位量词来修饰。

I don't like food which is too spicy.
我不喜欢食物太辣。

- prefer [prɪˈfɜːr] v 更喜欢
- exotic [ɪɡˈzɑːtɪk] a 异国风味的；奇特的 同 foreign [ˈfɔːrən] a 外国的
- cereal [ˈsɪriəl] n 谷物
- French toast phr 【美】法式吐司
- a big eater phr 大胃王
- single [ˈsɪŋɡl] a 单一的；个别的

Situation 3
你想劝劝朋友改掉坏习惯

Stop eating junk food! They do harm to your health.
不要再吃垃圾食物了！它们有害健康。

Smoking is <mark>forbidden</mark> in non-smoking restaurants.
无烟餐厅是禁止吸烟的。

> Grammar-7
> "forbid" 当成动词时，为 "禁止" 之意，其用法相当于 "ban（禁止；禁令）" 的动词用法。forbid 的动词三态：forbid - forbade - forbidden

Are you drunk?
你喝醉了吗？

- junk food phr 垃圾食物
- do harm to phr 有害……
- non-smoking [nɒn ˈsməʊkɪŋ] ad 不抽烟的；禁止吸烟的
- restaurant [ˈrestrɑːnt] n 餐厅

Situation 4
你肚子不是很饿时可以说

- I don't have the appetite for a big meal. I just want to have milk pudding.
  我没有胃口吃大餐。我只想吃牛奶布丁。

- I'm not too hungry, so I'll have an appetizer.
  我不是很饿,所以我点开胃菜就好了。

have an appetite for `phr` 有胃口吃……　　meal [miːl] `n` 一餐

 老外不会教你的小秘密

★ 除了"*delicious*(美味的)"这个词,你可以发挥创意,用感官动词"*taste*(尝起来)、*look*(看起来)、*smell*(闻起来)"等加上形容词来形容食物的味道或外观。例如:"*It tastes scrumptious.*(这个尝起来真美妙。)""*It looks fantastic.*(这个看起来真棒。)"或是"*It smells gross.*(这个闻起来很恶心。)"。

 不怕你学不会

1. My coffee is _____ sweet to drink. Please give me a new one.
2. Non-smoking restaurants impose a ban on smoking.
   = Smoking is _____ in non-smoking restaurants.
3. I eat steamed stuffed bun _____ today's breakfast.
4. My mom told me to buy a _____ of bread.
5. My boss loves to have a cup of latte _____ he is reading newspapers.

答案:1. too　2. forbidden　3. for　4. loaf　5. while

Unit 4 吃饱后该做的事
Check, please!

 原来老外这样记单词 / 老外从小到大学习单词的方法，就是看到什么就学什么！

broccoli [ˈbrɑːkəli]
n 西蓝花

eggplant [ˈegplænt]
n 茄子

lettuce [ˈletɪs]
n 莴苣

cucumber [ˈkjuːkʌmbər]
n 小黄瓜

carrot [ˈkærət]
n 红萝卜

其他衍生单词：

celery [ˈseləri] n 芹菜
spinach [ˈspɪnɪtʃ] n 菠菜
pea [piː] n 豌豆
onion [ˈʌnjən] n 洋葱
bamboo shoot phr 竹笋
potato [pəˈteɪtəʊ] n 马铃薯

老外最常用的单词
连这些单词都不会,你还敢说你学过英语吗?

好甜好吃的单词 ★★

syrup [ˈsɪrəp] n 糖浆

jelly [ˈdʒeli] n 果冻
candy [ˈkændi] n 糖果
caramel [ˈkærəmel] n 焦糖
moon cake phr 月饼
cotton candy phr 棉花糖
brown sugar phr 黑糖
pumpkin pie phr 南瓜派

让人肚子有点小饿的单词 ★★

fortune cookie phr 签语饼

peanut [ˈpiːnʌt] n 花生
yogurt [ˈjəʊɡərt] n 酸奶
onion ring phr 洋葱圈
bubble gum phr 泡泡糖
hash browns phr 薯饼
potato chips phr 薯片
scone [skɑːn] n 【英】司康饼;烤饼

有特别用途的单词 ★★

food coloring phr 食用色素

vitamin [ˈvaɪtəmɪn] n 维生素
mineral [ˈmɪnərəl] n 矿物质
gourmet [ˈɡʊrmeɪ] n 美食家
vegetarian [ˌvedʒəˈterɪən] n 素食主义者
station cook phr 烹饪操作间,厨房里烹调某种食物的工作区域

用英语聊天，原来这么简单
老外每天说的英语，其实就是这几句。

服务生：您要付现金还是刷卡？　邦德：刷卡，麻烦你了。

Situation 1
吃饱后，想称赞一下店家

- It's hard to find such delicious Vietnamese food in this city.
  在这个城市里要找到这么好吃的越南菜不容易。

- It's really delicious.
  真的很好吃。

- It deserves its❶ reputation.
  果真名不虚传！

  > **Grammar-1**
  > 句中的"its"为"it"之所有格形态，切记，不可以写成"it's"，后者为"it is"的缩写。

- I like the dish.
  我喜欢这道菜。

  deserve [dɪˈzɜːrv] Ⅴ 应受；该得
  reputation [ˌrepjuˈteɪʃn] n 名声 同 fame [feɪm] n 声誉；名声

Situation 2
结账时一定会这样说

- Does the price include service charge?
  这个价钱包含服务费吗？

- Please take the rest of my dish home in a doggie bag.
  请帮我用外带的袋子装剩下的食物。

Keep the change.
零钱不用找了。

Grammar-2
"change" 在这里当名词，为"零钱；找零"的意思，且为不可数名词，不可在字尾加上 s。

Grammar-3
"on" 为介词，其后所接为"宾格"。

It's on me!
我请客！

We're going to split the bill.
我们要各付各的。

Grammar-4
"split the bill" 为"分摊账单"的意思，亦可延伸为"各付各的"之意。和其相同用法的短语还有"Let's go Dutch!"、"Let's share the bill!" 或 "Let's go fifty-fifty!"

include [ɪnˈkluːd] v 包含；包括　　service charge phr 服务费

the rest of sth phr ……中剩下的……

doggie bag phr （剩食）外带食物的袋子

keep [kiːp] v 保留；保有

Situation 3
想介绍食物的做法

The Buffalo Wings is sauted and then grilled over an open flame.
水牛城辣鸡翅是嫩煎过后再直接火烤。

Grammar-5
"Buffalo Wings" 为专有名词，意思为"水牛城辣鸡翅"。是采用鸡翅的中下部，不裹面粉油炸，再以辣椒为原料的酱汁及其他调料调味而制成。

To make pizza, you will need flour, yeast powder and olive oil.
做比萨你会需要面粉、酵母粉和橄榄油。

There are tomato sauce, cheese, onions and pepper in it.
这里面有番茄酱、芝士、洋葱和胡椒。

Instant noodles are convenient to prepare, so I take them as meals when I am busy.
方便面很容易准备，所以忙碌的时候我都以它为食。

Grammar-6
"take A as B" 为"把 A 当作 B"的意思。

The dish could use more salt.
这道菜可以再加点盐。

Grammar-7
"mix A and B" 有"把 A 和 B 混合"的意思，其中 A 与 B 皆需要为名词。

He mixed lettuce and some raisins to make salad.
他把生菜和葡萄干混合做成沙拉。

Let the water boil first before putting in the pasta.
煮意大利面前先把水煮沸。

Follow every step in the recipes, and you can be a good home cook, too.
只要你按照食谱上的每个步骤做，你也可以是个好的家庭厨师。

Unit 4 吃饱后该做的事

Chapter 1 肚子饿了怎么办

- saute [soʊˈteɪ] v. 嫩煎；煸
- grill [grɪl] v.（用烤架等）烤
- flame [fleɪm] n. 火焰；火舌
- instant noodles phr 方便面
- convenient [kənˈviːniənt] a. 方便的；便利的
- raisin [ˈreɪzn] n. 葡萄干
- salad [ˈsæləd] n. 沙拉

Situation 4
聊中国美食

Have you ever tried stinky tofu?
你有吃过臭豆腐吗？

> Grammar-8
> "Have you ever...?" 这个句型通常用以询问，有"到目前为止是否有……"的意思。

Soybean milk **goes sour** after exposed to sunlight.
豆浆在阳光下曝晒后酸掉了。

> Grammar-9
> "go sour"为固定短语，即"变酸；令人失望"的意思，其中"go"有"变为；变成"的意思，也可以用"become"或"get"等来替换。

- stinky tofu phr 臭豆腐
- soybean milk phr 豆浆
- sth. be exposed to phr 某物暴露于……
- sunlight [ˈsʌnlaɪt] n. 日光

老外不会教你的小秘密

★ 当有人请你吃很奇怪的东西时，为了表示出修养，你可以说，"*It's interesting / unusual.*（这东西真是有意思／真特别。）"、"*I've never had anything like this before.*（我从来没吃过这样的东西。）"或是"*It's not really my thing.*（这不太合我口味。）"。另外，主人热情地请外国人吃当地食物，但因为味道太重或太臭，外国人一时无法接受时，可以礼貌地回应"*I guess it's an acquired taste.*（我想这是一种需要适应的口味。）"

不怕你学不会

1. I don't have the a_____e for a big meal.
2. That b_____y always has some free samples of handmade cookies.
3. Would you r_____d us your specialties?

答案：1. appetite 2. bakery 3. recommend

看看老外怎么学

来玩玩看老外最爱的填字游戏，边玩边学单词好轻松！

Wordpuzzle

down　1. After the meal, let's have some d_____ts.

　　　2. The s_____p is too hot.

　　　3. Do you think those cookies are e_____e?

cross　4. How would you like your s_____k, medium or well-done?

　　　5. How would you like to pay, by c_____h or by credit card?

　　　6. The cake is d_____s, isn't it?

答案：1. desserts（甜点） 2. soup（汤） 3. edible（可食用的） 4. steak（牛排） 5. cash（现金） 6. delicious（美味的）

Chapter 2 购物去
Go shopping

和朋友们的完美约会，当然就是大吃一顿后开始 shopping time！快进入这个 Chapter 学学老外的方法！

Unit 1	Unit 2	Unit 3	Unit 4
货比三家不吃亏	万能店员	最聪明的消费者	售后心得

Unit 1 货比三家不吃亏
Shopping around

原来老外这样记单词 老外从小到大学习单词的方法，就是看到什么就学什么！

agate [ˈæɡət]
n 玛瑙

pearl [pɜːrl]
n 珍珠

diamond [ˈdaɪəmənd]
n 钻石

jade [dʒeɪd]
n 翡翠

其他衍生单词：

crystal [ˈkrɪstl] n 水晶
coral [ˈkɔːrəl] n 珊瑚
ruby [ˈruːbi] n 红宝石
emerald [ˈemərəld] n 绿宝石
glitter [ˈɡlɪtər] v 闪闪发光
jewelry [ˈdʒuːəlri] n 珠宝

Unit 1 货比三家不吃亏

Chapter **2** 购物去

老外最常用的单词 / 连这些单词都不会，你还敢说你学过英语吗？

老外都爱逛这些店

antique shop phr 古董店
cafeteria [ˌkæfəˈtɪrɪə] n 自助餐；食堂
photographic studio phr 照相馆
stationery store phr 文具店
bakery [ˈbeɪkəri] n 面包店
chain store phr 连锁店
optical shop phr 眼镜店
barber shop phr 理发厅
beauty salon phr 美发院
children's department phr 童装部
food court phr 美食街

老外都爱去这里玩

bookstore [ˈbʊk stɔr] n 书店
bookstand [ˈbʊkstænd] n 书报摊
gym [dʒɪm] n 健身房
picnic [ˈpɪknɪk] n 野餐
countryside [ˈkʌntrɪsaɪd] n 郊外
amusement park phr 游乐园
beach party phr 海滩派对
night club phr 夜店
karaoke n 卡拉OK

可以逛一整天的地方

garage sale phr 二手物清仓拍卖
bazaar [bəˈzɑːr] n 市集
shopping mall phr 大商场
shopping district phr 商圈
flea market phr 跳蚤市场
night market phr 夜市
lost and found phr 失物招领处

用英语聊天，原来这么简单
老外每天说的英语，其实就是这几句。

玛丽：我们去逛街吧！ 安：好！我想买些冬天的衣物。

Situation 1
单纯在街上逛逛

- I saw a wonderful bicycle in the window display.
  我看到橱窗里展示了一辆很棒的自行车。

- I'm looking for some accessories to attend a wedding.
  我正在买参加婚礼需要的首饰。

- After you look at the garment, hang it back on a hanger and put them back on the rack.
  看完一件衣服之后，把它挂回衣架上并放回架子上。

- Where is the grocery store? I want to get some cheese.
  杂货店在哪里？我想买些奶酪。

wonderful ['wʌndərfl] a 极好的   window display phr 橱窗展示

garment ['gɑːrmənt] n （一件）衣服   hanger ['hæŋər] n 衣架；挂钩

rack [ræk] n 架子；挂物架

Situation 2
购物季到了！
准备去大采购

- The new department store downtown has a great summer sale; you'll find great bargains.
  市区里新百货公司有夏季大减价，你会找到物超所值的商品。

Unit 1 货比三家不吃亏

Chapter 2 购物去

Grammar-1
"be on sale" 为 "特价；减价出售" 的意思。要特别注意，和 "be for sale（出售中）" 的意思有所区别。

Grammar-2
buyer 当名词时为 "买家；顾客" 的意思，其用法和 "customer" 相当。

This armchair is on sale ❶ on Father's Day to attract more buyers ❷.
这款扶手椅在父亲节特价吸引了更多的买家。

Body lotions and hand creams are hot deals in winter season.
身体乳和护手霜是冬季的热销产品。

Grammar-3
"follow the trend" 为 "跟随潮流" 的意思，也有较负面的意思，为 "随波逐流"。

Rita always follows the fashion trend ❸.
瑞塔总是跟随时尚潮流。

During the Christmas season, there are many parents bringing their children to toy departments.
在圣诞季时，有很多父母会带着小孩到玩具部。

department store [phr] 百货公司   sale [seɪl] [n] 特卖会

bargain [ˈbɑːrɡən] [n] 便宜货；物超所值的商品

armchair [ˈɑːrmtʃer] [n] 扶手椅

lotion [ˈloʊʃn] [n] 乳液   hot deal [phr] 热销商品

trend [trend] [n] 趋势；流行

Situation 3
你和朋友的特殊购物习惯

You can buy clothes in the shopping mall.
你可以到购物中心买衣服。

Grammar-4
"goods" 当名词时，为 "商品；货物" 的意思；也可以换成 "products（产品）" 或是 "commodity（商品；日用品）" 等词。

Some big department stores only sell their own brand goods ❹.
有些大型的百货公司只会卖它们自有品牌的商品。

Grammar-5
"even though" 为 "即使" 的意思，其用法和 "although" 相同。

My dad likes to shop at a warehouse; my mom prefers to go to a retail store even though ❺ it is a bit more expensive. But for a good bargain, they both enjoy ❻ going to a thrift store.
我爸爸喜欢去批发店购物，我妈妈比较偏好去零售店购物，即便是有点贵。但为了买到好价位的商品，他们两个都喜欢到慈善商店里买东西。

Grammar-6
"enjoy" 为特殊词，其后所接的动词皆须以 v-ing 的形式呈现。

The special exhibition in the museum usually requires a separate ticket.
博物馆里的特展通常需要另购门票。

Elaine likes to shop till she drops ❼.
伊莱恩喜欢疯狂采购，买到手软为止。

Grammar-7
"to shop till sb. drops" 为 "买到手软" 的意思。

027

"used to +v" 为"过去常常做某件事"的意思。

I <mark>used to</mark> ❽ purchase newspapers in convenience stores, but now I watch news reports on TV.
我以前都到便利店买报纸，但现在我都看电视上的新闻报道。

Would you like to go to the convenience store with me?
你想要和我一起去便利商店吗？

own brand `phr` 自有品牌   warehouse ['werhaus] `n` 大型零售店

retail store `phr` 零售商店

thrift store `phr` 慈善商店 `同` charity shop `phr` 义卖商店

drop [drɑːp] `v` （因疲劳／受伤等）倒下

convenience store `phr` 便利商店

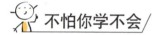

1. I want to buy something at the grocery store even though I don't have time.

    = I want to buy something at the grocery store _____ I don't have time.

2. Some big department stores only sell their own brand products.

    = Some big department stores only sell their own brand _____.

3. This armchair is on sale on Father's Day to attract more buyers.

    = This armchair is on sale on Father's Day to attract more _____.

4. I used to _____ milk in the morning, but now I drink coffee instead.

5. Andrew likes to shop till he _____.

答案：1. although 2. goods / commodities 3. customers 4. drink 5. drops

Unit 2 万能店员
We can do everything

原来老外这样记单词 / 老外从小到大学习单词的方法，就是看到什么就学什么！

scarf [skɑːrf]
n 围巾

dummy [ˈdʌmi]
n （橱窗中的）假人模特

jeans [dʒiːnz]
n 牛仔裤

layered skirt
phr 蛋糕裙

legging [ˈleɡɪŋ]
n 内搭裤

其他衍生单词：

wig [wɪɡ] n 假发
blouson [ˈblaʊsɑːn] n 宽身束腰女上衣
hot pants phr 热裤
fishnet stockings phr 网袜
cravat [krəˈvæt] n 领带；(旧式)领结
accessory [əkˈsesəri] n 配件

老外最常用的单词 / 连这些单词都不会，你还敢说你学过英语吗？

百货公司里会有这些东西

wall lamp `phr` 壁灯

elevator [ˈelɪveɪtər] `n` 电梯
escalator [ˈeskəleɪtər] `n` 电扶梯
attendant [əˈtendənt] `n` 服务员
elevator operator `phr` 电梯操作员
emergency exit `phr` 逃生门
display window `phr` 橱窗

商店里会有这些人事物

shop assistant `phr` 店员

discount [ˈdɪskaʊnt] `n` 折扣
sales slip `phr` 销货单
remittance slip `phr` 汇款单
No bargain `phr` 不讨价
value-based pricing `phr` 价值定价法
market-penetration pricing `phr` 市场渗透定价法
market-skimming pricing `phr` 市场吸脂定价法

用这些方法把东西卖出去

marketing strategy `phr` 行销策略

flyer [ˈflaɪər] `n` 传单
bonus [ˈbəʊnəs] `n` 红利
sample [ˈsæmpl] `n` 试用品
new arrival `phr` 新品上市
annual sale `phr` 周年庆
free shipping `phr` 免运费
gift voucher `phr` 礼券
marketing survey `phr` 市场问卷调查

Unit 2 万能店员

 用英语聊天，原来这么简单　老外每天说的英语，其实就是这几句。

Chapter **2** 购物去

店员：女士，这个商品真的很划算。　莎拉：让我想想。

Situation 1
各式各样的店家

Grammar-1
"offer" 当动词时，为"提供"的意思，其用法相当于"provide"或是"give"。另外，"offer" 在这里也可以用"sell（销售）"来替换。

Grammar-2
"weigh" 当动词，为"称重"的意思，拼法要和名词稍微区分一下，即"weight"。

Grammar-3
"sth. cost sb. an arm and a leg" 为"某物让某人所费不赀"的意思。

The florist shop offers ❶ expensive bouquets on Mother's Day.
花店在母亲节的时候出售昂贵的花束。

You can find many odd things in the flea market.
你可以在跳蚤市场找到很多奇特的东西。

Customers weigh ❷ the fruit and vegetables on the scale in the produce section of the supermarket.
在超市的农产品区里，顾客们使用秤来称水果和蔬菜的重量。

The best place in this neighborhood is the shopping mall.
这附近最好的地方是卖场。

If you buy something at this newly-opened boutique, it will cost you an arm and a leg ❸.
如果你在新开的精品店里买东西，将会让你所费不赀。

First, we will go to the grocery store to get some sugar, next to the delicatessen to get some fried rice, and then we will buy vegetables at the open market.
首先，我们会到杂货店里买些糖，接着到熟食店里买炒饭，然后再到自由市场里买蔬菜。

031

florist shop [phr] 花店　　bouquet [buˈkeɪ] [n] 花束

scale [skeɪl] [n] 天平；秤　　produce section [phr] 农产品区

newly-opened [phr] 新开张的　　boutique [buːˈtiːk] [n] 精品店

grocery [ˈɡrəʊsəri] [n] 食品杂货店

delicatessen [ˌdelɪkəˈtesn] [n] 熟食店

open market [phr] 自由市场

Situation 2
如果你是店员，要推销你们家的商品

Grammar-4
"discount" 当名词时，为"折扣"的意思；当动词时，为"打折；减价"的意思。

We can offer you a better price **discount** ❹ if you buy more than 10 items.
如果你购买10件以上的商品，我们就能给你更多的折扣。

Let me show you some popular styles of dress.
让我为你介绍一些受欢迎的连衣裙款式。

Grammar-5
"A go good with B" 为 "A 和 B 很搭" 的意思。

This beanie **goes good with** ❺ your white sweater.
这顶毛线帽跟你的白色毛线衣很搭。

price [praɪs] [n] 价格　　beanie [ˈbiːni] [n] 毛线帽

go with [phr] 伴随；相合　　sweater [ˈswetər] [n] 毛线衣

Situation 3
如果你是店员，要让客人倍感亲切可以这样说

The ladies clothing shop **is situated above** ❻ the jewelry store.
女装店在珠宝店的楼上。

Grammar-6
"be situated above" 为 "位于……上方" 的意思。

Do you want to buy the used one or the brand new one?
你想要买二手的还是全新的呢？

Grammar-7
"both A and B" 为 "A 和 B 两者都……" 的意思。

At the entrance of the shop, you will find **both** shopping carts **and** ❼ shopping baskets for your convenience.
在商店入口处，为了方便你可以找到购物车和购物篮。

You will find toothpastes and toothbrushes in Aisle 7.
你在卖场中的第7号过道会找到牙膏和牙刷。

Bruno Mars' new albums have arrived.
火星人布鲁诺的新专辑已经到货了。

Grammar-9
"help sb. with sth." 为 "帮助某人某事物……" 的意思，要注意其后所接的介词为 with。

Grammar-8
"salesperson" 当名词时，为 "销售员" 的意思，其用法和 "salespeople" 及 "salesclerk" 相同。

(**Salesperson** ❽) My name is Catherine. If you need any **help** ❾, I'd be happy to help you out in any way I can.
（销售员）我的名字是凯瑟琳。如果您需要帮忙，我很乐意提供任何协助。

Unit 2 万能店员

Chapter 2 购物去

Grammar-10
"import sth. from somewhere" 为 "从某处进口某物" 的意思，和其相反的用法则为 "import sth. into somewhere"，"将某物输入某国" 之意。

Most shoes in the shoe department are **imported from** Europe.
鞋类区的大部分鞋子都是从欧洲进口的。

This brand of chalk **is out of stock**. How about buying other brands?
这个品牌的粉笔缺货中。要不要先买其他品牌的呢？

Grammar-11
"be out of stock" 为 "缺货中；无现货" 的意思，相同的短语还有 "be sold out"。

You can try on all kinds of sunglasses to see which one **suits** you best.
你可以试戴每款太阳眼镜，看看哪一款最适合。

Grammar-12
"suit" 当动词时，为 "适合；相配；满足" 的意思；当名词时，为 "套装；诉讼；套房" 的意思。

lady clothing shop *phr* 女装店　　shopping cart *phr* 购物车

for one's convenience *phr* 为了某人的方便

toothpaste ['tu:θpeɪst] *n* 牙膏　　toothbrush ['tu:θbrʌʃ] *n* 牙刷

aisle [aɪl] *n* 通道；走道　　import ['ɪmpɔ:rt] *v* 进口；输入

Europe ['jʊərəp] *n* 欧洲　　chalk [tʃɔ:k] *n* 粉笔

How about...? *phr* 要不要……？　　try on... *phr* 试穿；试戴

sunglasses ['sʌnglæsɪz] *n* 太阳镜

不怕你学不会

1. The bakery sells chocolate cakes on Valentine's Day.
   = The bakery _____ chocolate cakes on Valentine's Day.

2. If you buy something at that antique shop, it will cost you an _____ and a _____.

3. I help my sister _____ her homework.

4. This brand of pens is out of stock.
   = This brand of pens is _____.

答案：1. offers / provides　2. arm, leg　3. with　4. sold out

最聪明的消费者
The smartest consumers

 原来老外这样记单词 / 老外从小到大学习单词的方法，就是看到什么就学什么！

cashier [kæˈʃɪr]
n 收银员

bill [bɪl]
n 账单；纸钞

credit card slave
phr 卡奴

invoice [ˈɪnvɔɪs]
n 发票

ATM card (= cash card)
phr 银行卡

其他衍生单词：

brand [brænd] n 商标、品牌　　**membership card** phr 会员卡　　**bar-code** n 条码

shopping list phr 购物清单　　**clerk** [klɜːrk] n 【美】店员，销售员　　**price scan** phr 扫描价钱

老外最常用的单词 / 连这些单词都不会，你还敢说你学过英语吗？

Chapter 2 购物去

老外都这样买

online shopping phr 线上购物

bid [bɪd] v 下标
shopaholic [ʃɑːpəˈhɔːlɪk] n 购物狂
POD (= pay on delivery) abbr 货到付款
installment payment phr 分期付款
window shopping phr 橱窗购物
in-store picking phr 到店取货

老外都买这些

electric toothbrush phr 电动牙刷

shampoo [ʃæmˈpuː] n 洗发液
soap [səʊp] n 肥皂
hairdryer [ˈheɪrdraɪər] n 吹风机
hair conditioner phr 润发乳；护发素
contact lens phr 隐形眼镜
hand cream phr 护手霜
porcelain [ˈpɔːrsəlɪn] n 瓷器

顾客至上

tip [tɪp] n 小费

client [ˈklaɪənt] n 顾客
consume [kənˈsuːm] v 花费
waste [weɪst] v 浪费
complain [kəmˈpleɪn] v 抱怨
deception [dɪˈsepʃn] n 欺诈
Consumer Protection Officer phr 消费者保护官
Keep the change! phr 不用找钱！

用英语聊天，原来这么简单 / 老外每天说的英语，其实就是这几句。

辛迪：妈妈，我想要买这把可爱的小伞。　　辛迪妈：可以，但你先试穿看看这件外套吧。

Situation 1
如果你买了新东西

- I bought a new hammer at the hardware store across from the tailor's shop.
  我在成衣店对面的五金店里买了一个新的铁锤。

- I would like to order ❶ a pair of toddler shoes for my little niece.
  我想要订购一双婴儿学步鞋给我的侄女。

  Grammar-1
  "order" 当动词时，为 "命令；订购；安排" 的意思；当名词时，则为 "顺序；秩序；订货" 的意思。在此句为 "订购" 之意。

- I bought the ancient coins in the antique shop.
  我在古董店里买到了古钱币。

  Grammar-2
  "out of order" 为 "故障" 的意思。

- My multi-function printer has been out of order ❷ continually, so I decided to buy a new one in a 3C store.
  由于我的多功能打印机屡屡故障，因此我决定到数码商品卖场买一台新的。

- Look at this jukebox! It really cost me a lot.
  看看这台点唱机！它真的花了我不少钱。

- I got my nails manicured in a beauty parlor.
  我到美容院修指甲。

Unit 3 最聪明的消费者

Chapter 2 购物去

hammer [ˈhæmər] n 铁锤
hardware store phr 五金店
tailor's shop phr 成衣店
toddler shoes phr 婴儿学步鞋
niece [niːs] n 侄女；外甥女
multi-function printer phr 多功能打印机
continually [kənˈtɪnjuəli] ad 一再地
get one's nails manicured phr 修指甲
beauty parlor phr 美容院

Situation 2
如果你想开口问问店员

Where is the children's department?
童装部在哪里？

Are there any electronic stores around?
这附近有电器行吗？

I would like to buy a casual shirt and dressy pants. Where is the men's clothing department?
我想要买一件便装和一件西装裤。男装部在哪里呢？

May I take a look at the jewelry over there?
我可以看看那边的珠宝吗？

How much do these pants cost❸?
(Look at the price tag.)
这条裤子多少钱呢？（看了一下价格标签。）

Grammar-3
"How much do/does/did... cost?" 为询问价钱的用法，要特别注意 cost 的主语须为"物品"；相同的句型还有 How much is it?（这个多少钱？）

Do I get any freebies for buying the refrigerator?
我买冰箱会送什么东西吗？

"Pardon❹, where are the fitting rooms?"
不好意思请问一下，试衣间在哪里呢？

Grammar-4
"pardon" 为口语用法，解释为"不好意思"，其用法和 "Excuse me!（对不起！抱歉！）" 相同。

Will this polka dot dress shrink in the wash?
这件圆点花纹的连衣裙下水洗过后会缩水吗？

The shoes are too loose for me. Can you give me one size smaller?
这双鞋对我来说太松了。可以给我小一号的吗？

Is there a seven-day trial period?
有 7 天试用期吗？

037

casual shirt `phr` 便装   dressy pants `phr` 西装裤

men's clothing department `phr` 男装部

price tag `phr` 价格标签   fitting room `phr` 更衣室

polka pot `phr` 圆点花纹   shrink [ʃrɪŋk] `v` 缩水

loose [luːs] `a` 松的；宽的   one size smaller `phr` 小一号的

Situation 3
顾客是上帝的理念

The cashier was very pleasant to all the customers despite the chaos in the store.
尽管商店里一片混乱，收银员还是对所有的客人很友善。

The salesperson was not helpful, so I asked to talk to the manager.
销售员没有帮助，所以我要求和经理谈谈。

The company has taken out an insurance policy for their newest product.
这家公司已经为他们最新的产品投保。

We provide free dust proof bags for customers who buy the briefcases.
我们给购买公文包的顾客提供免费的防尘袋。

despite [dɪˈspaɪt] prep. 不管；尽管

chaos [ˈkeɪɑːs] `n` 混乱；混乱的一团

helpful [ˈhelpfl] `a` 有帮助的   manager [ˈmænɪdʒər] `n` 经理

take out an insurance policy `phr` 投保   dust proof bag `phr` 防尘袋

 老外不会教你的小秘密

★ 每当逛街购物时，如果想要砍价，我们可以使用 "*If you knock the price down a little, I'll take it.* （如果你降一点价，我就买了。）" 的句子，或是用 "*I'm afraid that's out of my price range.* （那恐怕超出我的预算。）" 的句子。这两句一出口，相信会得到一点折扣。

★ 逛街购物，不管是买鞋子还是衣服，免不了要试穿一下，除了 "*try on sth.*" 的短语可以用之外，也可以用 "*throw on sth.*"，即 "随意穿上……；套上……" 的意思。

Unit 4 售后心得
After you bought...

原来老外这样记单词 / 老外从小到大学习单词的方法，就是看到什么就学什么！

- **bow tie** `phr` 蝶形领结
- **perfume** [pərˈfjuːm] `n` 香水
- **pocket watch** `phr` 怀表
- **quartz watch** `phr` 石英表
- **evening gown** `phr` 晚礼服

其他衍生单词：

- **luxury** [ˈlʌkʃəri] `n` 奢侈品
- **sheet** [ʃiːt] `n` 床单
- **overseas imports** `phr` 舶来品
- **suit** [suːt] `n` 西装
- **swallow-tailed coat** `phr` 燕尾服
- **bed cover** `phr` 床罩

老外最常用的单词
连这些单词都不会,你还敢说你学过英语吗?

买这些最文艺

gadget ['gædʒɪt] n 小玩意儿

magazine ['mægəziːn] n 杂志
novel ['nɑːvl] n 小说
geta ['getə] n (日本式)木屐
wallet ['wɑːlɪt] n 皮夹
jigsaw puzzle phr 拼图玩具
wrapping paper phr 包装纸
mascot ['mæskɑːt] n 吉祥物

买这些你最潮

villa ['vɪlə] n 郊区别墅

lottery ['lɑːtəri] n 彩票
handmade [ˌhænd'meɪd] a 手工的
exquisite [ɪk'skwɪzɪt] a 精致的
best-selling [best 'selɪŋ] a 最畅销的
waterproof ['wɔːtərpruːf] a 防水的
second-hand a 二手的
organic food phr 有机食品
delicate ['delɪkət] a 雅致的

偶尔会碰到的小状况

refund ['riːfʌnd] n 退款

glitch [glɪtʃ] n 小瑕疵;小故障
restocking fee phr 退货手续费
after-care service phr 售后服务
warranty ['wɔːrənti] n 保修
installation fee phr 安装费
surcharge ['sɜːrtʃɑːrdʒ] n 手续费
special delivery phr 快递

Unit 4 售后心得

用英语聊天，原来这么简单
老外每天说的英语，其实就是这几句。

Chapter 2 购物去

Did you see the stain? I require the refund.
Customer
Shop assistant
I apologize, but let me ask our manager first.

顾客：你看到这个污渍了吗？我想要退款。　店员：真的很抱歉，但我得先问过我们经理。

Situation 1
打折了！还不快用上这几句

There is a promotion at the drugstore❶. You can buy one bottle of shampoo and the second one is free.
药店里有促销活动，你买一瓶洗发水，就送一瓶。

They have a limited quantity of mouth wash on sale, so first come first served❷.
他们有少量的漱口水是特价，所以先到先得。

You can get 20% off❸ by using this coupon.
使用这张折价券可以享 8 折优惠。

promotion [prə'məʊʃn] n 促销；推销

limited quantity of phr 少量的　　mouth wash phr 漱口水

coupon ['ku:pɒn] n 优惠券；折价券

Grammar-1
"drugstore" 为"药店"的意思，其用法和"pharmacy（药房）"相同。

Grammar-2
"first come first served" 字面上的意思为先到的先被服务，也就引申为"先到先得"。

Grammar-3
"20% off" 为"20% 的折扣"，即"8 折"。

Situation 2
结账时一定会这样说

When we buy less than 12 items, we can go to the express lane to pay.
当我们购买的东西少于 12 件时，我们可以到快速结账通道付钱。

Will you pay cash❹, write a check❺, or use your credit card?
你要付现、开支票还是使用信用卡呢？

Grammar-4
"pay cash" 也可换成 "pay in cash"。

Grammar-5
开支票的正确写法为 "write a check"，而 "open a check" 为错误写法。

041

Grammar-6
"be included in..." 为"被包含在……"的意思；但在此句中仅留下过去分词当成被动的用法。

Grammar-7
"receipt"当名词时，为"收据"的意思。和"voucher（收据）"可以代换。

You could put this on layaway.
您可以分期付款。

Do you need a Tax ID included in your receipt?
你的发票需要税务登记号吗？

If there are any problems with the product, please bring it back with a receipt in seven days.
如果产品有任何问题，请在 7 天内将产品及发票带过来。

item ['aɪtəm] n 项目；品目

express lane phr （卖场）快速结账通道

cash [kæʃ] n 现金   credit card phr 信用卡   Tax ID 税务登记号

Situation 3
对商品不满

Grammar-8
"exchange"的用法和"change"相同，为"交换，更换"的意思；也可以使用"interchange"来代换，但是当名词解释时，为"立体交叉道"的意思。

Where is the return counter?
退货柜台在哪里？

We will provide you with after-sale service.
我们提供售后服务。

You will need the receipt if you wish to exchange the item.
如果你要换货，你需要提供收据。

You can return the product free of charge if you don't like it.
如果您不喜欢这个商品，您可以免手续费退回。

Grammar-9
"return A to B"为"把A退回或是还给B"的意思。

I cannot return it to the store because I bought it on a clearance sale.
我不能把这些东西退还给商店，因为我是在清仓大甩卖的时候购买的。

May I ask what's wrong with the product?
可以请问产品哪里有问题吗？

We offer a one-year warranty for free.
我们提供一年的保修。

Grammar-10
"lemon"当名词时，除了"柠檬"之外，还可解释为"瑕疵品；没有价值的东西"等意思。

Tony spent all of his savings buying a used car, but all he got is a lemon.
托尼花了所有的积蓄买了一台二手车，但他所购得的却是一辆瑕疵品。

I bought the wrong size. Could I exchange for the one of my size?
我买错尺寸了，请问我可以更换成我的尺寸吗？

Unit 4 售后心得

Chapter **2** 购物去

Sorry, but we have a no-return policy.
抱歉我们这里不能退货。

Grammar-11
"flaw"当名词时，为"瑕疵；缺点"的意思；当动词时，则为"使有瑕疵；使产生裂缝"的意思。

The miniskirt I bought yesterday was flawed ⑪. I want my money back.
我昨天买的迷你裙有瑕疵。我要退钱。

The pants I bought has a rip in it. I'd like my money back, please.
这条裤子上面有破洞，我想要退钱，谢谢。

The only thing we can do is give you store credit.
我们只能帮您换店内等值的商品。

clearance sale [phr] 清仓大拍卖　　savings ['sevɪŋz] [n] 积蓄；存款

but all one get(s) [phr] 却只得到……　　miniskirt ['mɪnɪskɜːt] [n] 迷你裙

Situation 4
小偷

She got caught shop lifting ⑫.
她因为顺手牵羊被抓了。

Grammar-12
"shop lifting"为固定短语，是"顺手牵羊"的意思，而"shop lifter"即为"扒手"之意。

caught [kɔːt] [v] 捕获（catch的过去分词）

不怕你学不会

1. That boutique shop is on sale now! _____ come _____ served.

2. May I have the receipt?
   = May I have the _____ ?

3. Do you want to _____ a check?

4. You will need the receipt if you wish to change the item.
   = You will need the receipt if you wish to _____ the item.

5. Excuse me, I want to return the skirts _____ the shop. What should I do now?

答案：1. First, first　2. voucher　3. write　4. exchange / interchange　5. to

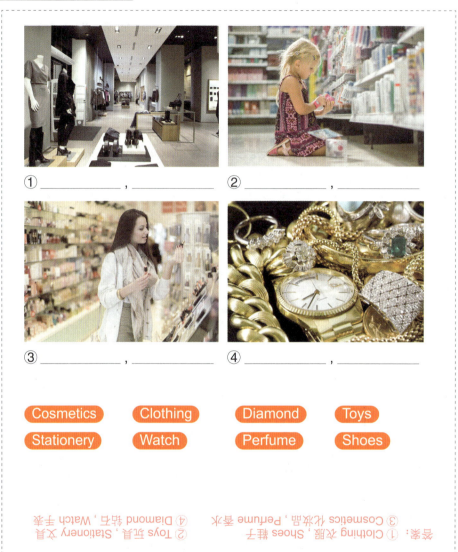

Chapter 3 庆祝时间

Let's celebrate

想知道如何向老外介绍超有特色的中国节日吗？想和朋友们一起在纽约时代广场，用英语倒计时数数吗？赶快一起来学学，一年365天都用得到，超High超实用的庆祝英语吧！

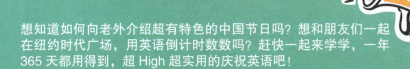

Unit 1	Unit 2	Unit 3
东方佳节	西方庆典	欢庆时光

Unit 1 东方佳节
Eastern festivals

原来老外这样记单词 / 老外从小到大学习单词的方法，就是看到什么就学什么！

firecracker [ˈfaɪərkrækər]
n 鞭炮

gold ingot
phr 金元宝

lucky money
phr 压岁钱

其他衍生单词：

rice cake phr 年糕　　reunion dinner phr 团圆饭　　lantern [ˈlæntərn] n 灯笼
radish cake phr 萝卜糕　　dragon and lion dance phr 舞龙舞狮　　mah-jong n 麻将

Unit 1 东方佳节

老外最常用的单词
连这些单词都不会，你还敢说你学过英语吗？

Chapter 3 庆祝时间

欢迎老外一起来过节 ★★

Double Ninth phr 重阳节
Ghost Festival phr 中元节
Father's Day phr 父亲节
Mother's Day phr 母亲节
Labor Day phr 【美】劳动节
Lantern Festival phr 元宵节

老外也懂端午节 ★★

rice dumpling phr 粽子

steam [sti:m] v 蒸；煮
calamus ['kæləməs] n 菖蒲
mugwort ['mʌg,wɜ:t] n 艾草
sachet [sæ'ʃeɪ] n 香包
bamboo leaf phr 竹叶
dried mushroom phr 干香菇
salted egg yolk phr 咸蛋黄
banyan twig phr 榕树枝
realgar wine phr 雄黄酒

中秋佳节必备 ★★★

barbecue ['bɑ:rbɪkju:] n 烤肉

sauce [sɔ:s] n 酱汁；调味酱
tongs [tɒŋz] n 钳子；夹具
charcoal ['tʃɑ:rkəʊl] n 木炭
aluminum foil phr 【美】铝箔纸
baste [beɪst] v （烤炙时）在……上涂油
basting brush phr 烤肉刷
Mid-Autumn Festival phr 中秋节

用英语聊天，原来这么简单
老外每天说的英语，其实就是这几句。

Situation 1
跟老外介绍中国的习俗

- People often go to temples to pray for a prosperous new year.
  人们常到庙里祈求新年运势昌隆。

- People go to temples to pay homage to the Gods on the New Year's Day of the lunar calendar.
  人们在大年初一的时候到寺庙里拜拜。

  > **Grammar-1**
  > "sth. be used to"为被动语态用法，即"某物被用来做……"的意思。

- In ancient times, sky lanterns were used to ❶ transmit messages. Nowadays sky lanterns are flown on the Lantern Festival as a celebration.
  在古代，天灯是用来传递信息的。现在我们放天灯来庆祝元宵节。

  > **Grammar-2**
  > "peace"当名词时，有"和睦；平静"的意思，其用法相当于"harmony"。

- We eat glutinous rice balls on Winter's Extreme to pray for peace ❷ and safety of the family.
  我们在冬至吃汤圆，目的是要祈求家庭的和谐和安全。

- People in China go tombstone sweeping on Tomb Sweeping Festival.
  中国人在清明节的时候去扫墓。

  > **Grammar-3**
  > "look forward to"表示"展望；期待"，后面接名词或动名词，一般表示以愉快的心情来等待或盼望某一事情的发生。

- Because they can get lots of red envelopes, all kids are looking forward to ❸ the coming of Chinese Lunar New year.
  因为可以领到很多红包，孩子们都期待中国农历新年的到来。

Unit 1 东方佳节

Chapter 3 庆祝时间

- pay homage to `phr` 向……致敬
- lunar calendar `phr` 农历
- transmit [trænsˈmɪt] `v` 传送；传达
- nowadays [ˈnaʊədeɪz] `ad` 现今；时下
- celebration [ˌselɪˈbreɪʃn] `n` 庆典
- glutinous rice balls `phr` 汤圆
- Winter's Extreme `phr` 冬至
- pray [preɪ] `v` 祈祷；祈求
- sweep [swiːp] `v` 清扫；打扫
- Tomb Sweeping Festival `phr` 清明节
- red envelope `phr` 红包
- Lunar New Year `phr` 农历新年

Situation 2
跟老外介绍中国节日

There is no school during Children's Day.
儿童节学校放假。

Do you know ❹ when is Ghost Festival?
你知道中元节是什么时候吗?

> Grammar-4
> "Do you know...?"为名词从句用法，即"你知道……吗?"的意思，其后若接另一个疑问句时，需以直述句来呈现。

We extol ❺ the greatest teacher, Confucius, on Teacher's Day.
我们在教师节赞颂伟大的教师——孔子。

> Grammar-5
> "extol"当动词时，有"赞美；颂扬"之意，其用法相当于"praise"或"exalt"。

Confucius [kənˈfjuːʃəs] `n` 孔子
Teacher's Day `phr` 教师节

Situation 3
跟老外介绍端午节

Have you ever seen ❻ dragon boat racing on Dragon Boat Festival?
你曾在端午节时看过龙舟赛吗?

> Grammar-6
> "Have you ever seen...?"即"你看过……吗?"的意思，表达从过去某个时间点一直到目前为止动作的进行时，可以用现在完成时来表达。

Does eating rice dumplings have something to do with ❼ Qu Yuan at this time of year?
在一年的这个时候要吃粽子是不是和屈原有关呢?

> Grammar-7
> "have something to do with"有"和……有些许关联"的意思，其中"something"若换成"nothing"时，则为"和……毫无关联"的意思。

The drummer at the front of the dragon boat helps everyone keep a tempo.
龙船上的鼓手是帮大家配合节奏的。

> Grammar-8
> "to"有"为了……"的意思，相同用法的短语为"in order to"，且to为不定式，后面所接的动词需以原形呈现。

To ❽ drive away evil spirits, people bind mugwort and calamus together with a red thread and hang them on the door.
为了驱邪，人们会用红线将艾草和菖蒲绑在一起并挂在门上。

It is said that someone who can make ❾ an egg stand on one end will have good luck for the rest of the year.
据说能把鸡蛋立起来的人整年都会有好运。

> Grammar-9
> "make"为使役动词，意思为"使……"，其后可以接上形容词或动词原形。

049

dragon boat race [phr] 龙舟赛　　Dragon Boat Festival [phr] 端午节

Qu Yuan [n] 屈原　　drummer [ˈdrʌmər] [n] 鼓手

keep a tempo [phr] 配合节拍（奏）　　evil [ˈiːvl] [a] 邪恶的

bind [baɪnd] [v] 捆；绑　　the rest of [phr] 剩下的；剩余的

Situation 4
跟老外介绍中秋节

Grammar-10
"bright" 当形容词时，有"明亮的"之意，其用法相当于"shining"或"glittering"。

The moon looks really big and **bright** on the Moon Festival.
中秋节时的月亮真的又大又亮。

The Moon Festival was originated from the Tang Dynasty.
中秋节起源于唐朝。

Grammar-11
"jade" 当名词时，意思为"翡翠；玉制品"；当形容词时，则有"玉制的"之意。

Do you believe that Chang-Er, Wu Gang and **Jade** Rabbit exist on the moon?
你相信嫦娥、吴刚和玉兔生活在月亮上吗？

How many days do you have off work for the Moon Festival?
你中秋节休几天？

the Moon Festival [phr] 中秋节　　originate [əˈrɪdʒɪneɪt] [v] 发源；来自

dynasty [ˈdaɪnəsti] [n] 朝代；王朝　　exist [ɪɡˈzɪst] [v] 存在；生存

on the moon [phr] 月球上

不怕你学不会

1. We extol Qu Yuan on the Dragon Boat Festival because he is very faithful to his country.

   = We _____ Qu Yuan on the Dragon Boat Festival because he is very faithful to his country.

2. A: The moon is so glittering tonight. B: Yeah, today is the Moon Festival.

   = A: The moon is so _____ tonight. B: Yeah, today is the Moon Festival.

3. In fact, barbecue has _____ to do with the Moon Festival.

答案：1. praise / exalt　2. bright / shining　3. nothing

Unit 2 西方庆典
Western holidays

原来老外这样记单词 / 老外从小到大学习单词的方法，就是看到什么就学什么！

ornament [ˈɔːrnəmənt]
n 装饰；装饰品

tinsel [ˈtɪnsl]
n 镶有闪光金属丝的织物

pinecone [ˈpɪnˌkɒn]
n 松果；松球

gingerbread [ˈdʒɪndʒərbred]
n 姜饼

candle [ˈkændl]
n 蜡烛

其他衍生单词：

candy cane phr 拐杖糖
mistletoe [ˈmɪsltəʊ] n 槲寄生
holly [ˈhɑːli] n 冬青；冬青属植物

poinsettia [ˌpɔɪnˈsetɪə] n 圣诞红；猩猩木
wreath [riːθ] n 花冠；花圈
Christmas [ˈkrɪsməs] n 圣诞节

老外最常用的单词 / 连这些单词都不会，你还敢说你学过英语吗？

万圣节 ★★★

Jack-o'-lantern [ˈdʒækə ˈlæntərn] n
南瓜灯；杰克灯

carve [kɑːrv] v 雕刻；切开
haunt [hɔːnt] v （鬼魂等）常出没于……
mummy [ˈmʌmi] n 木乃伊
tombstone [ˈtuːmstəun] n 墓碑；墓石
devil [ˈdevl] n 魔鬼；恶魔
goblin [ˈɡɑːblɪn] n （丑陋的）小妖精
spooky [ˈspuːki] a 令人毛骨悚然的
toffee apple phr 太妃糖苹果

圣诞节 ★★★

reindeer [ˈreɪndɪr] n 【动】驯鹿

gravy [ˈɡreɪvi] n （作调味用的）卤；肉汁
stuffing [ˈstʌfɪŋ] n （塞于鸡鸭腹中的）填料
decoration [ˌdekəˈreɪʃn] n 装饰品
sleigh [sleɪ] n （轻便）雪橇
snowman [ˈsnəumæn] n 雪人
moose [muːs] n 【动】麋鹿；北美麋
chimney [ˈtʃɪmni] n 烟囱
cranberry sauce phr 蔓越莓酱
mashed potato phr 马铃薯泥

土拨鼠目 ★★★

groundhog [ˈɡraundhɒɡ] n 【动】土拨鼠

rodent [ˈrəudnt] n 啮齿类动物
bunny [ˈbʌni] n 小兔子
hare [her] n 野兔
hibernation [ˌhaɪbərˈneɪʃn] n 冬眠；过冬
burrow [ˈbɜːrəu] n （兔/狐等的）洞穴；地道

用英语聊天，原来这么简单
老外每天说的英语，其实就是这几句。

Chapter 3 庆祝时间

Thank you, Ma'am!

Lacey: All of you are so cute! Here you go.

莱西：你们都打扮得好可爱呀！这给你们。 孩子们：谢谢女士！

Situation 1 过万圣节

When it comes to ❶ Halloween, orange and black come into my mind first.
一提到万圣节，我第一个想到橘色和黑色。

Grammar-1 句中一开头便出现"When it comes to"的短语，有"一提到……"的意思，其中的 to 为介词，后面需接 N 或 Ving。

I'm going to **dress up** ❷ as a fairy on Halloween.
我要在万圣节时装扮成仙女。

Grammar-2 "dress up"具有"盛装打扮"的意思，和其相同用法的短语有"go as + N"；后者为"装扮成……"的意思。

Let's buy **a great number of** ❸ candies and **hand** them **out** to the kids.
我们去买很多的糖果来分送给小朋友们吧。

Grammar-3 "a great number of"为"很多"的意思，和其相似的短语为"many""a lot of"。

mind [maɪnd] n 心；头脑

fairy ['feri] n 仙女 ▣ sprite [spraɪt] n 鬼怪；小妖精

hand out phr 分发

Situation 2 过感恩节

The first Thanksgiving was to thank the Indians for helping them **grow** ❹ foods.
第一个感恩节是为了要感谢印第安人教导他们种植食物。

Grammar-4 "grow"当动词时，有"种植；栽培"之意，其用法相当于"plant"或"cultivate"。

It's a tradition to **take turns** ❺ carving the turkey in our family at this time of the year.
每年的这个时候，在我们家有轮流切火鸡的传统。

Grammar-5 句中的"take turns"意指"轮流换班；替换"，后面可以接不定式，与"do sth. by turns"的意思相同。

🎧 053

Grammar-6
"be thankful for" 为"某人感谢某事物"的意思，和短语"give thanks for"相似，其意为"某人为某事物表达感谢之意"。

I am thankful for this big feast with my lovely family.
我很感谢可以和我这么可爱的家人一起共享丰盛的一餐。

Thanksgiving [ˌθæŋksˈɡɪvɪŋ] n 感恩节

Indian [ˈɪndɪən] n 印第安人

tradition [trəˈdɪʃn] n 传统；惯例 ≡ custom [ˈkʌstəm] n 习俗；惯例

carve [kɑːrv] v 切（肉、菜） turkey [ˈtɜːrki] n 火鸡

feast [fiːst] n 盛宴；宴席

lovely [ˈlʌvli] a 可爱的；美好的 ≡ delightful [dɪˈlaɪtfl] a 令人愉快的

Situation 3
过圣诞节

How are you going to spend Christmas this year?
你今年要如何度过圣诞节呢？

Grammar-7
"spend"当动词时，除了有"花费"的意思之外，还有"度假"的意思；也可用"go away for the holiday"的短语来替换。
spend 动词三态为：
spend - spent - spent

Did you buy any must-haves for the Christmas party?
你买了圣诞派对中一定要有的任何一样东西吗？

Stars are hung up on the top of the Christmas tree, and wrapped presents are put under it.
圣诞树的顶端摆星星，底下则摆包装好的礼物。

Grammar-8
"must-have"的意思为"一定要有的东西"。在此指在派对中如果少了其中一样气氛便会不同。

Every child expects Santa Claus's coming on Christmas Eve.
每个小孩在圣诞夜都期待圣诞老人的出现。

Grammar-10
句中提到"every"为形容词，后面需要接上单数名词，用以表示"每一个"。

My friends and I make gingerbread houses together during the Christmas season.
我朋友和我在圣诞季的时候都会做姜饼屋。

Grammar-9
"hang up"表示"把……挂起来"，也可指"挂断电话"。
hang 动词三态为：
hang - hung - hung

Grammar-11
"during + 一段时间"表示"在……期间内发生"的动作，但不一定自始至终。

Are we supposed to hang those stockings on the Christmas tree?
我们应该把那些长袜挂在圣诞树上吗？

Grammar-12
"be supposed to"有"期望；认为应该"的意思。

party [ˈpɑːrti] n 派对 ≡ celebration [ˌselɪˈbreɪʃn] n 庆祝活动

Christmas tree phr 圣诞树

wrapped [ræpt] a 包装好的；【俚】恋爱中的

present [ˈpreznt] n 礼物；赠品 expect [ɪkˈspekt] v 期待；预料

Santa Claus phr 圣诞老人 Christmas Eve phr 圣诞节前夕

gingerbread [ˈdʒɪndʒərbred] n 姜饼 season [ˈsiːzn] n 季节；节期

hang [hæŋ] v 把……挂起 stocking [ˈstɑːkɪŋ] n 长袜

Unit 2 西方庆典

Situation 4
过愚人节

Who on earth places a fake snake in my drawer? You can **dish it out** ⑬ , but you can't take it.
究竟是谁放了一条假蛇在我抽屉里？敢做不敢当。

Remember not to ⑭ trick me on April Fools' Day, or you'll get **a taste of your own medicine** ⑮ .
记住不要在愚人节时戏弄我，否则你会自食恶果的。

on earth phr 究竟　　fake [feɪk] a 假的；冒充的

drawer [drɔːr] n 抽屉

trick [trɪk] v 戏弄；愚弄；捉弄 同 beguile [bɪˈɡaɪl] v 欺骗；诓骗

April Fools' Day phr 愚人节

Grammar-13
"dish it out" 是指 "批评；指责" 的意思，而 take 则是指 "接受" 的意思；放在 "You can dish it out, but you can't take it." 句子中，便引申为 "敢做不敢当" 的意思。

Grammar-14
"remember not to + V" 句型省略掉了第二人称主语和助动词 do。

Grammar-15
"a taste of one's own medicine" 有 "自食恶果" 的意思，也引申为 "以其人之道，还治其人之身。" 也可以用 "I will get back at you.（我会报复你的。）" 来替换。

Situation 5
过复活节

Easter is to **commemorate** ⑯ the rebirth of Jesus Christ.
复活节是为了纪念耶稣的重生。

Kids **took part in a search** ⑰ to find the hidden eggs on Easter morning.
孩子们在复活节的早上寻找被藏起来的鸡蛋。

rebirth [ˌriːˈbɜːrθ] n 再生；复活　　Jesus [ˈdʒiːzəs] n 耶稣

hidden [ˈhɪdn] a 隐藏的

Grammar-16
"commemorate" 当动词时，有 "庆祝；纪念" 之意，其用法相当于 "celebrate" 一词。

Grammar-17
"take part in a search" 有 "加入搜索" 的意思，也可以将 "take part in" 替换为 "join" 或 "participate in"。

Chapter **3** 庆祝时间

老外不会教你的小秘密

★ 愚人节时，你是否会整人或是被别人整呢？我们来学学看相关的句子：

✦ *Don't pull my leg! I know today is April Fools' Day.*
别吓我！我知道今天是愚人节。

✦ *Do you play jokes on your friends on April Fools' Day?*
你在愚人节时会对朋友恶作剧吗？

✦ *Don't play a prank on me. I would never fall for a trick.*
不要耍我，我不会被那恶作剧骗到的。

以上这些说法，都是和恶作剧相关的表达方式。

Unit 3 欢庆时光 Party time

原来老外这样记单词
老外从小到大学习单词的方法，就是看到什么就学什么！

helium balloon phr 氦气气球

floating ['fləʊtɪŋ] a 飘浮的

noisemaker ['nɔɪzˌmeɪkə] n 高声喧闹的人

blowout ['bləʊaʊt] n 纸喇叭（可以卷曲伸缩）

其他衍生单词：

party poppers phr 礼花
streamer ['stri:mər] n 装饰用的彩纸带
resolution [ˌrezə'lu:ʃn] n 决心；解答

cuddle ['kʌdl] v 拥抱
hoax [həʊks] n 骗局
surprise [sər'praɪz] n 使人惊讶的事

Unit 3 欢庆时光

老外最常用的单词
连这些单词都不会，你还敢说你学过英语吗？

Chapter 3 庆祝时间

和老外一起狂欢 ★★

marching band phr 游行乐队

annual [ˈænjʊəl] a 一年一度的
carnival [ˈkɑːrnɪvl] n 嘉年华
firework [ˈfaɪərwɜːrk] n 烟火；烟火大会
horn [hɔːrn] n 喇叭
flagpole [ˈflæɡpəʊl] n 旗杆
parade [pəˈreɪd] n 游行；阅兵（典礼）
　　　　　　　v 在……游行
float [fləʊt] n （游行时用的）花车

虔诚老外会用到的字 ★★

mosque [mɑːsk] n 清真寺

church [tʃɜːrtʃ] n 教堂
crucifix [ˈkruːsəfɪks] n 十字架
pure [pjʊr] a 纯洁的；贞洁的
Bible [ˈbaɪbl] n 圣经
saint [seɪnt] n 圣人
Goddess [ˈɡɑːdəs] n 女神
Cupid [ˈkjuːpɪd] n 丘比特；爱神
Venus [ˈviːnəs] n 维纳斯女神
religious [rɪˈlɪdʒəs] a 虔诚的；宗教的

就是要黏腻腻甜蜜蜜 ★★

blind date phr 相亲

single [ˈsɪŋɡl] n 单身者（男子或女子）
bachelor [ˈbætʃələr] n 单身男子
spinster [ˈspɪnstər] n 未婚女子
truffle [ˈtrʌfl] n 松露巧克力
propose [prəˈpəʊz] n 求婚
adore [əˈdɔːr] v 崇拜；爱慕
Valentine's Day phr 情人节

057

用英语聊天，原来这么简单 / 老外每天说的英语，其实就是这几句。

Let's party all night!

彼得：让我们狂欢一整夜！

Situation 1
欢庆时光是最快乐的！

Happy New Year! New year **stands for** ❶ new beginnings!
新年快乐！新的一年代表新的开始。

Grammar-1
"stand for"和"stand by"都有"支持"之意，但区别是："stand for"多指"主张；拥护"；"stand by"则含"忠于；保护；捍卫"之意。

Many children are **looking forward to** ❷ Children's Day because they can take the day off and receive many presents.
许多小孩期待儿童节，因为他们可以放假而且可以收到很多礼物。

Grammar-2
"look forward to"有"期待"的意思，其后接上 N 或 Ving。

New Year phr 新年；元旦

beginning [bɪˈgɪnɪŋ] n 开始；开端 同 opening [ˈəʊpnɪŋ] n 开始；开头

Children's Day phr 儿童节   day off phr 休息日

receive [rɪˈsiːv] v 收到；接到

Situation 2
如果你有新鲜的庆祝想法想提出时

I need to think of something new to do on New Year's Eve.
我必须想个新鲜的方法来跨年。

In New York, Times Square **is** always **crowded with** ❸ people to see the ball drop for the New Year.
在纽约，时代广场总是挤满了人看新年的水晶球降落。

Grammar-3
"be crowded with"为"挤满……"的意思，和其相似用法的短语为"be full of"。

Unit 3 欢庆时光

Let's go watch the fireworks by ❹ the riverbank.
我们到河堤上看烟火。

Grammar-4
"by" 当介词词时，有 "经由；沿着" 之意；当副词时，则为 "经过；在旁边"。

Does your wife ache for ❺ your present on your wedding anniversary?
你太太会渴望结婚纪念日的礼物吗？

Grammar-5
"ache for" 有 "渴望" 的意思，和其相同用法的短语为 "yearn for"。

Let's buy a bouquet of carnations for ❻ Mom on Mother's Day, shall we?
我们在母亲节时，买一束康乃馨给妈妈，好吗？

Grammar-6
"buy sth. for sb." 即 "买某物给某人" 的意思，要特别注意其后所接介词须用 "for"。

- Times Square **phr** 时代广场
- drop [drɑːp] **v** 下降；终止
- firework ['faɪərwɜːrk] **n** 烟火；烟火大会
- riverbank ['rɪvərbæŋk] **n** 河堤；河岸
- wedding anniversary **phr** 结婚纪念日
- carnation [kɑːr'neɪʃn] **n** 康乃馨

Situation 3　节日富含的意义

The purpose of Grandparent's Day is to increase interactions between grandparents and grandchildren.
祖父母节的意义是增进祖父母和孙儿之间的互动。

Father's Day is on the eighth day ❼ of August.
父亲节在 8 月的第 8 天。

Grammar-7
"eighth" 的意思为 "第 8；1/8"，此时为名词；当形容词时，则解释为 "第 8 的；1/8 的"。

- purpose ['pɜːrpəs] **n** 目的；意图
- Grandparent's Day **phr** 祖父母节
- increase [ɪn'kriːs] **v** 增加；增强

Situation 4　浪漫的情人节

Wish you a merry ❽ Chinese Valentine's Day!
愿你有一个快乐的七夕情人节！

Grammar-8
"merry" 当形容词时，有 "愉快的；欢乐的" 之意，其用法与 "happy" 类似。

Danny has a crush on ❾ Kitty. He plans to propose to her on Valentine's Day!
丹尼迷恋凯蒂。他打算在情人节时向她求婚。

Grammar-9
"have a crush on sb." 有 "迷恋某人" 的意思，相似的短语有 "have fallen for sb."、"have a thing for sb." 和 "have fallen in love with sb."。

It's common sense to send a box of chocolate to the guys whom ❿ you like on Valentine's Day.
情人节时，送盒巧克力给你喜欢的人是常识。

Grammar-10
"whom" 为代名词，用以表示 "……的人"。

Grammar-11
"sth. cost sb. a lot" 即"某物花某人很多钱",此为常见的用法。

Wow! Leo must be smitten with you. Look at that bouquet of roses on the table. It surely cost him a lot ⓫.
哇!利奥真是为你魂牵梦萦。看看桌上的玫瑰花束。那一定花了他不少钱。

Grammar-12
"be one's steady" 为"稳定的对象",也就引申为"情人"的意思;可以用"Valentine"或"mine"来替换。

Please be my steady ⓬, I will love you with my heart and soul.
请当我的爱人,我会全心全意地爱你。

propose [prə'pəuz] v 求婚 同 make an offer of marriage phr 求婚

common sense phr 常识   smite [smaɪt] v 使神魂颠倒

bouquet [bu'keɪ] n 花束;恭维(或赞颂)的话

heart and soul phr 热心地;全心全意地

Situation 5
悠闲的时刻

What do you usually ⓭ do on weekends?
你周末的时候都在做些什么事?

Grammar-13
"usually" 通常置于助动词和 be 之后,及一般动词之前,偶尔也会置于句首。

Some people would choose to be no brainers in their leisure time, which means they don't use their brains on leisure activities.
有些人休闲的时候会选择当无脑人,也就是说他们休闲的时候不想用脑。

on weekends phr 每逢周末;假日 相 holiday ['hɑːlədeɪ] n 假日;【英】假期

choose [tʃuːz] v 选择;挑选   leisure ['liːʒər] n 闲暇

activity [æk'tɪvəti] n 活动

 老外不会教你的小秘密

★ 在中国有 *Chinese Valentine's Day*(农历七夕),在西方有 *Valentine's Day*(西方情人节),在这么重要的日子,男男女女都会向自己心仪的对象告白,但这是需要勇气的。因此,为了鼓励他人追求自己喜欢的男生或女生,我们可以说:

✦ *You should get up the nerve to woo my best friend, Yvonne.*
你应该鼓起勇气向我最好的朋友——伊冯求婚才是。

✦ *Why don't you have the nerve to go after that pretty girl?*
你为何不鼓起勇气来追求那位漂亮的女生呢?

Chapter 4
哥哥姐姐动起来

Get started

想要维持好身材,每日持续的运动是必不可少的!现在流行的健身运动有很多,赶快一起来加入吧!

Unit 1	Unit 2	Unit 3	Unit 4
来场刺激的	球来就打	地上跑 & 水里游	全民疯奥运

Unit 1 来场刺激的 Exciting games

原来老外这样记单词 / 老外从小到大学习单词的方法，就是看到什么就学什么！

back line phr 底线

hoop [huːp] n （篮球的）篮筐

backboard [ˈbækbɔːrd] n 篮板

scoreboard [ˈskɔːrbɔːrd] n 计分板

sideline [ˈsaɪdlaɪn] n （球场等的）界线

central line phr 中心线

three point line phr 三分线

其他衍生单词：

coach [kəʊtʃ] n 教练
referee [ˌrefəˈriː] n 裁判
linesman [ˈlaɪnzmən] n 边线裁判

cheerleader [ˈtʃɪrliːdər] n 【美】啦啦队长
mascot [ˈmæskət] n 吉祥物
bullpen [ˈbʊlpen] n 候补队员区

老外最常用的单词 / 连这些单词都不会,你还敢说你学过英语吗?

运动前需要先做这些

stretch [stretʃ] v 伸直;伸长

outstretch [aʊt'stretʃ] v 伸出、扩展
kneepad ['niː,pæd] n 护膝
helmet ['helmɪt] n 头盔
warm up phr 暖身
cool down phr 缓和运动
shoulder pad phr 护肩、垫肩

用这些展开健康人生

punching bag
phr (练习拳击用的)沙袋;吊袋

treadmill ['tredmɪl] n 跑步机
dumbbell ['dʌm,bel] n 哑铃
skateboard ['skeɪtbɔːrd] n 滑板
hula hoop phr 呼啦圈
yoga mat phr 瑜伽垫
exercise bike phr 健身自行车

让你从菜鸟变老鸟

starting point phr 起跑点;出发点

stopwatch ['staːpwaːtʃ] n 秒表;跑表
circuit ['sɜːrkɪt] n 巡回赛
tactic ['tæktɪk] n 战术;策略;手法
promotion [prə'məʊʃn] n 晋级
single ['sɪŋɡl] n 单打比赛
double ['dʌbl] n (网球等的)双打
semifinal [,semɪ'faɪnəl] n 半决赛
break shot phr 开球
live broadcast phr 实况转播
drug test phr 药物检验

Chapter 4 哥哥姐姐动起来

Unit 1 来场刺激的

用英语聊天，原来这么简单 / 老外每天说的英语，其实就是这几句。

乔治：加油啊英格兰队！　本：打倒他们！

Situation 1
看比赛时要用的句子

I'd like four front row tickets. How much do they cost?
我想要买4张前排座位的票。需要多少钱呢？

Thousands of ❶ fans came to the arena to support their team.
数以千计的粉丝为了支持他们的队伍来到运动场。

Grammar-1
"thousands of" 为固定短语，解释为"数以千计的"。

It is convenient to watch MLB playoffs on smartphones.
在智能手机上看美国职棒大联盟季后赛真方便。

front [frʌnt] a 前面的　　ticket ['tɪkɪt] n 票；券

arena [ə'ri:nə] n 比赛场；竞技场　同 stadium ['steɪdɪəm] n 运动场；体育场

support [sə'pɔ:rt] v 支持；拥护

convenient [kən'vi:nɪənt] a 方便的；便利的

MLB abbr 美国职业棒球大联盟 (=Major League Baseball)

playoff ['pleˌɔf] n 季后赛　　smartphone n 智能手机

Situation 2
和你的朋友讨论比赛

The competition will start at 7 o'clock on ❷ Saturday morning.
这场比赛将会在星期六早上7点开始。

Grammar-2
时间介词用法："at + 时间（通常是指几点几分）"；"on + 特定时间"。

064

How many **players** are there on the baseball field?
棒球场上有多少球员呢？

Mom always asks me which team is winning when I watch baseball games **on TV**.
妈妈总是在我看电视棒球比赛时问我哪一队赢了。

How much time **is left** in the game?
这场比赛还剩下多少时间呢？

competition [ˌkɑːmpəˈtɪʃn] n 比赛；竞赛

Grammar-3
"player" 当名词时，意思为"球员"，和其相同的词汇有"sportsman（运动员；运动家）"及"athlete（运动员；体育家）"。

Grammar-4
"on TV" 为"通过电视"之意，因此在表达看电视上的某一个节目时，不可以使用 on the TV 的用法！

Grammar-5
"be left" 中 "left" 为动词，是"leave"的过去分词形式。

Situation 3
揭晓比赛结果

Terry won the MVP this season.
泰瑞获选本赛季最有价值球员。

Last year's champion won the **trophy** again this year.
去年的冠军今年又再次赢得了奖品。

The best hockey team won the Stanley Cup.
最棒的曲棍球队赢得了斯坦利杯。

The game **ended in a draw**.
这场比赛最后以平手结束。

Eva won **first place** in the open championship.
伊娃在公开赛中获得冠军。

The host **delivered a speech** in the closing ceremony.
主持人在闭幕式时演讲。

MVP abbr 最有价值的球员 (=Most Valuable Player)

champion [ˈtʃæmpiən] n （竞赛的）优胜者；冠军

hockey [ˈhɑːki] n 曲棍球   Stanley Cup phr 斯坦利杯

game [ɡeɪm] n 运动；竞赛 同 contest [ˈkɑːntest] n 竞赛；比赛

open [ˈəʊpən] a 公开的   championship [ˈtʃæmpiənʃɪp] n 锦标赛

closing [ˈkləʊzɪŋ] a 结尾的；闭幕的

ceremony [ˈserəməʊni] n 仪式；典礼

Grammar-6
"trophy" 当名词时，为"奖品"的意思，其用法和"prize（奖赏；奖品）"及"award（奖品）"等相同。

Grammar-7
"end in a draw" 意思为"以平手结束"；和其相似的用法为"end in smoke"，有"以失败收场"的意思。

Grammar-8
"first place" 为名词，意思为"冠军"，其用法等同于"first prize"与"champion"等。

Grammar-9
"deliver a speech" 有"发表演讲"的意思，和其相同的短语为"give a speech"与"make a speech"。

Situation 4
讨论一场好比赛

Usually speaking, the home team has more advantages over the guest team.
一般而言，主队比客队拥有更多的优势。

> **Grammar-10**
> "usually speaking" 的意思为 "一般而言"，和其相同的短语为 "generally speaking"。

Every team has its own **signals** when playing in a race.
每一个队伍在比赛时都有它独特的暗号。

> **Grammar-11**
> "signal" 当名词时，解释为 "暗号；信号"，其用法相当于 "beacon"。

Our **opponents** played well, but we played better.
我们的对手打得很好，但我们更棒！

> **Grammar-12**
> "opponent" 当名词时，意思为 "对手；敌手"，和其相同的词汇有 "rival（匹敌者）" 及 "competitor（竞争者）"。

advantage [əd'væntɪdʒ] n 优点；优势
guest [gɛst] a 客人的
race [reɪs] n 比赛；竞赛

Sports agents **are responsible for** signing contracts with players.
球队经纪人负责和球员签约。

> **Grammar-13**
> "be responsible for" 有 "负责" 的意思，和其相同的短语为 "be held responsible for"。

sign [saɪn] v 签字；署名
contract ['kɑːntrækt] n 契约；合约书

不怕你学不会

1. Our opponents played well, but we played better.
   = Our _____ played well, but we played better.

2. Sports agents are responsible for signing contracts with players.
   = Sports agents are _____ responsible for signing contracts with players.

3. The competition will start _____ 4 o'clock _____ Friday afternoon.

4. The game ended in _____ . My teammates all felt very depressed very much.

5. The host delivered a speech in the closing ceremony.
   = The host _____ a speech in the closing ceremony.

答案：1. rivals / competitors 2. held 3. at, on 4. smoke 5. gave / made

Unit 2 球来就打
Get the ball rolling

原来老外这样记单词 / 老外从小到大学习单词的方法，就是看到什么就学什么！

forward [ˈfɔːrwərd]
n 前锋

center [ˈsentər]
n 中锋

guard [ɡɑːrd]
n 后卫

backcourt [ˈbækkɔːrt]
n 控球员

goalkeeper [ˈɡəʊlkiːpər]
n 守门员

其他衍生单词：

pitcher [ˈpɪtʃər] n 投手

shortstop [ˈʃɔrt,stɑp] n 【棒】游击手

rookie [ˈrʊki] n 【口】新入选选手

striker [ˈstraɪkər] n 【足】前锋

goal [ɡəʊl] v (足球等)攻门；射门得分

penalty area phr (足球)罚球区

067

老外最常用的单词
连这些单词都不会,你还敢说你学过英语吗?

风靡全球的球类运动

polo [ˈpəʊləʊ] n 马球
golf [ɡɑːlf] n 高尔夫球
rugby [ˈrʌɡbi] n 英式橄榄球
handball [ˈhændbɔːl] n 手球
softball [ˈsɔːftbɔːl] n 垒球
billiard [ˈbɪljəd] n 撞球
shotput [ˈʃɑːt pʊt] n 铅球
baseball [ˈbeɪsbɔːl] n 棒球
dodge ball phr 躲避球

让技巧进步再进步

block [blɑːk] v 拦网

hurdle [ˈhɜːrdl] n 跳栏
shoot [ʃuːt]
v 【足】射(门);【篮】投(篮)
screwball [ˈskruːbɔːl] n 螺旋球
sinker [ˈsɪŋkər] n 伸卡球
fake move phr 假动作
touch net phr 触网
grand slam
phr 【棒】满垒有人时的全垒打

比赛中的术语

strike [straɪk] n 【保】全倒

turnover [ˈtɜːrnoʊvər]
n 【篮】易手;失球
foul [faʊl] n v (比赛中)犯规
gutter ball phr 落沟球
home run phr 全垒打
foot fault phr
【网】【排】踩线越线犯规
bank shot phr 擦板
free throw phr 罚球
free kick phr 【足】任意球

Unit 2 球来就打

 用英语聊天，原来这么简单 / 老外每天说的英语，其实就是这几句。

父亲：跑步前记得绑好鞋带。 儿子：好的，爸爸。

Situation 1
开始运动前，记得先做这些事

Get the ball rolling. We will come help you.
开始吧，我们会帮助你的。

Make sure you properly warm up before you start your training.
开始训练前要确认做好热身运动。

Mom always **reminds** me **to** wear my protective gear before I go roller-blading.
妈妈总会提醒我在溜直排轮滑前要先穿戴好我的防护装备。

We have to rent bowling shoes to play in bowling alleys.
去保龄球馆打球时需要租保龄球鞋。

protective [prəˈtektɪv] a 保护的；防护的   rent [rent] v 租用

bowling alley phr 【美】保龄球馆

Grammar-1
"get the ball rolling"，有"开始进行……"的意思。

Grammar-2
此句中的"remind sb. to V..."有"提醒某人做某事"的意思。

Situation 2
也别忘了先搞懂游戏规则

Ping-pong is also called table tennis. We must use our paddles to hit the ball toward our opponent.
乒乓球也称为桌球，我们必须要使用球拍将球击打给对手。

I don't know how to **keep score** in bowling.
我不知道如何记录保龄球的分数。

Grammar-3
"keep score"有"记分"的意思，与其相同用法的词汇为"record（记录）"。

Grammar-4
"while" 在此的意思为"然而",其用来指明两种相反或不同的状况,有强调语气的功能。

Badminton, tennis, and squash are played with a racket and a ball, while in archery we use a bow and arrows.
羽毛球、网球和壁球是用球拍和球来打的;然而射箭则是使用弓和箭。

In relay races, we have to learn how to quickly pass the baton to our teammates.
在接力赛里,我们必须要学会快速地交棒给队友。

Sailing and rowing are water sports.
游艇比赛和划船都是水上运动。

Grammar-5
"most" 有两种用法,当 "most of + N" 时意为 "某群体中的大部分";"most + 复数名词" 则为 "大部分的……"。

Most sports are played in teams, but darts are played by only one player.
大部分的运动是以团队为主,但是标枪运动是由一名选手进行的。

ping-pong ['pɪŋ pɔːŋ] n 乒乓球;桌球

paddle ['pædl] n (桌球的)球拍

badminton ['bædmɪntən] n 羽毛球

squash [skwɑːʃ] n 壁球   archery ['ɑːrtʃəri] n 箭术;射箭运动

relay race phr 接力赛   baton [bəˈtɑːn] n 短棒

teammate ['tiːmmeɪt] n 队友   sailing ['seɪlɪŋ] n 航海;游艇比赛

rowing ['rəʊɪŋ] n 划船   dart [dɑːrt] n 标枪

Situation 3
到了运动场,你还可以说

Our old gymnasium received new equipment, such as running and cycling machines.
我们老旧的体育馆有新的装备,像是跑步机和单车等。

gymnasium [dʒɪmˈneɪzɪəm] n 体育馆

equipment [ɪˈkwɪpmənt] n 装备;设备

Grammar-6
"such as" 有 "比如;像是……" 的意思,在此也可以用 "like(像;如)" 来替换。

Situation 4
运动上的优秀表现就用这几句

That basketball player dunked the ball handsomely and won thunderous applause.
那位球员帅气的灌篮获得雷鸣般的掌声。

She made a perfect jump shot and won points for her team.
她完美的跳投为她的队伍得分了。

Grammar-7
"perfect" 当形容词时,有 "完美的;无缺的" 之意,其用法相当于 "flawless(无瑕疵的)"。

handsomely ['hænsəmli] ad 漂亮地

thunderous applause phr 雷鸣般的掌声　　jump shot phr 【篮】跳跃投篮

point [pɔɪnt] n 分数；（比赛等的）得分

 老外不会教你的小秘密

★ 篮球里，主客队每次上场都是 5 名球员，每个球员都会有自己要坚守的位置，而这样的问答句要如何表达呢？如："*A: What position do you play?*（你打什么位置呢？）*B: I'm the power forward.*（我是大前锋。）"在 B 的答句里，我们也可以用 "*play*" 来取代 "*be*" 的用法。当然，我们还有递补球员，也就是 "*I'm the Sixth Man.*（我是第六人。）" 的句子；那么候补球员呢？有没有注意到，候补球员是坐在板凳上呢？对了，我们就可以运用 "*I'm a bench player.*（我是候补球员。）" 来表示。

★ 有没有在篮球场上看过 1 对 1、3 对 3 的打球方式？这个时候，我们可以用 "*Do you want to play 1 on 1?*（你要不要单挑呢？）" 或是 "*Do you want to go 1 on 1?*（你要不要单挑呢？）" 的句子来邀约他人。而若要表达以多少分赢或输时，如："*The team won the game 97 to 76.*（这球队以 97 比 76 赢得了这场比赛。）"；相反地，输球时则将 "*won*（获胜）" 改为 "*lost*（输掉；失败）" 即可。

 不怕你学不会

1. Get the _____ rolling , and we will come help you.
2. I don't know how to _____ score in badminton.
3. Our old gymnasium received new equipment, such as running and cycling machines.
   = Our old gymnasium received new equipment, _____ running and cycling machines.

答案：1. ball　2. keep　3. like

Unit 3 地上跑 & 水里游
Land or water

原来老外这样记单词 老外从小到大学习单词的方法，就是看到什么就学什么！

swimming pool
phr 游泳池

lane rope
phr 水道绳

swim cap
phr 泳帽

goggles [ˈgɑːglz]
n 蛙镜

swimming wear
phr 泳衣

其他衍生单词：

swim [swɪm] v 游泳
breaststroke [ˈbreststrəʊk] n 蛙式
backstroke [ˈbækstrəʊk] n 仰式

dog paddle n 狗刨式游泳
butterfly stroke phr 蝶式
medley [ˈmedli] n 混合式

Unit 3 地上跑 & 水里游

 老外最常用的单词 连这些单词都不会，你还敢说你学过英语吗？

水上运动 ★★★

windsurf ['wɪndsɜːrf] n 风帆

surf [sɜːrf] v 冲浪
canoe [kəˈnuː] n 独木舟 v 划独木舟
dive [daɪv] v 跳水；潜水
water skiing phr 滑水
scuba-diving phr 水肺潜水
synchronized swimming
phr 水上芭蕾
kite surfing phr 风筝冲浪

Chapter 4 哥哥姐姐动起来

做这些练身体 ★★★

javelin throwing phr 掷标枪

discus [ˈdɪskəs] n 铁饼
marathon [ˈmærəθɑːn] n 马拉松
sprint [sprɪnt] n 短距离赛跑
weight lifting phr 举重
pole vault phr 撑竿跳
push-up [pʊʃ ʌp] n 【美】俯卧撑
sit-up [ˈsɪt ʌp] n 【体】仰卧起坐
yoga [ˈjəʊɡə] n 瑜伽

让人痴迷的运动 ★★★

gymnastics [dʒɪmˈnæstɪks]
n 体操；体育

fencing [ˈfensɪŋ] n 剑术
bullfight [ˈbʊlfaɪt] n 斗牛
karate [kəˈrɑːti] n 空手道
judo [ˈdʒuːdəʊ] n 【日】柔道
bodybuilding [ˈbɑːdibɪldɪŋ]
n 健身法（举重/柔软操等活动）
bungee jumping phr 高空弹跳
sport stacking phr 竞技叠杯
rock climbing phr 攀岩运动

073

用英语聊天，原来这么简单 / 老外每天说的英语，其实就是这几句。

教练：试着控制呼吸。吐气、吸气……

Situation 1
喜欢运动吗？

- I like to pass, shoot and dribble the ball, so ❶ I like to play basketball.
  我喜欢传球、投球和运球，所以我喜欢打篮球。

  My family prefers going mountain climbing to biking this weekend.
  我的家人这个周末想去爬山胜过去骑自行车。

  Edward loves to go jogging before playing a game of chess.
  爱德华喜爱在下棋比赛前先慢跑。

  pass [pæs] v. （球类运动中）传递　　dribble ['drɪbl] v.【体】运球

  go jogging phr 慢跑 ≈ go running phr 跑步　　chess [tʃes] n. 国际象棋

Grammar-1
"so"意思为"因此"，和其同义的词汇有"therefore（因此；所以）"、"thus（从而；因此）"及"thence（因此；由此）"，但注意"so"为连词，"therefore""thus""thence"为副词。

Situation 2
和朋友讨论运动习惯

- What's your workout routine?
  你平常的训练内容是什么？

  Becky drives to the stable ❷ to go horseback riding twice a week.
  贝基一星期两次开车到马厩骑马。

  Every morning I go jogging to build my vital capacity.
  我每天早上慢跑来训练我的肺活量。

Grammar-2
"stable"当形容词时，有"稳定的"的意思；但在此句中，则为名词，意思为"马厩"。

Unit 3 地上跑 & 水里游

To stay healthy, Chris does aerobics four times a week.
为了保持健康，克里斯一星期做 4 次有氧运动。

twice [twaɪs] ad 两次；两回　　aerobics [eˈroʊbɪks] n 有氧运动

Situation 3
不擅长运动

I can't run for too long.
我不能跑太久。

I'm a total landlubber; I know nothing about ❸ swimming.
我是个不折不扣的旱鸭子；我对游泳一窍不通。

I am afraid of water; I can't stand staying in water for an hour.
我很怕水，而且我无法忍受在水中待一个小时。

The man was in a bath of sweat ❹ after running for an hour.
那个男人跑步一小时后便汗如雨下。

I cannot tell the difference between ❺ Chinese martial arts and Japanese ones.
我无法分辨中国武术和日本武术之间的不同。

landlubber [ˈlændlʌbər] n 旱鸭子；不懂航海之人

martial art phr 武术

Grammar-3
"know nothing about" 有"一窍不通"的意思，和其相同的短语为"lack the slightest knowledge of"。

Grammar-4
"in a bath of sweat" 有"汗如雨下"的意思，和其相同的短语为"sweat profusely"。

Grammar-5
"tell the difference between" 为"区分；区别"的意思。

Situation 4
不小心受伤了

Contact sports such as boxing and judo are dangerous.
像拳击和柔道这类触身运动是很危险的。

My arms are all sore after boxing.
打完拳击后我胳膊酸痛。

The lifeguard gave the drowning girl an artificial respiration ❻.
救生员帮溺水的女生进行人工呼吸。

I didn't wear suitable ❼ skates, so I got hurt while skating.
因为我没穿合脚的溜冰鞋，所以在溜冰时受伤了。

It hurt very much when I crushed into another runner on the field.
我在跑道上撞到另一个跑者，很痛。

Rita sprained her ankle ❽ in a track and field competition.
丽塔在田径比赛时扭伤了脚踝。

Grammar-6
"give sb. an artificial respiration" 为固定短语，解释为"对某人进行人工呼吸"。

Grammar-7
"suitable" 为形容词，意思为"适当的"，其用法相当于"proper（恰当的；适合的）"和"fitting（合适的；相称的）"等词汇。

Grammar-8
"sprain one's ankle" 为固定短语，有"扭伤脚踝"的意思。

Chapter 4 哥哥姐姐动起来

075

boxing [ˈbɑːksɪŋ] n 拳击；拳术　　dangerous [ˈdeɪndʒərəs] a 危险的

lifeguard [ˈlaɪfɡɑːrd] n 救生员　　artificial respiration phr 人工呼吸

get hurt phr 受伤　　skating v 【体】滑冰（运动）

track and field phr 【体】田径运动

老外不会教你的小秘密

★ 你是游泳好手吗？你会几种游泳方式呢？来学学以下的对话：
- A: *What type of strokes do you know?* 你会游什么式呢？
- B: *I'm better at freestyle than any other strokes.* 我自由式游得比其他式好。

不怕你学不会

1. You should wear proper shoes when you go jogging.
   = You should wear _____ shoes when you go jogging.

2. Can you tell the difference _____ windsurfing and kite surfing?

3. My arms and legs are still sore now, so I may not go to the gym today.
   = My arms and legs are still sore now; _____ I may not go to the gym today.

答案：1. suitable　2. between　3. therefore / hence / thus

Unit 4 全民疯奥运 Olympics

 原来老外这样记单词 / 老外从小到大学习单词的方法，就是看到什么就学什么！

national flag phr 国旗

torch [tɔːrʃ] n 火炬；火把

audience [ˈɔːdɪəns] n 观众

podium [ˈpəʊdɪəm] n 颁奖台

field [fiːld] n 运动场

其他衍生单词：

- **glory** [ˈɡlɔːri] n 光荣，荣誉
- **Olympics** [ɒˈlɪmpɪks] n 奥林匹克运动会
- **decathlon** [dɪˈkæθlɒn] n 十项运动
- **triathlon** [traɪˈæθlən] n 【体】铁人三项（游泳／单车／赛跑）
- **gold medal** phr 金牌
- **world cup** phr 世界杯

老外最常用的单词 / 连这些单词都不会，你还敢说你学过英语吗？

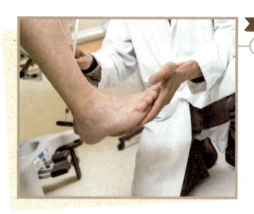

运动时还有这些好朋友

Achilles' heel `phr` 致命弱点

sponsor [ˈspɑːnsər] `n` 赞助商
athletics [æθˈletɪks]
`n` 体育运动；体育（课）
stadium [ˈsteɪdɪəm] `n` 体育场
sport lottery `phr` 运动彩券
physical education (= P.E.)
`phr` 体育课
sun visor `phr` 中空的遮阳帽

运动也要比行头

roller skate `phr` 轮式溜冰鞋

roller-blades [ˈrəʊlər bleɪdz]
`n` 直排轮式溜冰鞋
spike [spaɪk] `n`【俚】钉鞋
sneaker [ˈsniːkər] `n`【口】运动鞋
cleat [kliːt] `n` 鞋底上的防滑钉
pole [pəʊl] `n` 柱；竿
earphone [ˈɪrˌfəʊn] `n` 耳机
glove [glʌv] `n` 手套

随时注意身体状态

tennis elbow `phr` 网球肘

endorphin [enˈdɔːrfɪn] `n` 脑内啡
muscular [ˈmʌskjələr]
`a` 肌肉的；健壮的
vigorous [ˈvɪgərəs] `a` 精力充沛的
flexibility [ˌfleksəˈbɪləti]
`n` 弹性；灵活性
flexible [ˈfleksəbl] `a` 有弹性的；灵活的
body function `phr` 身体机能
explosive force `phr` 爆发力

Unit 4 全民疯奥运

 用英语聊天，原来这么简单 / 老外每天说的英语，其实就是这几句。

吉娜：我今天准备跑10千米。　肖恩：不错啊！

Chapter 4 哥哥姐姐动起来

Situation 1
和朋友们讨论奥运会！

- I can't wait for the Olympics to come.
  我快等不及奥运会了。

  Ice figure skating, speed skating and skiing are winter sports.
  花式滑冰、速度滑冰和滑雪都是冬季运动。

  At the London Olympics, China won altogether 88 medals: 38 gold, 27 silver and 23 bronze medals.
  在伦敦奥运会上，中国总共赢得88枚奖牌，有38枚金牌、27枚银牌和23枚铜牌。

  Taekwondo is a popular sport in China.
  跆拳道在中国是一项很流行的运动。

  Many nations take part in ❶ the Olympic Games, which are held quadrennially.
  很多国家参加了每4年举办一次的奥运会。

  It's my pleasure to serve as ❷ a torch carrier for this year's Olympic Games.
  能担任今年奥运的圣火传递者是我的荣幸。

Grammar-1
"take part in" 有"参加、参与"的意思，与其相同的词汇和短语有 "join（参加）" "participate in（参加）"。

Grammar-2
"serve as" 为固定短语，有"担任"的意思。

- ice figure skating **phr** 花式滑冰
- speed skating **phr** 速度滑冰
- ski [skiː] **v** 滑雪
- altogether [ˌɔːltəˈɡeðər] **ad** 全部；合计

079

medal ['medl] n 奖章；勋章　　bronze [brɑːnz] n 青铜 a 青铜色的

nation ['neɪʃn] n 国家　　quadrennially [kwɒ'drenɪrli] ad 4 年一次的

pleasure ['pleʒər] n 愉快；乐事

Situation 2
破纪录

This new player just **broke the record** ❸ for the 100-meter dash.
这名新选手刚刚破了 100 米短跑的纪录。

> **Grammar-3**
> "break the record" 有 "打破纪录" 的意思，和其相同的短语有 "make the new record"，字面上的意思为 "刷新纪录"，也引申为 "打破纪录"。

Situation 3
边运动边减肥

I sweat a lot when I go cycling.
我骑自行车时流了很多汗。

Oats are one of the best fat-burning foods.
燕麦是最好的瘦身食物之一。

You should have a balanced diet and do exercise.
你应该摄取均衡的饮食和运动。

If you want to lose weight, then go on this exercise menu.
如果你想减肥，请遵守这个运动菜单。

oat [əʊt] n 燕麦　　fat-burning food phr 燃脂食物；瘦身食品

Situation 4
边运动边练肌肉

You should do some exercise if you want to get stronger.
你想变强壮的话就该做点运动。

How much weight can you lift?
你可以举多重？

> **Grammar-4**
> "keep in shape" 有 "维持身材" 的意思。

Many celebrities employ fitness instructors to help them **keep in shape** ❹.
许多名人聘请健身教练来帮助他们维持身材。

Weight lifting is a great way to relieve stress.
举重是疏解压力的好方法。

celebrity [sə'lebrəti] n 名人；名流

Situation 5
运动有进步

> **Grammar-5**
> "amateur" 当形容词时，有 "业余的" 之意，其用法相当于 "nonprofessional（非专业的）" 一词。

Originally, he was just an **amateur** ❺ player; he is now a successful professional player.
原本他只是一个业余选手，现在他是一位成功的专业选手。

You look more muscular than before.
你现在看起来比以前更强壮了。

I found my body is getting refined.
我发现我的身体变壮实了。

I felt refreshed after I went to the aerobics class.
我上完有氧课觉得精神变好了。

successful [sək'sesfl] **a** 成功的；胜利的

professional [prə'feʃnəl] **n** 职业选手 **a** 职业（上）的

 老外不会教你的小秘密

★ 在英语中，要表示"打"球的动词都是"*play*"，但是打篮球也可以用"*shoot hoops*"来表达。想想看，打篮球有"*hoop*"为"篮筐"的意思，而"*shoot*"就是"投球"的意思。因此，下次邀人打篮球时，不妨试试"*Do you want to shoot some hoops with me?*（你要不要和我一起去投几球呢？）"的句子！

★ 在比赛里，我们都会以"*Go! Go! Go!*（加油！加油！加油！）"的英语句子来表达。但是要表明自己想要支持的队伍时，则是用"*root for*"！也就是"*I'm going to root for China.*（我要给中国队加油。）"

 不怕你学不会

1. John has taken part in marathon competition for four years. Of course he won't miss it this year.

   = John has _____ marathon competition for four years. Of course he won't miss this year.

2. He was just an amateur player, but now he becomes a successful professional player.

   = He was just a _____ player, but now he becomes a successful professional player.

3. You should do some exercise if you want to _____ in shape.

答案：1. joined / participated in 2. nonprofessional 3. keep

看看老外怎么学 / 一起来测测你的运动知识够不够吧！

_____ 1. What can you see on the tennis games?

    a. tee b. volley c. traveling d. bunt

_____ 2. Who is the God of basketball?

    a. Chris Davis   b. Eldrick "Tiger" Woods

    c. Martina Hingis   d. Michael Jordan

_____ 3. Which sport can't play on land?

    a. golf b. tennis c. snorkeling d. shot-put

_____ 4. What kind of sport can you play in the sky?

    a. skydiving   b. badminton

    c. baseball   d. bungee jumping

_____ 5. Which belongs to Decathlon?

    a. pump iron b. discus c. windsurfing d. soccer

答案：1.b 2.d 3.c 4.a 5.b

I wonder the answer is … !

Chapter 5 健康很重要

The most important thing

近年来,健康及保健成为国人最关心的问题;如何活得健康?吃得健康?快来一起学习与健康相关的英语知识吧!

Unit 1	Unit 2	Unit 3	Unit 4
到处都在痛	心痛的感觉	用药须注意	关注健康

Unit 1 到处都在痛
Get hurt

原来老外这样记单词 老外从小到大学习单词的方法，就是看到什么就学什么！

melancholy [ˈmelənkɑːli]
n 忧郁

edema [ɪˈdiːmə]
n 【医】浮肿；水肿

cavity [ˈkævəti]
n （牙齿的）蛀洞

wrinkle [ˈrɪŋkl]
n 皱纹

anorexia [ˌænəˈreksɪə]
n 【医】厌食症

其他衍生单词：

periodontal disease phr 牙周病
insomnia [ɪnˈsɑːmnɪə] n 失眠
bulimia [buˈlɪmɪə] n 贪食症

amnesia [æmˈniːʒə] n 【医】失忆症
insanity [ɪnˈsænəti] n 精神错乱
mental deficiency phr 智力缺陷

Unit 1 到处都在痛

老外最常用的单词
连这些单词都不会，你还敢说你学过英语吗？

这些地方有问题 ★★★

osteoporosis [ˌɑːstɪəʊpəˈrəʊsɪs]
n 【医】骨质疏松

nyctalopia [ˌnɪktəˈləʊpɪr] n
【医】夜盲（症）
glaucoma [ɡlaʊˈkəʊmə] n 【医】青光眼
cerebral contusion phr 脑挫伤
retinal detachment phr
【医】视网膜剥离
muscular atrophy phr 肌肉萎缩症
heat stroke phr 【医】中暑

Chapter **5** 健康好重要

外面痛里面也痛 ★★

bloated [ˈbləʊtɪd] a 胀气的

symptom [ˈsɪmptəm] n 症状；征兆
cramp [kræmp] n （腹部）绞痛
paralysis [pəˈræləsɪs] n 麻痹；瘫痪
morning sickness phr 孕妇晨吐
brain injury phr 脑部损伤
heart attack phr 心脏病发作
toothache [ˈtuːθeɪk] n 牙痛
stomachache [ˈstʌməkˌek] n 胃痛

要小心的问题 ★★★

smallpox [ˈsmɔːlpɑːks] n 【医】天花

epidemic [ˌepɪˈdemɪk]
n 流行病 a 传染的
atavism [ˈætəˌvɪzəm] n 【生】隔代遗传
favism [ˈfɑːvɪzm] n 蚕豆症
food poisoning phr 食物中毒
avian influenza (= bird flu)
phr 禽流感
myocardial infraction
phr 【医】心肌梗死

用英语聊天，原来这么简单 / 老外每天说的英语，其实就是这几句。

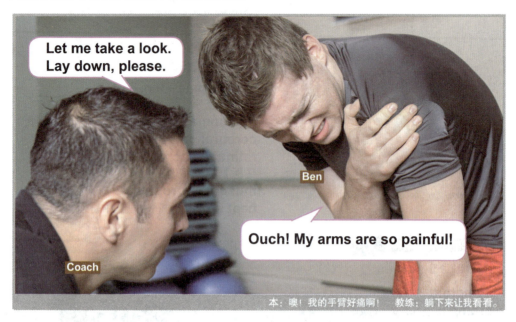

本：噢！我的手臂好痛啊！　教练：躺下来让我看看。

Situation 1
有人受伤

I only got a bruise, but my friend got a deep cut.
我只是瘀青而已，但是我朋友的伤口却很深。

I felt a piercing pain in my left arm after getting a bee sting.
我的左手臂被蜜蜂蜇完后感到刺痛。

bruise [bru:z] n 伤痕；青肿　　deep [di:p] a 深的

cut [kʌt] n 伤口；刻痕　　piercing ['pɪrsɪŋ] a 锐利的

sting [stɪŋ] n 蜇；叮

Situation 2
身体不舒服

Joe felt unwell in the morning; he complained of ❶ an earache.
乔在早上的时候感到不适，他抱怨耳朵痛。

You look terrible. Get some rest!
你的脸色很可怕，休息一下吧！

I have had a sore throat ❷ for two days.
我喉咙已经痛了两天了。

My forehead is really hot. I think I caught a cold.
我额头很烫，我想我感冒了。

> Grammar-1
> "complain" 当动词时，意思为"抱怨"，其后面可以接上的介词有"of""to""about"，或用"that 从句"来衔接。

> Grammar-2
> "have a sore throat" 的意思为"喉咙痛"，此为固定短语。

Unit 1 到处都在痛

Grammar-3
用来表示"(哪一个部位)不舒服",可以用"have pain in + 部位"的句型来表达。

The child has pain in the abdomen ❸ ; he might have a stomachache.
这个孩子腹部疼痛,他可能是胃痛。

unwell [ʌnˈwel] a 不舒服的　　earache [ˈɪreɪk] n 耳朵痛

sore [sɔːr] a 疼痛发炎的　　throat [θrəʊt] n 喉咙

abdomen [ˈæbdəmen] n 腹部

Grammar-4
"be kept + adj."有"被维持着……的状态"的意思。

Situation 3
生病了

The child with an infectious disease was kept isolated ❹.
这个带有感染疾病的孩子被隔离了。

I'm running a high temperature. Could I take a day off?
我体温变高了,我可以请假一天吗?

Roger, who had a high level of sugar in his diet since his childhood, is now battling diabetes.
罗杰从儿童期时饮食上就摄取高糖分,现在正在和糖尿病做斗争。

infectious [ɪnˈfekʃəs] a 感染的;传染性的 同 contagious a 接触传染性的

disease [dɪˈziːz] n 疾病　　diet [ˈdaɪət] n 饮食;食物

battle [ˈbætl] v 为……而搏斗;为……而奋战

diabetes [ˌdaɪəˈbiːtiːz] n 糖尿病

Situation 4
心理上有些不对劲

I'm suffering from insomnia. I haven't slept well for a week.
我最近失眠,我已经一个星期没睡好了。

His mental status is not stable. That is to say ❺, he may be normal this moment but become abnormal the next moment.
他的精神状况不稳定。也就是说,他可能这一刻是正常的,但下一刻就变得不正常了。

Grammar-5
"That is to say..."的意思为"也就是说……",和其相同的短语为"in other words..."。

Her personality changed dramatically after she survived a disaster ❻.
她的性格在经历过一场灾难后产生了剧变。

Grammar-6
"survive a disaster"的意思为"从灾难中幸免"。

Grammar-7
"A is as important as B"的意思为"A 和 B 一样重要",其中,A 和 B 要放入相同词性的词汇。

Mental health is as important as ❼ physical health.
心理健康和生理健康一样重要。

mental [ˈmentl] a 精神的;心理的

stable [ˈsteɪbl] a 稳定的 反 unstable a 不稳定的

normal ['nɔːrml] a 正常的   abnormal [æb'nɔːrml] a 反常的

personality [ˌpɜːrsə'næləti] n 人格

dramatically [drə'mætɪkli] ad 戏剧性地   physical ['fɪzɪkl] a 身体的

Situation 5
紧急状况发生时

One of the victims was rushed to the ER at the closest hospital, and was immediately put in the ICU.
其中一个受难者被紧急送到最近医院的急诊室且立刻被送入了加护病房。

When the ambulance arrived at the site of the accident, the paramedics saw that a volunteer had already given first aid care to the victims.
当救护车抵达车祸现场时，护理人员看到一位志愿者已经在急救受难者了。

ER abbr 急诊室 (=Emergency Room)

immediately [ɪ'miːdiətli] ad 直接地；马上 同 instantly ['ɪnstəntli] ad 立即；马上

ICU abbr 加护病房 (=Intensive Care Unit)

paramedic [ˌpærə'medɪk] n 护理人员；医务辅助人员   first aid phr 急救

victim ['vɪktɪm] n 遇难者；受害者

 老外不会教你的小秘密

★ 我们都知道摄入过多的糖分不只会变胖，有时候甚至会引起糖尿病，要表达减少糖分的摄取量该怎么说呢？我们可以用"*cut down on* 减少（食物等的）摄取"的短语，例如："*You should cut down on high-sugar foods for the sake of your health.*（为了你的健康，你应该减少高糖分食物的摄取。）"。当然，我们可以将"*high-sugar*（高糖分）"用下列词汇来替换：
  ✦ *high-calorie*（高热量）
  ✦ *high-salt*（高盐分）

★ 一个人如果因为工作或课业压力大而无法睡着时，除了可以用"*I suffered from insomnia last night.*（我昨晚失眠了。）"的句子来表达，也可以用"*I didn't sleep a wink last night.*（我昨晚睡得不好。）"的句子，此句子的意思为"连眼睛都没眨"，等同于"一直睁着眼睛"！

Unit 2 心痛的感觉
See the doctor

原来老外这样记单词 / 老外从小到大学习单词的方法，就是看到什么就学什么！

consulting room
phr 【医】诊疗室

patient ['peɪʃnt]
n 病人

pediatrics [ˌpiːdɪˈætrɪks]
n 儿科

bandage [ˈbændɪdʒ]
n 绷带 v 用绷带包扎

stethoscope [ˈsteθəskəʊp]
n 【医】听诊器

其他衍生单词：

clinic [ˈklɪnɪk] n 诊所　　　**physician** [fɪˈzɪʃn] n 内科医生　　　**outpatient medicine** phr 门诊医疗

transfer [trænsˈfɜːr] v 转诊　　　**auscultation** [ˌɔːskəlˈteɪʃn] n 听诊法　　　**internal medicine** phr 内科

老外最常用的单词 / 连这些单词都不会,你还敢说你学过英语吗?

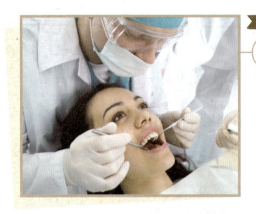

去医院就是为了看他们

orthodontist [ˌɔːrθəˈdɑːntɪst]
n 牙齿矫正医生

acupuncturist [ˈækjʊpʌŋktʃərɪst]
n 针灸医生
psychiatrist [saɪˈkaɪətrɪst] **n** 精神科医生
dermatologist [ˌdɜːrməˈtɑːlədʒɪst]
n 皮肤科医生
pharmacist [ˈfɑːrməsɪst] **n** 药剂师
obstetrician [ˌɑːbstəˈtrɪʃn] **n** 产科医生
anesthetist [əˈnesθɪtɪst] **n** 麻醉师

医生们的重要帮手

chiropractor
[ˈkaɪərəʊpræktər] **n** 脊椎按摩师

nurse [nɜːrs] **n** 护士 **v** 看护;照料
eugenicist [juːˈdʒiːnɪst] **n** 优生学家
dietician [ˌdaɪəˈtɪʃn] **n** 营养师
wheelchair [ˈwiːltʃer] **n** 轮椅
blood transfusion **phr** 输血
intravenous drip
phr 打点滴(静脉注射)

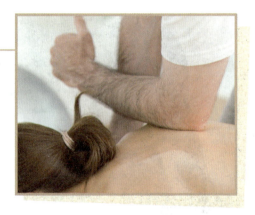

检查身体时会看到的单词

MRI (= magnetic resonance image) **phr** 【医】核磁共振摄影

urinalysis [ˌjʊrəˈnæləsɪs] **n** 验尿
BMI (= Body Mass Index)
phr 体重指数
physical examination
phr 身体检查;体检
CT scan **phr** 电脑断层扫描
weight scale **phr** 体重计
medical history **phr** 病史

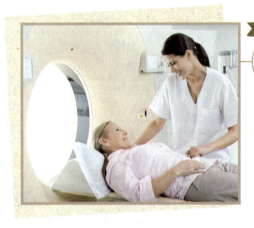

用英语聊天，原来这么简单 / 老外每天说的英语，其实就是这几句。

护士：早安！你准备好要进行今天的手术了吗？ 萨莉：是的。虽然还有点紧张，不过我想还行。

Situation 1
要进行手术

My grandmother will undergo ❶ a surgery on Thursday.
我的祖母将在星期四接受外科手术。

The surgeon is going to operate on ❷ my grandfather.
外科医生将要为我的祖父开刀。

The dentist performed a root canal treatment ❸ on one of my front teeth.
牙医在我其中一颗门牙上做了根管治疗。

Kevin is going to ❹ have a laser surgery to cure his myopia.
凯文将要接受激光手术来治疗他的近视。

The doctors are discussing whether to perform intubation on that critical patient or not ❺.
医生们正在讨论是否要对那位重症病患进行插管。

Grammar-1
"undergo" 当动词时，有"接受（治疗或检查等）"的意思，可以用"go through（经历；遭受）"来替换。

Grammar-2
"operate on / for" 其意思为"为……开刀"，后面通常接上所要开刀的对象。

Grammar-3
"a root canal treatment" 意思为"（牙齿的）根管治疗"。

Grammar-4
"be going to" 有"将要；将会"的意思，此为将来时句型。

Grammar-5
"whether or not" 的意思为"是否"，用以引导出两种非此即彼的可能性。

surgery ['sɜːrdʒəri] n （外科）手术 ⇔ operation [ˌɑːpə'reɪʃn] n 【医】手术

surgeon ['sɜːrdʒən] n 外科医生　　dentist ['dentɪst] n 牙医

perform [pər'fɔːrm] v 执行；完成；做　　front [frʌnt] a 前面的

laser ['leɪzər] n 激光

myopia [maɪˈəʊpɪə] n 【医】近视 反 hyperopia [ˌhaɪpəˈrəʊpɪə] n 【医】远视

discuss [dɪˈskʌs] v 讨论；商谈   critical [ˈkrɪtɪkl] a 危急的

Situation 2 检查身体

The radiologist took an X-ray of the outpatient's legs.
放射科医生用X光来照射病患的双腿。

To get a better diagnosis, we might have to take a blood sample ❻.
为了有更完整的诊断，我们必须要采取血液样本。

Grammar-6
"take a blood sample" 有 "采取血液样本" 的意思。

My father checks his blood pressure every day because he has high blood pressure.
我父亲每天检测他的血压，因为他有高血压。

Grammar-7
"量体温" 的表达方式为 "take temperature"。

The student nurse uses ear thermometer to take the patients' temperature ❼.
实习护士拿体温枪替病患量体温。

The results of the tests would be back in a month. Please be patient.
检查结果会在一个月内出来。请保持耐心。

radiologist [ˌreɪdɪˈɑːlədʒɪst] n 放射科医生

X-ray [ˈeks reɪ] n 【口】X光检查

outpatient [ˈaʊtpeɪʃnt] n 门诊病人

diagnosis [ˌdaɪəgˈnəʊsɪs] n 诊断

have to phr 必须 同 be obliged to phr 感激；被迫

blood pressure phr 血压   high blood pressure phr 高血压

thermometer [θərˈmɑːmɪtər] n 温度计

Situation 3 听懂医生的说法

What seems to be the problem and how long?
你哪里不舒服？持续多久了？

Please come back for a check-up after three days.
请在3天后复诊。

The psychologist declared that the patient has ADD.
心理学家说这位病患有注意力集中障碍。

Unit 2 心痛的感觉

Grammar-8
"be diagnosed with"
即"被诊断出患有某疾病"的意思。

This patient was diagnosed with ❽ acute ❾ leukemia, so a bone marrow transplantation is desperately needed.
这名病患被诊断出急性白血病,因此急需骨髓移植。

psychologist [saɪˈkɑːlədʒɪst] n 心理学家

declare [dɪˈkler] v 宣布;宣告

ADD abbr 注意力集中障碍(=Attention Deficit Disorder)

Grammar-8
"acute"为形容词,有"急性的"之意,其反义词为"chronic(慢性的)"。

leukemia [luːˈkiːmɪə] n 【医】白血病

bone marrow transplantation phr 骨髓移植

desperately [ˈdespərətli] ad 【口】极度地

Situation 4
小朋友最爱玩的医生游戏

The two little children had fun ❿ playing doctor by pretending to change bandages on their dog's leg.

Grammar-10
"have fun"的意思为"玩得开心",若后面接上动词,需以 Ving 的形式来呈现。

这两个小孩开心地玩着扮演医生的游戏来帮他们的小狗更换脚上的纱布。

pretend [prɪˈtend] v 假扮;假装

老外不会教你的小秘密

★ 住院时,不管是医生还是护士在查房时都会询问病患的状况,如果要表达还是很不舒服除了"*I'm not feeling well.*(我不舒服。)"或"*I feel ill.*(我不舒服。)"之外,还有"*I've been better.*(我好多了。)"。

不怕你学不会

1. My mother will undergo a surgery next Wednesday. I already took a day off from my school to keep accompany with her.

   = My mother will _____ a surgery next Wednesday. I already took a day off from my school to keep accompany with her.

2. She broke down when hearing that she was diagnosed _____ leukemia.

答案:1. go through 2. with

Unit 3 用药须注意
Medicine & Prescription

原来老外这样记单词 老外从小到大学习单词的方法，就是看到什么就学什么！

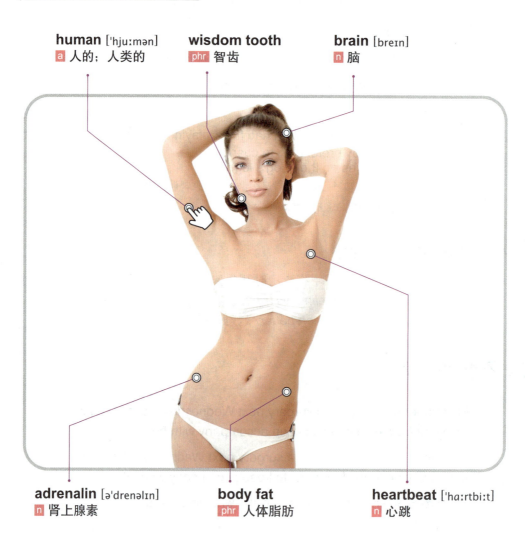

human [ˈhjuːmən]
a 人的；人类的

wisdom tooth
phr 智齿

brain [breɪn]
n 脑

adrenalin [əˈdrenəlɪn]
n 肾上腺素

body fat
phr 人体脂肪

heartbeat [ˈhɑːrtbiːt]
n 心跳

其他衍生单词：

hippocampus [ˌhɪpəˈkæmpəs] n （脑部结构）海马体
lymphatic system phr 【医】淋巴系统
calcium [ˈkælsɪəm] n 【化】钙

cholesterol [kəˈlestərɔːl] n 胆固醇
aspirin [ˈæsprɪn] n 阿司匹林
breathe [briːð] v 呼吸

老外最常用的单词
连这些单词都不会,你还敢说你学过英语吗?

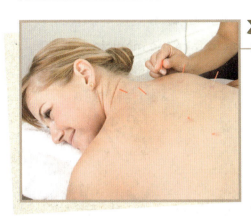

这些方法就不用怕

alternative therapy
phr 民间疗法
cure [kjʊr] v 治疗
remedy [ˈremədi] n v 治疗
genetics [dʒəˈnetɪks] n 遗传学
otolaryngology [ˌəʊtəʊlærɪŋˈgɑːlədʒi]
n 耳鼻喉科学
geriatrics [ˌdʒerɪˈætrɪk] n 老人医学
OT (= Occupational Therapy)
phr 职业治疗
diet regimen phr 饮食疗法

身上的小零件

canine [ˈkeɪnaɪn] n 犬齿 ad 犬齿的

vein [veɪn] n 静脉;血管
subconsciousness [ˌsʌbˈkɒnʃəsnɪs]
n 潜意识
respiratory [ˈrespərətɔːri] a 呼吸的
periodontal [ˌperɪəˈdɑːntl] a 牙周的
metabolism [məˈtæbəlɪzəm] n 新陈代谢
organ [ˈɔːrɡən] n 器官
blood sugar phr 血糖

治病的关键单词

vaccinate [ˈvæksɪneɪt] v 接种疫苗

antibiotic [ˌæntɪbaɪˈɑːtɪk]
n 【微】抗生素
antidepressant [ˌæntɪdɪˈpresnt]
n 抗忧郁剂
placebo [pləˈsiːbəʊ] n 安慰剂;宽心丸
ointment [ˈɔɪntmənt] n 药膏;软膏
aspirin [ˈæsprɪn] n 阿司匹林
coughing syrup phr 咳嗽糖浆
side effect phr 副作用
whooping cough phr 百日咳
eye drops phr 眼药水

用英语聊天，原来这么简单 / 老外每天说的英语，其实就是这几句。

格雷丝：该吃药了，老伴。 布莱恩：我知道。

Situation 1
你熟悉自己的身体

Our cerebellum is in charge of sense of the equilibrium.
我们的小脑掌管平衡感。

Some genes may mutate during^❶ cell division.
有些基因在细胞分裂的时候会产生突变。

Grammar-1
"during"为时间介词，用以表示"在特定的期间内"。

Our pupils become bigger when we enter dark rooms.
我们的瞳孔在进入黑暗的房间时会变大。

According to ^❷ the human biological clock, people have the lowest body temperature at 4:30 a.m. in the morning.
根据人类的生理钟，人的体温在凌晨 4 点半时最低。

Grammar-2
"According to..."的意思为"根据……"，和其相同的短语为"on the basis of（基于……）"。

A body fat monitor can indicate your basal metabolic rate.
体脂计可以显示你的基础代谢率。

cerebellum [ˌserəˈbeləm] n 小脑　　in charge of phr 管理；负责

equilibrium [ˌiːkwɪˈlɪbrɪəm] n 平衡；均衡

gene [dʒiːn] n 【生】基因；遗传因子

mutate [ˈmjuːteɪt] v 产生突变；变化

Unit 3 用药须注意

cell division **phr** 细胞分裂
biological clock **phr** 生理钟
basal metabolic rate **phr** 基础代谢率
pupil ['pjuːpl] **n** 瞳孔；学生
indicate ['ɪndɪkeɪt] **v** 指出；表明

Situation 2
打针

The general practitioner gave an injection and painkillers ❸ to my little sister after the jellyfish stung her.
这位医生在我妹妹被水母蜇之后，帮她打了一针并给了止痛剂。

Grammar-3
"painkiller"当名词时，有"止痛剂"的意思，也可以用"pain reliever"来替换。

The nurse asked if ❹ I was allergic to penicillin.
护士问我是否对青霉素过敏。

general practitioner **phr** 全科医生；普通医生
injection [ɪn'dʒekʃn] **n** 注射
jellyfish ['dʒelɪfɪʃ] **n** 水母
penicillin [ˌpenɪ'sɪlɪn] **n** 青霉素

Grammar-4
"if"当连词时，有"是否"的意思，其用法和"whether...(or not)"相同。

Situation 3
买药、吃药、处方笺

Do I need to take any medicine?
我需要吃药吗？

Be careful when ❺ using over-the-counter medicine; not all of them are safe.
使用非处方药品要小心，因为并非所有的药品都是安全的。

Grammar-5
"when"为从属连词，后面需要接上从句；或可以改为介词用法，但需省略主语，动词一律以 Ving 来呈现。

Stay in bed, take one of these pills after every meal and before bed, and then drink lots of ❻ water.
躺在床上，饭后和睡前服用一颗这个药丸并多喝水。

Grammar-6
"lots of"可用来修饰可数名词或不可数名词；亦可代换成"a lot of"或"much"来修饰后面的 water。

I have to take medicine three times a day.
我每天要吃 3 次药。

You'd better take some medicine as prescribed.
你最好按照处方笺吃药。

Grammar-7
"be sure to"有"记得"的意思，其用法和"remember to V（记住；牢记）"相同。

Be sure to ❼ follow my prescription to the letter.
记得要遵照我处方笺上所有的建议。

A large section of the population prefers traditional Chinese medicine to Western medicine.
大部分的人喜欢中药胜过西药。

Grammar-8
"lose weight"的意思为"减重",其反义短语为"gain weight",即为"增重"的意思。

Grammar-9
"misuse"可当动词或名词,其有"滥用;虐待"的意思;但当"滥用"之意时,其用法相当于"overuse(对……过度使用)"。

Many women take slimming drugs as a measure to lose weight ❽ quickly.
许多女性把服用减肥药当作一个快速减重的方法。

It's not appropriate to misuse ❾ tranquilizers.
滥用镇静剂是不恰当的。

over-the-counter [ˌəʊvəðə'kaʊntɚ] a. (药品等)非处方的

medicine ['medsn] n. 药;内服药

prescription [prɪ'skrɪpʃn] n. 处方笺

letter ['letɚ] n. 字母;文字   population [ˌpɑːpju'leɪʃn] n. 人口

traditional Chinese medicine phr 中医

Western medicine phr 西医;西药   slimming ['slɪmɪŋ] n. 减肥

drug [drʌg] n. 药品   appropriate [ə'prəʊprɪət] a. 适当的;恰当的

tranquilizer ['træŋkwəlaɪzɚ] n. 镇静剂

 老外不会教你的小秘密

★ 你有过敏的症状吗?我们可以使用短语"*be allergic to* + *N*"或"*have / has an allergy to* + *N*"的用法。如:"*Sharon is allergic to meat.*(莎伦对肉过敏。)"或"*Sharon has an allergy to meat.*(莎伦对肉过敏。)";两者的差别为"*allergy*(名词)"和"*allergic*(形容词)"词性上的差异。

不怕你学不会

1. I wouldn't let my children take painkillers when they are still little.
   = I wouldn't let my children take _____ when they are still little.

2. The best way to cure your sore throat is to drink a lot of water.
   = The best way to cure your sore throat is to drink _____ water.

答案:1. pain relievers   2. much / lots of

Unit 4 关注健康
Last but not least

原来老外这样记单词 / 老外从小到大学习单词的方法，就是看到什么就学什么！

capsule [ˈkæpsl]
n 胶囊

vitamin [ˈvaɪtəmɪn]
n 维生素

powder [ˈpaʊdər]
n 药粉

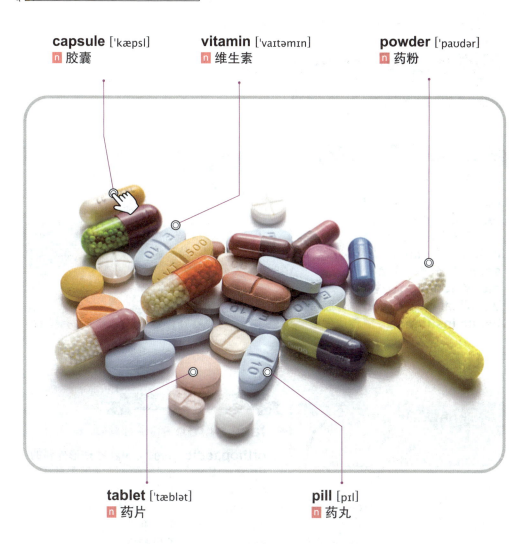

tablet [ˈtæblət]
n 药片

pill [pɪl]
n 药丸

其他衍生单词：

- **gallipot** [ˈgælɪˌpɒt] n 药罐
- **pharmacy** [ˈfɑːrməsi] n 药店
- **generic drug** phr 非专利药
- **dispenser bottle** phr 压式的罐子
- **agonist** n 兴奋剂
- **cough drop** phr 止咳药片

老外最常用的单词
连这些单词都不会,你还敢说你学过英语吗?

吃这些有益健康

ginseng [ˈdʒɪnseŋ] n 人参(制品)

nourishment [ˈnɜːrɪʃmənt] n 营养品
anthocyanin [ˌænθəˈsaɪənɪn] n 花青素
essence of chicken phr 鸡精
balanced diet phr 均衡膳食
cod liver oil phr 鱼肝油
bee propolis phr 蜂胶

关心身体外也要关心的事物

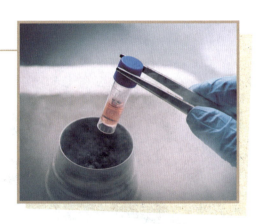

stem cell phr 干细胞

calorie [ˈkæləri] n 卡路里
rehabilitation [ˌriːəˌbɪlɪˈteɪʃn] n (病残人的)康复
nutrition [nuˈtrɪʃn] n 营养;营养学
safety [ˈseɪfti] n 安全
blood donation phr 捐血
umbilical cord blood phr 脐带血
health insurance phr 健康保险

让你改头换面的单词

face scrub phr 脸部磨砂

orthopaedic [ˌɔːrθəˈpiːdɪk] a 整形外科的
liposuction [ˈlɪpəʊsʌkʃn] n 【医】抽脂
elastin [ɪˈlæstɪn] n 弹力蛋白
implant [ɪmˈplænt] n 移植
wax [wæks] n 蜡 v 用蜡除毛
skin care phr 肌肤护理
blepharoplasty n 眼睑整容手术
adipose tissue phr 脂肪组织

用英语聊天，原来这么简单 / 老外每天说的英语，其实就是这几句。

凯瑞：我皮肤最近好干。 艾玛：你应该去做点皮肤护理。

Situation 1
食物是健康的基础

Make sure that you eat foods containing❶ a variety of vitamins and minerals.
确保你吃的食物里包含了各种维生素和矿物质。

Grammar-1
"containing"为分词构句的用法，我们可以还原成关系从句的用法，即"which contains…"的句子。

You can take some vitamins and have a balanced diet to keep in shape.
你可以吃些维生素，均衡饮食以保持身材。

Grammar-2
"bother"当动词时，意思为"困扰"，其用法和"annoy（困扰；惹恼）"相同。

I can't breathe well because my asthma is bothering❷ me. I drink basil leaves juice with honey to get instant relief.
我因为气喘发作而呼吸不顺畅。我喝蜂蜜罗勒汁来获得即时的舒缓。

Nowadays, more and more people drink herbal tea to stay healthy❸ .
现今有越来越多的人喝花草茶来保持健康。

Grammar-3
"stay healthy"有"保持健康"的意思，其中的"stay"也可使用"keep"替换。

You should go on this calorie diet if you want to lose weight.
你若要减肥，就必须坚持这个卡路里饮食法。

a variety of phr 各式各样的   mineral ['mɪnərəl] n 矿物；矿物质

asthma ['æzmə] n 【医】气喘（病）；哮喘

basil ['bæzl] n 罗勒   relief [rɪ'liːf] n （痛苦或负担等的）缓和

nowadays ['nauədeɪz] **ad** 时下；现今 **同** today [tə'deɪ] **ad** 现今；在当代

herbal tea **phr** 花草茶

Situation 2
劝阻朋友的坏习惯

Don't be so picky about food; otherwise you will **suffer from** malnutrition.
不要那么挑食，否则你会受营养失调之苦。

Grammar-4
"suffer from" 有 "遭受……之苦" 的意思，和其相同的短语为 "be in pain from"。

Ryan's lungs have become **much** healthier since he kicked his smoking habit.
自从瑞安戒掉抽烟的习惯之后，他的肺更加健康了。

Grammar-5
"much" 为程度副词，通常用来修饰比较级，也可以用 "far"、"even" 或 "still" 替换。

picky ['pɪki] **a** 挑剔的 **同** fastidious [fæ'stɪdɪəs] **a** 爱挑剔的

lung [lʌŋ] **n** 肺

Situation 3
预防胜于治疗

It is said that lanolin oil is very useful to avoid frostbite.
据说绵羊油对预防冻伤很有效。

Grammar-6
"It is said that..." 有 "据说" 的意思，通常置于句首。

You **had better** use band-aids to prevent your wound from bacterial infection.
你最好使用创可贴来预防细菌感染。

Grammar-7
"had better" 有 "最好……" 的意思，后接不带 to 的不定式，没有时态的变化，用于 "提出建议" 和 "发出间接的命令"。

avoid [ə'vɔɪd] **v** 避免；防止   frostbite ['frɔːstbaɪt] **n** 冻伤

prevent from **phr** 预防；阻止   bacterial [bæk'tɪrɪəl] **a** 细菌的

infection [ɪn'fekʃn] **n** 传染；影响

Situation 4
终于久病将愈

You will be happy to hear that after receiving an **IV drip** for a few days, the victim recovered very well.
你得知这名患者在接受静脉滴注几天后恢复状况良好将会开心。

Grammar-8
"IV drip" 意为 "静脉点滴"，其中 "IV" 为 "Intravenous（静脉内的）" 的缩写形式。

The girl walks downstairs with crutches slowly and carefully.
那个女孩拄着拐杖缓慢小心地走下楼梯。

recover [rɪ'kʌvər] **v** 恢复   crutch [krʌtʃ] **n** 拐杖

Situation 5
称赞健康的人

My older brother exercises daily; that is **why** he is fit.
我哥哥每天运动，这就是他这么健壮的原因。

Grammar-9
"why" 在此为关系副词的用法，相当于 "the reason that"。

fit [fɪt] **a** 健康的；强健的 **同** strong [strɔːŋ] **a** 强壮的 **同** healthy ['helθi] **a** 健康的

Unit 4 关注健康

Situation 6
怀孕生产

Grammar-10
"spend" 当动词时，意为"花费时间"，最重要的是主语需为"人"，且后面衔接的动词需以 Ving 来呈现。当然，我们也可以替换成 "sth. + take(s) + sb. + time" 的句型。

The dad-to-be <mark>spent</mark> ⑩ long hours pacing in the waiting room, waiting for the arrival of his new-born babe.
这位准爸爸在等候室中来回踱步好几个小时，等待新生儿的到来。

I went to see my new baby sister in the <mark>nursery</mark> ⑪, but my mother was in the maternity ward.
我到育婴室里看我妹妹，但是我妈妈还在产房里。

Grammar-11
"nursery" 当名词时，有"育婴室"的意思，也可以替换成 "baby's room"。

pace [peɪs] v 踱步于……   maternity [məˈtɜːrnəti] n 产科病房 a 产妇的

ward [wɔːrd] n 病房；病室

Situation 7
配眼镜

The optician has prescribed my aunt a new pair of glasses.
配镜师已经为我姑姑开了配一副新眼镜的处方笺。

optician [ɑːpˈtɪʃn] n （眼镜的）配镜师

prescribe [prɪˈskraɪb] v 为……开药方；开药方

 老外不会教你的小秘密

★ 青春期，脸上免不了长痘，此时，要如何表达脸上长痘呢？其实我们可以用 "*break out*" 这个短语，后面不需要再接 "*acne*（粉刺）" "*pimple*（面疱）" 等就可以清楚表达。如：" *You will break out if you stay up late.*（如果熬夜，你会长痘的。）"。

不怕你学不会

1. Don't be so picky about food; otherwise you will be in pain from malnutrition.

   = Don't be so _____ about food; otherwise you will _____ from malnutrition.

2. The dad-to-be spent long hours pacing in the waiting room.

   = It _____ the dad-to-be long hours to pace in the waiting room.

答案：1. fastidious, suffer   2. took

Chapter 5 健康好重要

看看老外怎么学

请对照图片,将身体各部位可能产生的疾病填入空格处。

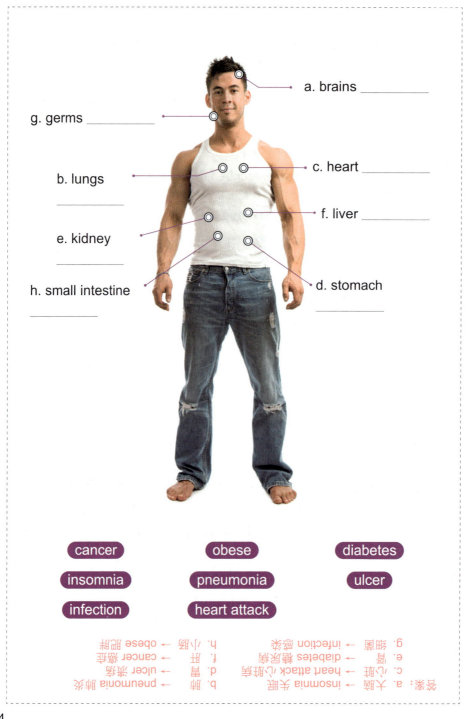

- a. brains _____
- g. germs _____
- b. lungs _____
- c. heart _____
- f. liver _____
- e. kidney _____
- d. stomach _____
- h. small intestine _____

cancer　　obese　　diabetes
insomnia　　pneumonia　　ulcer
infection　　heart attack

答案:
- a. 大脑 → insomnia 失眠
- b. 肺 → pneumonia 肺炎
- c. 心脏 → heart attack 心脏病
- d. 胃 → ulcer 溃疡
- e. 肾 → diabetes 糖尿病
- f. 肝 → cancer 癌症
- g. 细菌 → infection 感染
- h. 小肠 → obese 肥胖

Chapter 6 快乐去上学
Go to school

是否总是觉得上课好无聊、补习好累人、作业好烦人……如果可以逃走该有多好呢？那就来体验不一样的学生时光吧！

Unit 1	**Unit 2**	**Unit 3**	**Unit 4**
我要考第一名	校园风云榜	学校这个地方	各种重大日子

Unit 1 我要考第一名
First place in my class

原来老外这样记单词 / 老外从小到大学习单词的方法，就是看到什么就学什么！

dictionary [ˈdɪkʃəneri]
n 字典

blackboard [ˈblækbɔːrd]
n 黑板

whiteboard [ˈwaɪtbɔːrd]
n 白板

chalk [tʃɔːk] n 粉笔

marker [ˈmɑːrkər]
n 白板笔

其他衍生单词：

eraser [ɪˈreɪsər] n 橡皮擦；板擦
magnet [ˈmæɡnət] n 磁铁；磁石
globe [ɡloʊb] n 地球；地球仪
podium [ˈpoʊdiəm] n （放讲稿的）讲台；交响乐指挥台
platform [ˈplætfɔːrm] n 讲台；（铁路等的）月台
homeroom [ˈhoʊmruːm] n 【美】同年级学生定期集会接受导师指导的教室

Unit 1 我要考第一名

 老外最常用的单词 / 连这些单词都不会，你还敢说你学过英语吗？

看遍上课百态 ★★

doze [dəʊz] v 打盹；打瞌睡

absent-minded [ˌæbsənt ˈmaɪndɪd] a 心不在焉的
rote [rəʊt] n 死记硬背
underline [ˌʌndərˈlaɪn] v 在……的下面画线
preview [ˈpriːvjuː] v 预习
review [rɪˈvjuː] v 复习；温习
textbook [ˈtekstbʊk] n 教科书

请大家乖乖来上课 ★★

absent [ˈæbsənt]
a 缺席的；不在场的

absence [ˈæbsəns] n 缺席
presence [ˈprezns] n 出席；在场
present [ˈpreznt] a 出席的；在场的
dismiss [dɪsˈmɪs] v 让……离开
leave of absence phr 准假；休假
send off phr 送行
skip class phr 逃课

Chapter **6** 快乐去上学

这些行为要注意 ★★

tutorial [tuːˈtɔːrɪəl]
ad 个别指导的 n 导师的个别指导

detention [dɪˈtenʃn] n 课后辅导；滞留
guidance [ˈɡaɪdns] n 辅导；咨询
supervise [ˈsuːpərvaɪz] v 监督；指导
violate [ˈvaɪəleɪt] v 违反；妨碍
after-school help
phr 课后帮助、课后辅导
private class phr 私人课程

用英语聊天，原来这么简单 / 老外每天说的英语，其实就是这几句。

伊丽莎白：老师你看我画的！　老师：伊丽莎白，你画得真好！

Situation 1
上课的表现

Grammar-1
"take up"后面接名词或动名词，表示"开始某项活动／爱好"，在此句中有"占用"的意思。

Class participation <u>takes up</u> ❶ a big portion of your final grades. That means you are <u>encouraged</u> to share your ideas in class.
课堂参与占期末成绩中很大的比例。这就是说老师鼓励你在课堂上分享你的意见。

If you listen carefully in class, you should find the test easy enough.
如果你上课专心听讲，就会觉得考试很简单的。

Shirley gets very <u>nervous</u> when she gets <u>cold called</u> in class.
雪莉每次课堂上被提问都很紧张。

I didn't understand anything we learned today. I will be falling behind.
今天学的我没有一样听得懂，我会落后的。

participation [pɑ:r,tɪsɪ'peɪʃn] n 参加；参与

portion ['pɔ:rʃn] n （一）部分　　encourage [ɪn'kɜ:rɪdʒ] v 鼓励；促进

nervous ['nɜ:rvəs] a 紧张不安的 ≈ worried ['wɜ:rid] a 担心的

cold call phr 意外访问；抽问

Situation 2
要不要去上课呢

This professor does the roll call almost every class. You had better ❷ not skip class.
这位教授几乎每堂课都点名，你最好不要逃课。

Jack has skipped this course for three weeks; he will surely fail this course.
杰克已经在这门课上逃课3个星期了；他一定会不及格。

He skips class constantly. ❸ No wonder he was expelled from school.
他经常逃课，难怪他会被学校退学。

Grammar-2
"had better" 表示 "最好；还是……为好"，后面接不带 to 的不定式；虽然用了 "better" 一词，但并无比较意思，也不是说做这件事要比做别的事好。

Grammar-3
"constantly" 当副词时，有 "经常地" 之意，其用法相当于 "frequently" 和 "repeatedly"。

- professor [prəˈfesər] n 教授
- roll call n 点名
- skip [skɪp] v （故意）不出席；不参加
- course [kɔːrs] n 课程；科目
- fail [feɪl] v 失败；不及格
- no wonder phr 难怪
- expel [ɪkˈspel] v 驱逐；赶走

Situation 3
下课的时光

Mary often takes a nap during class breaks.
玛莉通常在下课时小睡一会儿。

I'm hungry enough to eat a horse after ❹ studying all day. Let's go out and eat something.
结束一天的课程之后，我饿到可以吃掉一匹马了。我们出去吃点东西。

I know you guys are eager to go back home. Let's call it a day!
我知道你们都迫不及待回家了，我们今天的课程就上到这里！

Students on duty are responsible for ❺ erasing the blackboard and sweeping the floor.
值日生负责擦黑板和扫地。

Grammar-4
句中的 "after" 作为连词，意思为 "在……之后"。

Grammar-5
"responsible for" 和 "in charge of" 都具有主动意义，可用来修饰主语和主语补语，而 "responsible for" 还可以表示前者是造成后者的原因。

- nap [næp] n 午睡
- break [breɪk] n 暂停；休息
- eager [ˈiːɡər] a 渴望的；急切的
- call it a day phr 结束一天的工作
- on duty phr 值日
- floor [flɔːr] n 地板；地面

Situation 4
教师的评价

Ms. Black is a strict ❻ teacher. She demands her students to study hard.
布莱克女士是一位严格的老师，她要求学生努力读书。

Grammar-6
"strict" 当形容词时，有 "严格的；严厉的" 之意，相当于词汇 "severe" 与 "stern"。

- demand [dɪˈmænd] v 要求；请求
- hard [hɑːrd] a 努力的

Situation 5
可怕的考试

I didn't study anything at all. It's too late to start now.
我什么都还没学，现在开始有点太晚了。

Grammar-7
"for the sake of" 即 "为了……（的利益或好处）" 的意思，同义短语为 "for the benefit of"。

I always stay up late before the final exam for the sake of getting good grades.
我总在期末考试来临前熬夜到很晚，为的就是能取得好成绩。

I can't go out this weekend. I have two exams next week.
我这周末不能出去了，我下星期有两个考试。

It's an open-book exam, so students can bring their textbooks with them.
这是开卷考试，同学们可以带课本来考。

Grammar-8
"however" 为连词，可放于句首或句中，需要加上逗号才能与后面的句子相连。

Open-book tests are considered easier than closed-book ones. However, open-book tests can sometimes be very difficult.
开卷考试被认为比闭卷考试简单。然而，开卷考试有时候也很难。

Grammar-9
"put down" 表示 "把……放下"，当及物动词时，宾语可以在中间也可以在后面。

Time is up. Put down your pens, or you'll get a zero on the test.
时间到了，把笔放下，否则以零分计算。

stay up [phr] 熬夜　　grade [greɪd] [n]【美】成绩；评分

consider [kənˈsɪdər] [v] 认为；把……视为

老外不会教你的小秘密

★ 面对考试，有人欢喜有人忧：
欢喜的人会说：
- *It was a piece of cake.* 真是太容易了。
- *It was a walk in the park.* 真是简单极了。

愁的人却会说：
- *I didn't know any of the answers.* 我一道题的答案都不知道。
- *I definitely flunked it.* 我铁定不及格了。
- *I am dead meat.* 我死定了。

Unit 2 校园风云榜
Classmates

 原来老外这样记单词 / 老外从小到大学习单词的方法，就是看到什么就学什么！

bookworm [ˈbʊkwɜːrm]
n 书呆子

straight-A student
phr 优等生

study group
phr 读书会

diligent [ˈdɪlɪdʒənt]
a 勤奋的；费尽心血的

其他衍生单词：

hands-on phr 亲自动手做
mnemonic [nɪˈmɑːnɪk] ad 有助于记忆的 n 记忆方法
group project phr 小组计划

adaptive learning phr 适应学习
study skills phr 读书技巧
note [nəʊt] n 笔记 v 记下、加注释

老外最常用的单词 / 连这些单词都不会,你还敢说你学过英语吗?

这些人也是你的同学们

mentor ['mentɔːr] n 良师益友

nerd [nɜːrd] n 【俚】讨厌的人;笨蛋
hard-working [hɑːrd 'wɜːrkɪŋ]
a 勤勉的;努力工作的
talented ['tæləntɪd]
a 天资高的;有才能的
clever ['klevər] a 聪明的;机敏的
brainy ['breɪni] a 脑筋好的
genius ['dʒiːniəs] n 天才;天资
class clown phr 班上的开心果

求学历程的几个阶段

undergraduate [ˌʌndər'grædʒuət]
n 大学生

sophomore ['sɑːfəmɔːr] n (大学/高中的)二年级学生
junior ['dʒuːniər] n 三年级生
senior ['siːniər] n (大学)四年级生
repeater [rɪ'piːtər] n 留级生
transfer [træns'fɜːr] n 转校(生)
preppy ['prepi]
n 【美俚】预备学校的学生或毕业生
graduate student phr 研究生

应对考试的万用单词在此

cheat [tʃiːt] v 作弊

peep [piːp] v 偷看
resit ['riːsɪt] v 重(考);补(考)
flunk [flʌŋk] v 失败;不及格
midterm [ˌmɪd'tɜːrm] n 期中考
final ['faɪnl] n 期末考
certification [ˌsɜːrtɪfɪ'keɪʃn] n 证书
essay ['eseɪ] n 论文
hired gun phr 考试枪手
test-taker phr 考生
pop quiz phr 【美】随堂考

Unit 2 校园风云榜

 用英语聊天，原来这么简单 / 老外每天说的英语，其实就是这几句。

娜塔莎：我昨晚熬夜准备今天的考试。我现在好累。
桑迪：我也是！我害怕我下一节打瞌睡。
汤姆：什么？今天有考试？你们在开玩笑吧？

Chapter 6 快乐去上学

Situation 1
进教室里的话题

I **am out of** ❶ whiteout. Can you lend me yours?
我的修正液用完了。可以把你的借给我吗？

Do you know where is the cashier?
你知道收银台怎么走吗？

Is the seat occupied? If not, may I sit **next to** ❷ you?
这个座位有人坐吗？如果没有的话，我可以坐你旁边吗？

Are you guys familiar with the campus? Which part do you like most?
你们都熟悉校园了吗？你最喜欢哪个部分？

How about ❸ forming a study group? We can share what we have read with each other.
成立一个读书会如何？我们可以彼此分享所读的东西。

Do you want to row canoes with me in the lake?
你想跟我去湖里划独木舟吗？

Grammar-1
"be out of" 即 "……用完了" 的意思，和其相同用法的短语为 "run out of"。

Grammar-2
"next to" 表示 "在……旁边"，后面接表示具体意义的名词。

Grammar-3
"How about..." 的用法与 "What about" 相同；用于征求意见、询问消息或提供建议。

whiteout [ˈwaɪtˌaʊt] n 修正液
seat [siːt] n 座位
occupied [ˈɑːkjupaɪd] a 已占用的
form [fɔːrm] v 组织；成立
share [ʃer] v 分享；分担

Situation 2
校园风云人物

Jenny is intelligent and diligent. She is the teacher's pet.
珍妮聪明且勤奋。她是老师宠爱的学生。

Joshua loves to sit and read on the grass.
乔许喜欢坐在草地上读书。

I was elected chairman of the student association last year.
我去年被选为学生会的会长。

intelligent [ɪnˈtelɪdʒənt] a 聪明的   teacher's pet phr 老师的宠儿

elect [ɪˈlekt] v 推选   chairman [ˈtʃeəmən] n 会长

association [əˌsəʊsɪˈeɪʃn] n 学生会

Situation 3
和同学的小矛盾

John's sister was bullied by her classmates.
约翰的妹妹遭到她同学的欺凌。

If you need any help with schoolwork or interpersonal relationships, you can turn to your homeroom teacher for help.
如果你在课业或人际上需要任何帮助，你可以找班主任帮忙。

Grammar-4
"be bullied by" 的意思为"被……欺凌"，此句子为被动语态，be 需依照时态来做变化。

Grammar-5
"turn to" 解释为"向……求助"，后面接上人，表示求助之人。

bully [ˈbʊli] v 威吓；胁迫   schoolwork [ˈskuːlwɜːrk] n 学校作业

interpersonal relationship phr 人际关系

Situation 4
交换生

Tom is an exchange student from Australia. Everyone wants to make friends with him.
汤姆是从澳洲来的交换生。每个人都想跟他交朋友。

Grammar-6
"make friends" 表示"交朋友；结为朋友"，"friends" 之后可以接上"with"，再接名词，表明与何人结为朋友。

exchange student phr 交换生   Australia [ɔːˈstreɪljə] n 澳大利亚

Situation 5
社团活动时间

Which kind of societies will you participate in?
你想参加哪一类的社团？

Did you join any clubs in the university?
你在大学时参加了任何社团吗？

I'm in the biology and movie club.
我参加了生物社和电影社。

club [klʌb] n 社团

Situation 6
做报告

I am busy preparing for my oral presentation. Please don't disturb me.
我正忙于准备口头报告，请不要打扰我。

Grammar-7
"be busy + Ving" 即"忙碌于……"的意思，要特别注意的是，其后所接的动词需以 Ving 来呈现。

Sam only wants to be a free rider when doing group presentation. That is, he doesn't contribute anything to his group.
山姆只想在做报告的时候搭便车。也就是说，他对小组没有贡献任何东西。

Grammar-8
"contribute to" 的意思为"帮忙；贡献"。

Never copy your report from the Internet; otherwise you would have to drop out of school.
永远不要从网上抄袭报告，否则你会被学校退学。

Grammar-9
"never"为频率副词，意思为"从未；永不"，其反义词为"ever"和"always"。

Professors are provided with anti-copy software. Therefore, they can check if students copy someone's homework.
教授有防抄袭软件，所以他们可以检查学生是否抄袭别人的作业。

Grammar-10
"homework"为不可数名词，当"家庭作业"的意思，且没有复数形态；相同的词汇为"assignment"，复数形态在词尾加上"s"。

This book report requires five pages, double spaced, and font size 10.
这份读书报告需要 5 页，2 倍行距，字数大小为 10 号。

oral [ˈɔːrəl] **a** 口头的
presentation [ˌpriːzenˈteɪʃn] **n** 上演；演出
disturb [dɪˈstɜːrb] **v** 妨碍；打扰
free rider **phr** 搭便车的人；免费受益者
group [gruːp] **n** 团体
copy [ˈkɑːpi] **v** 抄袭；模仿
report [rɪˈpɔːrt] **n** 报告
drop out **phr** 退出（学校等）
provide [prəˈvaɪd] **v** 提供；供给
software [ˈsɔːftwer] **n** 【电脑】软件
require [rɪˈkwaɪər] **v** 需要
font [fɑːnt] **n** 【电脑】字形；字体

不怕你学不会

1. Samantha doesn't contribute anything _____ her group. She just wants to be a free rider.

2. I really want to make friends _____ Natalie. She is so cute.

3. Judy is busy _____ (study) for the test tomorrow, so we need to be quiet.

答案：1. to 2. with 3. studying

Unit 3 学校这个地方
The place called school

 原来老外这样记单词 / 老外从小到大学习单词的方法，就是看到什么就学什么！

belfry [ˈbelfri]
n 钟楼

flag [flæg]
n 国旗

flag-raising ceremony
phr 升旗典礼

school house
phr 校舍

school grounds
phr 学校土地

pole [pəʊl]
n 旗杆

其他衍生单词：

bulletin board phr 公布栏
overhead projector phr 投影机
lightning rod phr 避雷针
locker [ˈlɑːkər] n 置物柜
attic [ˈætɪk] n 阁楼
lawn [lɔːn] n 草地

老外最常用的单词 / 连这些单词都不会，你还敢说你学过英语吗？

展开校园大探险

academic [ˌækəˈdemɪk] a 学术的

course [kɔːrs] n 课程；科目；路线
credit [ˈkredɪt] n 【美】学分
office of academic affairs phr 教务处
office of general affairs phr 总务处
cashier section phr 出纳组
discipline section phr 纪律组
lecturing section phr 教学组
registrar section phr 注册组

学校里的大人物

instructor [ɪnˈstrʌktər]
n 【美】大学讲师

principal [ˈprɪnsəpl] n 校长
faculty [ˈfæklti] n （任何学校的）全体教员
substitute [ˈsʌbstɪtuːt] n 代课老师
tutor [ˈtuːtər] n 家庭教师
intern [ɪnˈtɜːrn] n 实习老师
counselor [ˈkaʊnsələr] n 辅导老师
recruiter [rɪˈkruːtər] n 招聘人员
subject teacher phr 任课老师

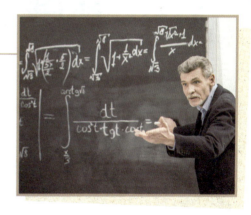

这些地方也是学校

kindergarten [ˈkɪndərɡɑːrtn]
n 幼儿园

university [ˌjuːnɪˈvɜːrsəti] n 大学
day care phr 日间托儿所
graduate school phr 研究生院
elementary school phr 小学
cram school phr 补习班
community college phr 社区大学

用英语聊天，原来这么简单 / 老外每天说的英语，其实就是这几句。

蒂芙妮：你看我的课表！多满啊！　康妮：我想你这学期要更努力用功了。

Situation 1
学校的规矩

Chewing gum is forbidden on campus ❶.
校园内禁止嚼口香糖。

Grammar-1
"campus" 有"校园"的意思，当要表达"校园内"时，以介词 on 来做引导，即为"on campus"。

Grammar-2
"carry out" 即"举行；实现"的意思，和其相同用法的有"hold"及"come off"。

Many universities carry out ❷ orientation to help students get accustomed to the new environment quickly.
许多大学举办新生训练以便学生尽早适应新环境。

Tuition fee is going to rise by 15% next year. Many parents are complaining about the heavy economical burden ❸.
学费明年将上调 15%。许多家长都在抱怨沉重的经济负担。

Grammar-3
"burden" 的意思为"负担；重担"，其用法相当于"load"一词。

chewing gum phr 嚼口香糖

forbidden [fərˈbɪdn] a 被禁止的 同 prohibited [prəˈhɪbɪt] a 被禁止的

orientation [ˌɔːriənˈteɪʃn] n （对新生的）情况介绍

accustomed [əˈkʌstəmd] a 习惯的；适应的

environment [ɪnˈvaɪrənmənt] n 环境

rise [raɪz] v 增加　　complain about phr 抱怨

economical [ˌiːkəˈnɑːmɪkl] a 经济的

Situation 2
最重要的选课

I'm looking at the course list. I have a busy schedule this semester.
我正在看课程表，我这学期选了很多课。

One of my roommates' major is finance. The other roommate's major is music.
我的一位室友主修财经，另一位室友则主修音乐。

Grammar-4
"sth. is all Greek to sb." 的意思为"某人对某事物一窍不通"。

I am going to drop this psychology course because it is all Greek to me ⑤.
我想退选心理学课程，因为我对它一窍不通。

Grammar-5
"whether or not" 与 "whether or no" 语义上没有区别，但使用中常将 "whether or not" 分成 "whether...or not" 并在它们中间插入两项选择中的前者。

I have no idea whether to minor in accounting or not ⑤.
我不知道到底要不要辅修会计。

How many credits do you need this semester?
这学期你需要多少学分呢？

The course number of Japanese is 2222, and it is three credits.
日语课的课程编号为2222，它有3个学分。

Grammar-6
"because" 为连词，用以连接两个从句，而它所连接的从句可以放于句首也可以放在后面。

I love taking courses in different departments because ⑥ I can study with students from different departments.
我喜欢修不同学院的课，因为可以跟不同学院的学生一起念书。

This course is three credits, and I'm only two credits short this semester.
这门课有3学分，而我这学期只差2学分。

Grammar-7
"audit a course" 为"旁听课程"的意思，相同用法的短语有"sit in a class"。

It's polite to get the professor's permission if you want to audit that course ⑦.
如果你想旁听这门课，先得到教授的允许比较有礼貌。

College students could arrange their own class schedule. They can choose whether to take certain courses or not.
大学生可以安排他们自己的课表。他们可以选择是否要修某一门课。

roommate ['ru:mmeɪt] n 室友

major ['meɪdʒər] n （大学中的）主修科目

finance ['faɪnæns] n 财政；金融   drop [drɑːp] v 停止；终止

psychology [saɪˈkɑːlədʒi] n 心理学   minor in phr 副修

accounting [əˈkaʊntɪŋ] n 会计；会计学 audit [ˈɔːdɪt] n 审计；查账

credit [ˈkredɪt] n 【美】学分

department [dɪˈpɑːrtmənt] n （大学的）系　　polite [pəˈlaɪt] a 有礼貌的

permission [pərˈmɪʃn] n 允许；许可　反 prohibition [ˌproʊhɪˈbɪʃn] n 禁止

arrange [əˈreɪndʒ] v 安排　　certain [ˈsɜːrtn] pron 某些；某几个

Situation 3
户外教学

Annie is so excited about ❽ the field trip that she cannot fall asleep.
安妮对于户外教学太兴奋以至于睡不着觉。

> Grammar-8
> "be excited about" 为 "对……感到兴奋" 的意思，其主词为人，情绪动词需以过去分词来修饰。

Situation 4
与人沟通的场合

Our resident assistant is hard to communicate with. She never takes in ❾ others' advice.
我们的宿舍管理员很难沟通，她从不采纳别人的意见。

Do you mind ❿ changing beds with me? I prefer the one against the wall.
你会介意跟我换床吗？我比较喜欢靠墙的那张床。

> Grammar-9
> "take in" 表示 "理解" 时，后面一般接事物；表示 "欺骗" 时为非正式用法，采用被动语态，主语一般是人。

> Grammar-10
> "mind" 在句中的意思为 "介意；反对"，后面通常加上 Ving。

field trip phr 户外教学；远足　　fall asleep phr 睡着

communicate [kəˈmjuːnɪkeɪt] v 沟通　　advice [ədˈvaɪs] n 忠告

against [əˈɡenst] prep. 倚；靠

老外不会教你的小秘密

★ 在学校，学生除了平常用功读书之外，每到期中或是期末考试时，图书馆里的学生比平日多很多，咖啡店里或 24 小时的食物连锁店里都会看到学生们在读书，有的甚至会熬夜，隔天看到了对方的熊猫眼不禁会问：
  ✦ *Did you burn the midnight oil?* 你熬夜了吗？
  ✦ *I need to pull an all-nighter for the final test.* 我必须要为了期末考试来开夜车了。
  ✦ *How could I stay up all night for the paper? I'm so sleepy now.*
    我要如何熬夜赶报告呢？我现在好困。
  看完了以上的句子，会不会心有戚戚焉呢？为了顺利通过考试，平时累积比临时抱佛脚更有用！

★ 开学了，有必修课程或是选修课程，那么 "*take a required course*" 就可以表达 "选择必修课程" 的用法；相反地，也会遇到不合适自己的课程或是 "*double book*（重复选课）"，要退选的时候，我们可以说 "*drop a course*"，即为 "退选" 的意思。

Unit 4 各种重大日子 Calender

原来老外这样记单词 / 老外从小到大学习单词的方法，就是看到什么就学什么！

graduation [ˌɡrædʒʊ'eɪʃn]
n 毕业典礼

tassel ['tæsl]
n 流苏

headwear ['hɛd,wɛr]
n 头饰

diploma [dɪ'pləʊmə]
n 毕业证

gown [ɡaʊn]
n 礼服

graduate ['grædʒʊət]
n 应届毕业生

其他衍生单词：

academic dissertation phr 学位论文
commencement [kə'mensmənt] 【美】学位授予典礼
graduation trip phr 毕业旅行

academic degree phr 学位
valedictorian [ˌvælɪdɪk'tɔːrɪən] n 在校生代表
salutatorian [səˌluːtə'tɔːrɪən] n 毕业生代表

老外最常用的单词 / 连这些单词都不会,你还敢说你学过英语吗?

入校第一天会听到的单词

gang [gæŋ] v 成群结队

beginner [bɪ'gɪnər] n 初学者
freshman ['freʃmən] n (大学等的)新生
enroll [ɪn'rəʊl] v 注册;入学
register ['redʒɪstər] v 登记;注册
entrance ['entrəns] n 入学许可
clique [kliːk] v 结党
crossing guard phr 交通协管员

还有这些也重要

scholarship ['skɑːlərʃɪp] n 奖学金

semester [sɪ'mestər] n 一学期;半学年
anniversary [ˌænɪ'vɜːrsəri] n 周年纪念
yearbook ['jɪrbʊk] n 年鉴;毕业纪念册
coursework ['kɔːrswɜːrk] n 按照学校课表上课,修完所有学分即可毕业
encaenia [en'siːnɪr] n (牛津大学)校庆典礼
study period phr 学习期间

学习不设限!

distance education phr 远程教育

library ['laɪbreri] n 图书馆
home environment phr 家庭环境
further education phr 【英】进修
home education phr 家庭教育
computer lab phr 电脑实验室
mother nature phr 大自然

Unit 4 各种重大日子

用英语聊天，原来这么简单 / 老外每天说的英语，其实就是这几句。

Happy graduation! Woo-Hoo!

Students

学生们：毕业快乐喔！耶！

Chapter **6** 快乐去上学

Situation 1
开学日

- Take a look at the syllabus for this semester. Raise your hand if ❶ you have any questions.
看一下这学期的教学大纲。如果有任何疑问请举手。

Grammar-1
句中的"if"为从属连词，意思为"假如"。

I am looking at the campus map. The library is a little bit far away from here.
我正在看校园地图，这里离图书馆有点远。

I'm a freshman here. This campus is so huge that I get lost.
我是这里的新生，校园太大导致我迷路了。

take a look at phr 看一看　　syllabus ['sɪləbəs] n 教学大纲

Situation 2
需要协助的话

- Professor White wants to employ a teaching assistant; maybe ❷ you can give it a try.
怀特教授想聘请一位助教，或许你可以试试看。

Grammar-2
"maybe"当副词时，有"或许；也许"之意，用法相当于"perhaps"。

Mr. Watson, could I ask for some extra tutoring during your office hours?
沃森老师，我可以请您在上班时间为我做辅导吗？

employ [ɪm'plɔɪ] v 雇用　　assistant [ə'sɪstənt] n 助教

give it a try phr 试试看

🎧 123

Situation 3
住宿舍也是一种人生历练

We've come to the dormitory. It's the end of our campus tour.
我们到宿舍了。这是我们的校园之旅最后一站。

The dormitory is a great place to meet other students.
宿舍是认识其他学生的好地方。

My roommates and I usually watch cable TV in the common room. We enjoy the programs a lot.
我和我室友常常到公共休息室看有线电视。我们非常喜欢电视节目。

I live with three other students. One of them sleeps early, so I have to be really quiet.
我和其他三位学生住一起。其中一位睡得早，所以我必须很小声。

Grammar-3
"regulation" 当名词时，有"规则；调节"的意思，其用法相当于 "rule"；当形容词时，则有"正规的；标准的"之意。

According to the dormitory regulation ❸, 11 p.m. to 6 a.m. is quiet hours. Boarders have to make as little noise as possible.
根据宿舍规定，晚上11点到早上6点为安静时段。住宿生尽可能不要制造噪音。

dormitory [ˈdɔːrmətɔːri] n 宿舍　　program [ˈproʊɡræm] n 节目

according to phr 根据　　boarder [ˈbɔːrdər] n 住宿生

Situation 4
代表学校争取荣誉

Zoe won first prize in the spelling bee. Her teachers and classmates are proud of ❹ her.
佐伊在拼字比赛中得了第一名。她的老师和同学都以她为荣。

Felix's essay got first place in class. His mother was very happy about it.
菲力克斯的作文拿到班上的第一名，他妈为此非常高兴。

Grammar-4
"be proud of" 有"以……为荣"的意思，与其相似的短语为"be one's pride"。

spelling bee phr 拼字比赛

Situation 5
凤凰花开的日子

The graduation ceremony will be held ❺ next Friday.
毕业典礼将在下星期五举行。

Grammar-5
句中的"hold"为及物动词，有"举办"的意思。

I have to finish my graduation thesis by ❻ April 30th. That is to say, the deadline is April 30th.
我必须在4月30日前完成毕业论文，也就是说，最后期限是4月30日。

Grammar-6
句中的"by"为一时间介词，用以表达"到……之时"的意思。

graduation [ˌɡrædʒuˈeɪʃn] n 毕业

ceremony [ˈserəmoʊni] n 仪式；典礼　　finish [ˈfɪnɪʃ] v 结束；完成

thesis [ˈθiːsɪs] n 论文　　deadline [ˈdedlaɪn] n 截止期限

Situation 6
出国继续进修

I have dreamt of studying **abrord** ❼ for many years.
我好几年前就开始梦想着去国外读书。

> **Grammar-7**
> "abroad" 当副词时, 有"在国外"的意思, 与 "overseas" 的用法相同。

I **got along well with** ❽ my host family when I studied in the United Kingdom.
我在英国读书的时候和寄宿家庭相处融洽。

> **Grammar-8**
> "get along with" 后面接表示人的名词或代词时, 用以表达"与……相处"。

I applied for five schools in the U.S.A., and I'm still waiting for the results.
我申请了 5 所美国的学校, 而我还在等回音。

host family phr 寄宿家庭

老外不会教你的小秘密

★ "赢在起跑点上"这样的话, 我们常常听到, 用英语可以这样表达:
  + *Get a head start, and you can get good grades.* 早一点起步念书, 你就会有不错的成绩。
  + *I need to get a jump on my competitor.* 我必须要比我的竞争者早一点开始念书。

不怕你学不会

1. Maybe you can take part in the speech contest, it is a good chance to hone in on your speaking skills.

   = _____ you can take part in the speech contest, it is a good chance to hone in on your speaking skills.

2. We are so proud of Nancy. She is the first girl who won the student wrestle competition.

   = Nancy _____ our _____. She is the first girl who won the student wrestle competition.

答案: 1. Perhaps 2. is, pride

看看老外怎么学 / 请将各科目对应的内容，填入图片中的框框里

- Napoléon
- harmonica
- cathode
- metaphor
- sketch
- diameter
- Mount Everest

答案：1. 数学 → diameter 直径 2. 文学 → metaphor 隐喻；象征 3. 艺术 → sketch 素描 4. 音乐 → harmonica 口琴 5. 科学 → cathode【电】阴极 6. 历史 → Napoléon 拿破仑 7. 地理 → Mount Everest 珠穆朗玛峰

Chapter 7 马路如虎口
Terrible traffic

出国旅游、商务出差、留学打工……，除了搞好人际关系之外，最重要的莫过于交通了！这些要如何开口表达呢？赶快一起来学学看吧！

Unit 1 行人要注意

Unit 2 驾驶要小心

Unit 3 上班族们

Unit 4 特殊交通方式

Unit 1 行人要注意
Watch out

 原来老外这样记单词 / 老外从小到大学习单词的方法，就是看到什么就学什么！

ramp [ræmp]
n 坡道

arrow ['ærəʊ]
n （指示方向等的）箭号，箭头

milepost ['maɪlpəʊst]
n 里程碑（标）

interchange ['ɪntətʃeɪndʒ]
n （高速公路上的）交流道

warning ['wɔːrnɪŋ]
n 警告；告诫

crash barrier
phr （公路上的）防撞护栏

其他衍生单词：

tunnel ['tʌnl] n 隧道；地道
stop sign phr 停止信号
rest area phr 休息站
barricade [ˌbærɪ'keɪd] n 路障；障碍物
do not enter phr 禁止进入
divider [dɪ'vaɪdər] n 分隔岛

老外最常用的单词 / 连这些单词都不会，你还敢说你学过英语吗？

走过路过别忘了注意这些 ★★

overpass [ˈəʊəpæs]
n 天桥；高架桥

underpass [ˈʌndərpæs]
n 【美】地下通道
route [ruːt] n 路线；航线
hydrant [ˈhaɪdrənt] n 消防栓
railway [ˈreɪlweɪ] n 铁路；铁道
streetlight [ˈstriːtˌlaɪt] n 路灯
zebra crossing phr 【英】斑马线
railroad crossing phr 平交道口

危险动作请勿模仿 ★★

speeding [ˈspiːdɪŋ]
a 高速行驶的

accident [ˈæksɪdənt] n 事故、意外
jaywalk [ˈdʒeɪwɔːk]
v 不守交通规则横穿马路
carjacking [ˈkɑːrdʒækɪŋ] n 武力劫车
suspend [səˈspend] v 暂缓执行（刑罚）
road rage phr 路怒症
drunk driving phr 酒后驾车

Chapter **7** 马路如虎口

收拾好行囊 ★★

hitchhiker [ˈhɪtʃhaɪkə]
n 搭便车的旅行者

car-pool [kɑːr puːl]
n 私人汽车轮流共用；拼车
board [bɔːrd]
v 登上（船／飞机／汽车等）
sidewalk [ˈsaɪdwɔːk] n 【美】人行道
pavement [ˈpeɪvmənt] n 【英】人行道
pedestrian [pəˈdestrɪən] n 行人
pedestrian crossing phr 行人穿越道

用英语聊天，原来这么简单
老外每天说的英语，其实就是这几句。

妈妈：小心点，艾伦。你过马路时应该两边都仔细看。 艾伦：我知道了，妈妈。

Situation 1
走在路上

Grammar-1
"out of order"表示"发生故障；乱七八糟；不合适"，一般用于beV后面当主词补语。

- Nearly half of the streetlights on the pavement are out of order ❶.
  人行道上近一半的路灯都出故障了。

- Nancy jaywalked and was bumped by a speeding motorcycle.
  南希随意穿越马路被一台超速的摩托车撞上。

nearly [ˈnɪrli] ad 几乎；差不多　　streetlight [ˈstriːt‚laɪt] n 路灯

motorcycle [ˈmoʊtərsaɪkl] n 摩托车

Situation 2
遇到需要帮助的行人

- Let me take you to the museum.
  我带你去博物馆吧。

- Go straight on Riverside Drive, turn left on Michigan Avenue, and the parking lot is on your right.
  河岸路直走，在密西根大道左转，停车场就在你的右边。

- You're at the intersection of Renmin East Road and Jiefang South Road.
  你现在在人民东路和解放南路的交叉口。

- When you come to the traffic light, turn right.
  当你碰到红绿灯后，向右转。

Unit 1 行人要注意

turn [tɜːrn] v 转向；转弯   parking lot n 停车场

Situation 3
乘出租车

Please take me to this address in fifteen minutes.
请在十五分钟内载我到这个地址。

We need to merge onto the highway as soon as possible.
我们必须尽快上高速公路。

address [əˈdres] n 住址；地址

Situation 4
交通规则

It is everyone's duty ❷ to follow the traffic rules.
遵守交通规则是大家的义务。

Howard got ticketed because he ran through the red light.
霍华德因闯红灯而被开罚单。

The police are now clamping down on drag-racing.
警方正在取缔飙车族。

traffic [ˈtræfɪk] n 交通

rule [ruːl] n 规则   ticket [ˈtɪkɪt] v 对……开出交通违规罚单

run through phr 快速地穿过   red light phr 红灯

police [pəˈliːs] n 警察   clamp down on phr 取缔；镇压

drag-racing phr 飙车

Grammar-2
"duty" 当名词时，有"任务；责任；义务"的意思，与其相同的词汇为"business"和"responsibility"。

Chapter **7**
马路如虎口

Situation 5
有意外发生

Do we have insurance? I hope they will pay for this.
我们有保险吗？希望他们会给付。

A car accident took place yesterday. Three people got seriously injured and were rushed to the hospital immediately.
昨天发生了车祸。三个人受重伤并立刻被送往医院。

Watch out! You almost hit that car in front of you!
小心点！你差点撞到前面那辆车。

Accidents on the level crossing delayed the train for one hour.
平交道上的意外使火车延误了 1 小时。

The motorcycle just came out of nowhere.
那辆摩托车不知道从哪儿冲出来的。

🎧 131

> **Grammar-3**
> "bump into" 后面接名词，表示"偶然碰上；撞到"的意思。

The driver **bumped into** ❸ the electric pole after the car brake was broken.

驾驶员在刹车失灵后撞上电线杆。

Are you alright? I'll call the ambulance. Try to relax.

你还好吗？我会叫救护车。试着放轻松点。

Due to the accident, the police **channelized** the traffic at the intersection.

由于事故的原因，警察在十字路口疏导交通。

seriously [ˈsɪrɪəsli] a 严重地；危急地   rush [rʌʃ] v 赶紧；仓促行动

hospital [ˈhɑːspɪtl] n 医院   level crossing phr 平交道

delay [dɪˈleɪ] v 耽搁；延误 ◎ postpone [pəʊˈspəʊn] v 延迟；延缓

driver [ˈdraɪvər] n 驾驶；司机 ◎ motorman [ˈməʊtəmən] n 司机

brake [breɪk] n 刹车   channelize [ˈtʃænəlˌaɪz] v 疏导

intersection [ˌɪntərˈsekʃn] n 十字路口 ◎ crossing [ˈkrɔːsɪŋ] n 交叉；十字路口

 老外不会教你的小秘密

★ 有没有为了赶车而跑得满身大汗的经验呢？赶车的说法有很多种，我们来学一下吧！最简单的说法是"*I run to catch the bus.*（我跑步赶公交车。）"；学英语不能只停留在初级的阶段，现在来说说看以下的句子：

✦ *I made a dash for the bus this morning.* 今天早上我跑步赶公交车。

✦ *I sprinted to the train.* 我跑步赶上火车了。

 不怕你学不会

1. The traffic lights are all _____ of order so we can't move right now.

2. Taking care of those kids is not my responsibility.

    = Taking care of those kids is not my _____.

答案：1. out 2. duty / business

Unit 2 驾驶要小心 Be careful

原来老外这样记单词 / 老外从小到大学习单词的方法，就是看到什么就学什么！

steering wheel phr 方向盘

air conditioner phr 空调

chauffeur [ʃəʊˈfɜːr]
n （私家车的）汽车司机

turn signal
phr 方向灯

radio [ˈreɪdɪəʊ]
n 收音机

其他衍生单词：

seat belt phr 安全带	**fender** [ˈfendər] n 挡泥板	**dashboard** [ˈdæʃbɔːrd] n 汽车仪表板
cup holder phr 置杯架	**odometer** [əʊˈdɑːmɪtər] n 里程表	**accelerator** [əkˈseləreɪtər] n 油门

老外最常用的单词 / 连这些单词都不会，你还敢说你学过英语吗？

这些单词都是车子

trolley [ˈtrɑːli] n 【美】有轨电车

wagon [ˈwæɡən]
n （送食品／饮料的）推车
convertible [kənˈvɜːrtəbl] n 敞篷车
carriage [ˈkærɪdʒ]
n 四轮马车；【美】婴儿车
dolly [ˈdɑːli] n （搬运重物用的）手推车
tram [træm] n 有轨电车；吊车
vehicle [ˈviːəkl] n 车辆
ox-driven cart phr 牛车

驾驶不可不知的单词

breath test phr 呼吸测试器（酒测）

detour [ˈdiːtʊr] n 绕道
alight [əˈlaɪt] v （从车辆／马背等）下来
bypass [ˈbaɪpæs] n 支路
layover [ˈleɪəʊvər] n 中途下车
tailgate [ˈteɪlɡeɪt] v 紧跟着（前车）行驶
cyclist [ˈsaɪklɪst] n 骑自行车者
motorcyclist [ˈməʊtərsaɪklɪst] n 骑摩托车者
flee [fliː] v 逃逸

停放爱车的所在

boom gate phr 收费闸门

entrance [ˈentrəns] n 入口；门口
exit [ˈeksɪt] n 出口；通道
collector [kəˈlektər]
n 收取款项（或东西）的人
garage [ɡəˈrɑːʒ] n 车库
handicapped space phr 残障停车位
parking lot phr 停车场

用英语聊天，原来这么简单 / 老外每天说的英语，其实就是这几句。

Son, before you start the engine, take a look at your surroundings first.

爸爸：儿子，在你发动引擎前，先注意一下四周。

Situation 1
成为一位好驾驶员

James finally got his driving license after several attempts.
詹姆斯在好几次的尝试后终于取得驾照。

Drivers usually **look at** ❶ the rear view mirror when making U turns.
驾驶车通常在掉头的时候会看一下后视镜。

Do you know **how** ❷ to drive a stick? Or we should rent an automatic?
你知道如何开手动挡车吗？还是我们要租一辆自动挡车呢？

Grammar-1
"look at"当及物动词时，后面接名词，如：人、物体等，用以表示"看"。

Grammar-2
"how（如何）"接不定词，可以在句子中当名词短语使用。

finally [ˈfaɪnəli] ad 最后；终于　　license [ˈlaɪsns] n 许可证

attempt [əˈtempt] n 尝试

usually [ˈjuːʒəli] ad 通常地 ⓢ routinely [ruːˈtiːnli] ad 常规地

turn [tɜːrn] n 转弯；折回　　stick [stɪk] n 手动挡车

automatic [ˌɔːtəˈmætɪk] n 自动排档汽车

Situation 2
要和朋友炫耀车子

Mike **would like** ❸ to buy a car which has a sunroof.
迈克想要买一辆有天窗的车。

Grammar-3
"would like"表示"想要；愿意"后面接上不定词，表示"某人想要做某事"。

I need car window stickers that are UV proof.
我需要防紫外线的车窗隔热纸。

GPS does benefit a person who has no sense of direction.
卫星导航系统给没有方向感的人很大的帮助。

Car video recorder records the paths you drive along ❹.
行车记录仪记录你所经过的道路。

Grammar-4
"along" 在此为介词，其意思为"沿着"。

sunroof [ˈsʌnruːf] n 天窗
sticker [ˈstɪkər] n 贴纸
proof [pruːf] a 能抵挡的
GPS abbr 全球定位系统 (=Global Positioning System)
benefit [ˈbenɪfɪt] v 有益于 同 profit [ˈprɑːfɪt] v 有益；有利
sense of direction phr 方向感
path [pæθ] n 道路，途径

Situation 3
驾车上路

I bought a new helmet yesterday because the old one was broken.
我昨天买了一顶新的安全帽，因为旧的已经坏掉了。

Fasten your seat belt, or ❺ I won't start the engine.
系好安全带，否则我不启动引擎。

Grammar-5
"or" 为连词，它所连接的两个单词有相同的词性；连接句子时，可以表示转折语气，意为"否则"。

The speed limit of this county road is fifty kilometers per hour.
此条县道限速为每小时 50 千米。

broken [ˈbroʊkən] v 毁坏；弄坏
fasten [ˈfæsn] v 系紧
start [stɑːrt] v 启动
engine [ˈendʒɪn] n 引擎
speed limit phr 限速
county [ˈkaʊnti] n 【美】郡
kilometer [ˈkɪləmiːtər] n 千米

Situation 4
劝诫危险驾驶

Didn't you see ❻ that sign? It says "No passing!"
你没有看到那标志吗？它的意思是"不能超车！"

Grammar-6
"see（看见）"为动词，后接宾语，再接动词不定式或 Ving 形式。

It is dangerous to use smartphones when ❼ you're driving.
开车的时候使用手机是非常危险的。

Grammar-7
"when（当……时候）"可以作从属连词，用以引导从句，和主句连接成复合句。

Kelly was so impatient that she kept ❽ overtaking other cars.
凯莉非常没耐心，所以她不断超别人的车。

Grammar-8
"kept"是"keep"的过去分词，在此句中有"继续不断"的意思，其后面需要接上 Ving 的动词。

He was sentenced to jail after he did a hit and run.
他肇事逃逸后被判入狱。

Grammar-10
"never" 可以表示"从不；从未；决不"；在句中有不同的位置，通常 never 在句中可以放在 be 或助动词的后面，一般动词的前面。

Never ⁹ drive a car when you are drunk. It's very dangerous and may cause tragedies.
永远不要酒后驾车。那很危险而且可能会酿成悲剧。

sign [saɪn] n 标志；招牌 ⓒ signal [ˈsɪgnəl] n 信号；标志

pass [pæs] v 超过　　impatient [ɪmˈpeɪʃnt] a 没耐心的

overtake [ˌoʊvərˈteɪk] v 超过；追上 ⓡ outdistance [ˌaʊtˈdɪstəns] v 把……抛在后头

sentence [ˈsentəns] v 宣判；判决

jail [dʒeɪl] n 监狱 ⓒ prison [ˈprɪzn] n 监狱；拘留所

drunk [drʌŋk] a 喝醉（酒）的

tragedy [ˈtrædʒədi] n 悲剧性事件；惨案

老外不会教你的小秘密

★ 当汽车仪表板的指针快到 E 这个字母时，就代表快没油了，这时我们可以用：
  ✦ *I need to stop for gas.* 我需要停下来加油。
  ✦ *I need to get gas.* 我需要加油。
★ 在国内加油真的很方便，有服务人员会给予协助；车子一旦停好了，想要将车子加满油时，我们可以说：
  ✦ *Fill up, please.* 请加满。

不怕你学不会

1. If you were drunk driving, you would be sentenced to jail.
   = If you were drunk driving, you would be sentenced to _____ .

2. He kept _____ (speed) and wouldn't slow down.

答案：1. prison　2. speeding

Chapter 7 马路如虎口

Unit 3 上班族们
The commuters

原来老外这样记单词 / 老外从小到大学习单词的方法，就是看到什么就学什么！

support ring
phr 拉环

subway [ˈsʌbweɪ]
n 地铁

passenger [ˈpæsɪndʒər]
n 乘客

seat [siːt]
n 座位

其他衍生单词：

ticket [ˈtɪkɪt] n 车票	**sleeping car** phr （火车）卧铺	**ticket examiner** phr 检票员
one-way ticket phr 单程车票	**priority seat** phr 优先座	**Tube** [tuːb] n 【英】地下铁（道）

老外最常用的单词 连这些单词都不会,你还敢说你学过英语吗?

交通运输相关的单词

double-decker bus phr 双层巴士

circulation [ˌsɜːrkjəˈleɪʃn] n 循环;运行
elevator [ˈelɪveɪtər] n 【美】电梯
lift [lɪft] n 【英】电梯
escalator [ˈeskəleɪtər] n 手扶梯
timetable [ˈtaɪmteɪbl] n (火车等的)时刻表
long-distance bus phr 长途巴士

水面上的船舰

aircraft carrier phr 航空母舰

liner [ˈlaɪnər] n 邮轮
ferryboat [ˈfɛriˌbot] n 渡轮
yacht [jɑːt] n 快艇;游艇
kayak [ˈkaɪæk] n 小艇
canoe [kəˈnuː] n 独木舟
fishing craft phr 渔船
cruise ship phr (带餐厅/酒吧的)游艇

天空中的小伙伴们

control tower
phr (机场)控制塔;塔台

airbus [ˈerbʌs] n 空中巴士
airship [ˈerʃɪp] n 飞艇;飞船
vessel [ˈvesl] n 飞机(特指水上飞机)
jumbo jet phr 巨型喷气式客机
aerial tramway phr 空中缆车
cable car phr 缆车

Chapter 7 马路如虎口

用英语聊天，原来这么简单 / 老外每天说的英语，其实就是这几句。

薇薇安：你现在要去哪一站？　埃莉莎：我下一站要下车。

Situation 1
上班族

Grammar-1
"plan to" 意思为"计划……"，后面接动词原形。

Grammar-2
"around" 为副词，有"到处；在周围；大约"的意思，常与动词构成短语。

- The government is planning to ❶ build BRT to improve the traffic situation.
  政府正计划兴建快速公交来改善交通状况。

- I can rush to the Tube in three minutes.
  我可以 3 分钟内赶去地铁站。

- The train was first invented in the 19th century.
  火车最早发明于 19 世纪。

- My girlfriend and I took a cable car to appreciate the breathtaking scenery around ❷ the amusement park.
  我和我女朋友乘缆车欣赏游乐场周边令人叹为观止的景色。

- I am already late, so I think I would just take a taxi.
  我已经迟到了，所以我想干脆坐出租车。

- You can take No. 222 or 223 to reach your destination.
  你可以搭 222 号或 223 号公交车到你的目的地。

- The Subway is fast and convenient.
  地铁既快速又方便。

Unit 3 上班族们

Commuters can save much money if they buy **monthly** tickets.
如果上班族买月票的话会省下很多钱。

Grammar-3
"watch out for" 后面接要当心的人或事。

Watch out for ❸ the platform gap when you're getting onto trains.
上火车的时候注意月台间的空隙。

Oh no! I should have taken the sea line train, but I took the mountain line train instead.
不！我应该搭海线的火车，结果我搭成山线了。

I **got on the** ❹ wrong train.
我搭错火车了。

Grammar-4
"get on the + 交通工具"，为"搭乘……"的意思，与其相同的用法有"be on the + 交通工具"及"board the + 交通工具"。

Grammar-5
"Oh, man!" 即"天呐！"的意思，相同的短语还有"Oh, my!" 或 "Oh, my god!"。

Oh, man! ❺ The seats on the bus are all occupied.
天呐！公交车上都没有空位了。

I'd like to buy a one-way ticket to New York.
我想买一张到纽约的单程车票。

Is there a ticket for a sleeping car to Venice?
还有到威尼斯的卧铺车票吗？

government [ˈɡʌvərnmənt] n 政府

invent [ɪnˈvent] v 发明；创造   century [ˈsentʃəri] n 世纪

appreciate [əˈpriːʃieɪt] v 欣赏；体会

breathtaking [ˈbreθteɪkɪŋ] a 惊人的   reach [riːtʃ] v 抵达；到达

destination [ˌdestɪˈneɪʃn] n 目的地；终点

convenient [kənˈviːnɪənt] a 方便的

commuter [kəˈmjuːtər] n 通勤者   monthly [ˈmʌnθli] a 每月的

platform [ˈplætfɔːrm] n 月台

gap [ɡæp] n 间隔；差距   line [laɪn] n 航线；铁路线

wrong [rɔːŋ] a 错误的 同 incorrect [ˌɪnkəˈrekt] a 不正确的

occupied [ˈɑːkjupaɪd] a 已占用的   Venice [ˈvenɪs] n 威尼斯

Chapter 7 马路如虎口

Situation 2
乘飞机出行

We are presently flying at an altitude of 35000 feet.
我们现在的飞行高度是 35000 英尺。

All the flights were cancelled due to ❻ the bad weather.
所有的航班都因为恶劣的天气而取消了。

Grammar-6
和句中"due to"相似用法的短语为"owing to""on account of"和"because of",皆是"由于；因为"的意思。

Ladies and gentlemen, you are free to move in the cabin now.
各位先生女士，现在可以自由在机舱内移动了。

Can I use my electronic devices now?
我现在可以使用电子产品了吗？

The helicopter delivered relief supplies to disastrous areas.
直升机运送救济物资到灾区。

flight [flaɪt] n （飞机的）班次　　cancel ['kænsl] v 取消；中止

weather ['weðər] n 天气　　helicopter ['helɪkɑːptər] n 直升机

relief [rɪ'liːf] n 救济物品　　disastrous [dɪ'zæstrəs] a 灾害的

 老外不会教你的小秘密

★ 身为一个上班族，节省钱的出行方式就是使用公交卡搭乘交通工具，如果"*go through the turnstile*（通过闸门）"时，闸门哔哔作响，那就代表你必须要"*top up your Easycard*（充值公交卡）"了；充值成功后，再一次"*scan the card*（刷卡）"便可以成功通过闸门搭车！

想要在站牌前拦下公交车或是出租车，需要熟记以下的短语，如：

✦ *flag down...* 挥手拦下……

✦ *hail down...* 挥手拦下……

✦ *call out to...* 大叫拦下……

所以，要拦下出租车或是公交车时就可以说：

✦ *Flag down a cab.* 拦出租车。

✦ *Hail down a taxi.* 拦出租车。

✦ *Call out to a bus.* 拦公交车。

Unit 4 特殊交通方式
Special means of transportation

 原来老外这样记单词 / 老外从小到大学习单词的方法，就是看到什么就学什么！

bow [baʊ]
n 船头；艏

deck [dek]
n 甲板

stern [stɜːrn]
n 船尾

life preserver
phr 【美】救生用具

propeller [prəˈpelər]
n 螺旋桨；推进器

其他衍生单词：

captain [ˈkæptɪn] n 船长；舰长

cabin [ˈkæbɪn] n （船的）客舱

oar [ɔːr] n 桨；橹

sailor [ˈseɪlər] n 船员；水手

crew [kruː] n 全体船员

anchor [ˈæŋkər] n 锚；锚状物

老外最常用的单词
连这些单词都不会，你还敢说你学过英语吗？

港口边的五光十色

pier [pɪr] n 码头

- **portside** [ˈpɔːtsaɪd] n 左舷；港口地区
- **starboard** [ˈstɑːrbərd] n （船／飞机的）右舷
- **lighthouse** [ˈlaɪthaʊs] n 灯塔
- **marina** [məˈriːnə] n 小艇码头；小艇船坞
- **bulwark** [ˈbʊlwɜːrk] n 防波堤
- **abutment** [əˈbʌtmənt] n 桥墩
- **cargo container** phr 货柜

工程车也出动

tow [toʊ] v 拖；拉

- **excavate** [ˈekskəveɪt] v 挖掘
- **patch** [pætʃ] v 修补
- **recondition** [ˌriːkənˈdɪʃn] v 修理；重建
- **resurface** [ˌriːˈsɜːrfɪs] v 重铺路面
- **pothole** [ˈpɑːthoʊl] n 路面上的坑洞
- **sewer** [ˈsuːər] n 下水道
- **gutter** [ˈɡʌtər] n （路旁边的）排水沟
- **jolt** [dʒoʊlt] n 颠簸

如何保养您的爱车

breakdown [ˈbreɪkdaʊn] n （机器等的）故障；损坏

- **maintenance** [ˈmeɪntənəns] n 维修；保养
- **gasoline** [ˈɡæsəliːn] n 汽油
- **muffler** [ˈmʌflər] n 消音器
- **kickstand** [ˈkɪkstænd] n 支架
- **loudspeaker** [ˌlaʊdˈspiːkər] n 扬声器
- **unleaded gasoline** phr 无铅汽油
- **exhaust pipe** phr （汽车等的）排气管

Unit 4 特殊交通方式

用英语聊天，原来这么简单 / 老外每天说的英语，其实就是这几句。

雪莉：呃……我们该先打给警察吗？ 海德：好，我也会打给我的保险公司。

Situation 1
古人的交通工具

In ancient times, people used horses and cattle as ❶ means of transportation.
古时候，人们把马和牛当成交通工具。

ancient ['eɪnʃənt] a 古代的；古老的　　cattle ['kætl] n 牛

transportation [ˌtrænspɔːr'teɪʃn] n 运输工具

Grammar-1
"as"在此为介词，用来表示"和……一样；作为"的意思。

Situation 2
很酷的交通工具

I have never ❷ taken submarines.
I hope that I could take it someday.
我从来没有坐过潜水艇。我希望有一天能坐。

Grammar-2
"sb. have never..."表示"某人从未……"。

That container ship was loaded with precious wood imported from Indonesia.
货柜船里载满了从印尼进口的珍贵木材。

I would go off-roading in my Jeep.
我要开我的吉普车去野外。

submarine [ˌsʌbmə'riːn] n 潜水艇　　someday ['sʌm,deɪ] ad 有朝一日

container ship phr 货柜船　　precious ['preʃəs] a 贵重的；宝贵的

import ['ɪmpɔːrt] v 进口；输入

Situation 3
想要租车

I want to rent a jeep **for** three days. How much does it cost?
我想要租吉普车三天，费用多少呢？

Grammar-3
"for" 表示持续的一段时间

rent [rent] v. 租用　　jeep [dʒiːp] n. 吉普车　　cost [kɔːst] v. 花费

Situation 4
驾驶习惯

He used to drive his car to work, but now he goes to work by bike **in order to** save the costs on gasoline.
他过去习惯开车去工作，但他现在为了省油钱而骑自行车去工作。

I can't actually parallel park well.
我不太会平行停车。

Grammar-4
"in order to（为了）" 与其相同的词汇或短语为 "to" 及 "so as to"，后面接原形动词。

I prefer scooters to motorcycles because the former is lighter than the latter.
我喜欢轻型摩托车胜过于普通摩托车，因为前者比后者轻便。

Grammar-5
"give way" 表示 "顺从；让步；妥协；屈服"；当不及物动词，后面可以接 to，再接宾语，表示 "向……屈服或让步"。

It's good manners to **give way** as you see the pedestrians walking across the street.
当你看见行人要穿越马路时，礼让是一个很好的礼仪。

save [seɪv] v. 节省；省去　　scooter [ˈskuːtər] n. 小轮摩托车

former [ˈfɔːrmər] a. （两者中）前者的

manner [ˈmænər] n. 态度；礼貌；规矩

street [striːt] n. 街道；（相对于人行道的）车道

Situation 5
随时注意路况

Listen carefully to the traffic report on the radio.
注意听广播的路况报道。

I always get caught in traffic jams during rush hour.
我总在高峰时段被困在车流里。

The tunnel is so dark that I need to turn on my headlights.
隧道太暗了，我必须打开车头灯。

Grammar-6
"It's + convenient + to v." 为 "……是很方便的" 的意思。

It's convenient and cheap **to** use the e-tag on the highway.
使用公路电子收费器既方便又便宜。

traffic jam phr. 交通堵塞　　rush hour phr. （上下班时）高峰时间

highway [ˈhaɪweɪ] n. 公路

Situation 6
维修爱车

The tire of the truck came off because the bolts were rusted.
货车的轮胎脱落了，因为螺丝生锈了。

My speedometer is broken. Sorry about that, officer.
我的时速表坏了。抱歉，警官。

You need to check your fuel gauge and polish the chrome.
你应该要检查看看你的燃油表，还有擦亮铬合金。

tire ['taɪər] n 轮胎　　truck [trʌk] n【美】卡车　　rust [rʌst] v 生锈

 老外不会教你的小秘密

★ 对于早上出门上班和傍晚下班回家的上班族来说，最怕遇到"rush hour（高峰时段）"；所以，当我们要说堵车的时候，除了可以用：
- *traffic jam* 堵车
- *gridlock* 交通大堵塞

也可以替换成下列句子：
- *The traffic is heavy.* 交通十分繁忙。
- *There is traffic congestion.* 交通拥挤。
- *The traffic hasn't moved at all.* 交通拥堵。

 不怕你学不会

1. He used to drive his car to work, but now he goes to work by bike so as to save the costs on gasoline.

   = He used to drive his car to work, but now he goes to work by bike _____ save the costs on gasoline.

2. Tim has never _____ (take) an airplane before, so he is a little nervous now.

答案：1. to / in order to　2. taken

Chapter **7** 马路如虎口

看看老外怎么学
将选项的单词分类后，搭配到对应的图片旁边吧

- biplane
- sedan
- clipper
- subway
- hot-air balloon
- limousine
- raft
- submarine
- monorail
- double-decker bus

答案：天上飞的 → biplane（双翼飞机）, hot-air balloon（热气球）
水里游的 → clipper（飞速帆船）, submarine（潜水艇）, raft（筏）
地上跑的 → sedan（轿车）, subway（地铁）, limousine（小型巴士）, double-decker bus（双层巴士）, monorail（单轨铁路）

Chapter 8
让你财源滚滚
Make lots of money

不管你是打工族、还是职场新人或是即将升职的老鸟，英语能力都是你工作上的拿分重点！快来用老外的方法学一学！

Unit 1
先找个工作吧

Unit 2
工作上的大小事

Unit 3
行行出状元

Unit 1 先找个工作吧
Find a job

原来老外这样记单词 / 老外从小到大学习单词的方法，就是看到什么就学什么！

job seeker
phr 求职者

competitiveness [kəmˈpetətɪvnəs]
n 竞争力

candidate [ˈkændɪdət]
n 应聘者、候选人

resume [rɪˈzuːm]
n 履历

applicant [ˈæplɪkənt]
n 申请人、申请者

其他衍生单词：

CV abbr 履历 (=curriculum vitae)
headhunter [ˈhedhʌntər] n 猎头
expertise [ˌekspɜːrˈtiːz] n 专业技术；专长
interviewer [ˈɪntərvjuːər] n 面试官
interviewee [ˌɪntərvjuːˈiː] n 面试者
job hopping phr 跳槽

Unit 1 先找个工作吧

老外最常用的单词 连这些单词都不会，你还敢说你学过英语吗？

创业相关的单词

partnership ['pɑːtnəʃɪp] n 合伙

boss [bɔːs] n 老板、上司
SOHO abbr 居家办公室
(= Small Office, Home Office)
teamwork ['tiːmwɜːrk] n 团队合作
cultural creativity industry
phr 文创产业
start from scratch phr 白手起家
business plan phr 商业计划

不同的职业 PART 1

chef [ʃef] n （餐馆等的）主厨

plumber ['plʌmər] n 水电工人
driver ['draɪvər] n 司机
housekeeper ['haʊskiːpər] n 女管家
nanny ['næni] n 保姆
waitress ['weɪtrəs] n 女服务生
vendor ['vendər] n 小贩
businessman ['bɪznəsmæn] n 商人
bricklayer ['brɪkleɪər] n 泥瓦匠
real estate agent phr 【美】房地产经纪人
bond trader phr 证券交易员

不同的职业 PART 2

barman ['bɑːrmən] n 酒吧男招待

detective [dɪ'tektɪv] n 侦探
caretaker ['keɪteɪkər] n 看护
goldsmith ['gəʊldsmɪθ] n 金匠
hairdresser ['heɪrdresər] n 美发师
waiter ['weɪtər] n 服务生
typist ['taɪpɪst] n 打字员
locksmith ['lɑːksmɪθ] n 锁匠
bodyguard ['bɑːdɪgɑːrd] n 保镖
tour guide phr 导游

Chapter 8 教你财源滚滚来

151

用英语聊天，原来这么简单 / 老外每天说的英语，其实就是这几句。

Welcome, Miss Lin. You are our new staff now!

Oh, my goodness! Thank you very much!

人力资源主管：林小姐，欢迎。你现在是我们的新员工了！　　林：哦，我的天啊，谢谢你！

Situation 1
有职位空缺

- The airline company is now **hiring** ❶ elites to fill posts in their new overseas office.
  航空公司正在聘用人才，让他们在海外的新公司任职。

  Grammar-1
  "hire"当动词时，有"雇用；租借"的意思，其用法相当于"employ（雇用）"及"recruit（聘用）"等词汇。

- I am sure Linda **is qualified for** ❷ this position.
  我确定琳达有资格胜任这个职位。

  Grammar-2
  "be qualified to + v."有"具备必要条件的；胜任的"的意思，还可以用"be qualified for + N"的方式来表达。

- Which shift do you prefer, day shift or night shift?
  你喜欢哪个工作时段，日班还是夜班？

- Interviewer: What is your educational background?
  面试官：你的学历背景是什么呢？

- What is your **previous** ❸ work experience?
  你之前的工作经验是什么呢？

  Grammar-3
  "previous"当形容词时，有"以前的"的意思，其用法相当于"earlier（早先的）"和"former（前任的；早前的）"。

- Would you like a part-time or a full-time position? We can offer you many fringe benefits with the full-time position.
  你想要兼职还是全职的工作呢？我们的全职工作可以提供你许多额外的福利。

---

elite [eɪˈliːt] n 人才；精英　　overseas [ˌoʊvərˈsiːz] a （在）海外的

office [ˈɔːfɪs] n 办公室　　qualified [ˈkwɑːlɪfaɪd] a 胜任的

position [pəˈzɪʃn] n 职位 (相) capacity [kəˈpæsəti] n 资格；职位

Unit 1 先找个工作吧

educational [ˌedʒʊˈkeɪʃənl] a 教育的

background [ˈbækɡraʊnd] n （包括学历在内的）经历

work experience phr 工作经验

part-time phr 兼职的；兼任的 反 full-time phr 专任的；全职的

fringe benefit phr 额外福利

Situation 2
找工作

You can find some good jobs on human resource websites.
你可以在人力资源网站中找到一些好工作。

Grammar-4
"fear" 当动词时，有"害怕；恐惧"的意思，也可以替换成"be afraid / fear of ＋ N"或"fear that ＋ 句子"。

I fear ❹ I will fail the job interview.
我怕我面试会失败。

I have to know what my target is, and then go to find a job.
我得先找到我的目标，然后再去找工作。

Grammar-5
"a piece of cake"字面上的意思为"一块蛋糕"，引申为"小事一桩"。

It is not a piece of cake ❺ to find a satisfying job.
要找到一个令人满意的工作并不容易。

How about getting an academic job?
不如找学术界的工作试试？

Steven landed a well-paid job at the bank.
史蒂文在银行里找到一份待遇不错的工作。

I want to pick up another job at night.
我想在晚上再找一份工作。

I feel confident that I am qualified for this post.
我信心十足，我能胜任这个职位。

I sent you my resume last week.
我上星期将我的履历表寄给您了。

Grammar-6
degree 是指学位，比如学士、硕士等；而 diploma 指文凭。

I believe I can hunt a good job with my doctorate diploma ❻.
我相信我能以博士的文凭找到好的工作。

fail [feɪl] v 失败   job interview phr 面试

satisfying [ˈsætɪsfaɪɪŋ] a 满意的；充分的

land [lænd] v 【口】弄到；捞到   well-paid [ˈwelˈpeɪd] a 待遇优厚的

Chapter **8** 教你财源滚滚来

153

confident [ˈkɑːnfɪdənt] a 有信心的   post [pəʊst] n 职位；职守

send [send] v 发送；寄   hunt [hʌnt] v 搜寻；寻找

doctorate [ˈdɑːktərət] n 博士学位

Situation 3
和同事周旋

I bend over backwards to please my manager, but he is still not happy.
我尽全力地讨好我的经理，但他还是不高兴。

Grammar-7
"co-worker" 当名词时，有"同事"的意思，其等同于"colleague（同事；同僚）"的用法。

Do you get along well with co-workers ❼ ?
你和同事相处得愉快吗？

please [pliːz] v 讨好   manager [ˈmænɪdʒər] n 经理

Situation 4
下班了

Let's call it a day ❽ and go out for a meal together.
我们结束一天的工作，然后一起外出吃饭吧！

go out phr 外出   together [təˈɡeðər] ad 一起；共同

Grammar-8
"call it a day" 有"结束一天的工作"的意思，常用的口语解释则为"决定或同意暂时停止（进行某事物）"。

Situation 5
加班

Can you work overtime tonight to finish all this paper work?
你今晚可以加班完成所有的文书工作吗？

work overtime phr 加班

Situation 6
请假

May I take a day off ❾ tomorrow?
I have an appointment at the doctor's.
我明天可以请一天假吗？我要去看医生。

appointment [əˈpɔɪntmənt] n （会面的）约定

Grammar-9
"take off" 的意思为"请假"。

Situation 7
被开除了

Allen got fired because his boss caught him sleeping ❿ on the job.
艾伦被解雇了，因为他的老板抓到他在工作中睡觉。

I lost my job. I need a new job immediately.
我失业了。我急需一份新的工作。

fire [ˈfaɪər] v 解雇 同 dismiss [dɪsˈmɪs] v 开除；免职

on the job phr 在工作中 同 at work phr 在工作

Grammar-10
"catch someone + Ving" 意思为"抓到某人正在做某事"。

Unit 2 工作上的大小事
Lots of work

原来老外这样记单词 / 老外从小到大学习单词的方法，就是看到什么就学什么！

- **secretary** [ˈsekrəteri] n 秘书
- **creativity director** phr 创意执行总监
- **white collar** phr 白领阶层
- **model** [ˈmɑːdl] n 模型
- **project supervisor** phr 专案主任

其他衍生单词：

- **blue-collar** [ˈbluːˌkɑlɚ] a 体力劳动者
- **special assistant** phr 特别助理 (= SA)
- **account executive** phr 业务员 (= AE)
- **account director** phr 客户总监 (= AD)
- **marketing representative** phr 销售代表
- **management consultant** phr 管理顾问

老外最常用的单词 / 连这些单词都不会,你还敢说你学过英语吗?

应该有的保障不能少

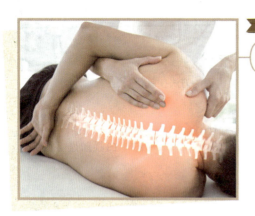

occupational accident
phr 职业伤害

retire [rɪˈtaɪər] v 退休
pension [ˈpenʃn] n 退休金
raise [reɪz] n 【美】加薪
labor insurance phr 劳动保险
annual leave phr 年假
year-end bonus phr 年终奖金
welfare allowance phr 福利津贴
basic wage phr 基本薪资;底薪

公司内的职位

operator [ˈɑːpəreɪtər] n 接线员

moonlighting [ˈmuːnˌlaɪtɪŋ] n 兼职
receptionist [rɪˈsepʃənɪst] n 接待员
auditor [ˈɔːdɪtər] n 查账员;审计员
general manager phr 总经理
market analyst phr 市场分析员
trainee manager phr 培训部经理
financial controller phr 财务主任
maintenance engineer phr 维修工程师

这些铁饭碗

career soldier phr 职业军人

president [ˈprezɪdənt] n 总统
diplomat [ˈdɪpləmæt] n 外交官
mayor [ˈmeɪər] n 市长
mail carrier phr 邮差
civil servant phr 公务员
prison officer phr 狱警

Unit 2 工作上的大小事

 用英语聊天，原来这么简单 / 老外每天说的英语，其实就是这几句。

Let's talk about the sales plan next year.
Does anybody have a good idea?

约翰：我们来讨论明年的销售计划吧。有人有好点子吗？

Chapter **8** 教你财源滚滚来

Situation 1
工作状况

One of my son's work is on a farm, one works in an office, and my third son is in the military.
我的一个儿子在农场工作，一个在办公室上班，而我的三儿子在服兵役。

Be at your desk ❶ at 9 sharp every morning from Monday to Friday.
从星期一到星期五的早上 9 点整上班。

Grammar-1
"be at your desk" 有"在位置上"之意，引申为"上班"的意思。

This responsibility doesn't fall under my job description.
这个责任不属于我的工作范围。

I have finished all the projects you gave me; do you have additional work for me?
我已经完成你交付给我的所有任务。还有额外工作要给我吗？

Please contact the manager. Let him help customers deal with the questions.
请联系你的管理人，并请他处理你的客人们遇到的问题。

military ['mɪləteri] n 军队　　responsibility [rɪ,spɑːnsə'bɪləti] n 责任；义务

job description phr 工作说明；职务说明　　project ['prɑːdʒekt] n 项目

additional [ə'dɪʃənl] a 额外的；添加的

157

Situation 2
帮别人留言

Mr. Martin will be unavailable for the next two weeks. ==May I take a message?== I will forward it to him on the first occasion.

马丁先生接下来两个星期都没有空。要帮你留言吗？我会在第一时间帮你转达。

Grammar-2
当对方询问 "May I take a message?"，意思是 "需要帮你留言吗？"。

- unavailable [ˌʌnəˈveɪləbl] a 没空的
- forward [ˈfɔːrwərd] v 转交；递送
- occasion [əˈkeɪʒn] n 时刻

Situation 3
准备升迁

He might be able to quickly move up the career ladder. He wants to work hard for advancement.

他想要快点往上爬。他为了晋升而努力工作。

Grammar-3
"be able to + V" 有 "可以……；能够……" 的意思，其用法等同于 "be capable of + Ving"。

There will be a general assembly on Wednesday night to discuss the new promotion. Please arrive promptly.

星期三晚上将有个全体代表会议，是为了讨论新的晋升问题。请准时出席。

- move up phr 提升
- career ladder phr 职业晋升阶梯
- advancement [ədˈvænsmənt] n 晋升
- general assembly phr 全体代表会议
- discuss [dɪˈskʌs] v 讨论；商谈
- promotion [prəˈmoʊʃn] n 晋升
- promptly [ˈprɑːmptli] ad 准时地

Situation 4
薪水的增减

==Due to== the economic crisis, all the employees will take a 20% pay cut for the next two months.

因为经济危机，所有员工在下两个月里将会减 20% 的薪水。

Grammar-4
"Due to..." 有 "由于……" 的意思，和其相同用法的短语有 "as a result of" "because of" 和 "owing to"。

I will give a ==bonus== to the first employee who doubles his sales quota.

我将发给第一个销售业绩翻倍的员工红利。

Grammar-5
"bonus" 当名词时，有 "红利；奖金" 的意思，而红利的种类有 "cash bonus（现金的）" 或 stock bonus（股票的）"。

Mr. Jones, I ==have been working== here for many years already, may I get a raise?

琼斯先生，我在这工作已经很多年了，我可以加薪吗？

Grammar-6
"have been working" 为现在完成进行时，用以说明从以前到现在持续的事情或动作。

- economic crisis phr 经济危机
- employee [ɪmˈplɔɪiː] n 员工
- sales [seɪlz] a 售货的；销售的
- quota [ˈkwoʊtə] n 限额；配额
- already [ɔːlˈredi] ad 已经；先前

Unit 2 工作上的大小事

Situation 5
客户都爱听的话

Next week, our biggest client will go to the factory for a visit. We need to make sure that he will renew his contract with us.
下星期，我们的最大客户将要到工厂参观。我们必须确保他会更新合约。

I have a potential client on the phone who would like to speak to the manager.
我电话上有一位潜在客户想要跟经理说话。

Grammar-7
"pay"为动词，有"支付"的意思，动词三态为"pay - paid - paid"。

How do I handle Mr. Yang's case? He still hasn't paid ⑦ his last two bills.
我要如何处理杨先生的案子呢？他还没有支付前两笔款项。

client ['klaɪənt] n 客户
factory ['fæktri] n 工厂
make sure phr 确信；把……弄清楚
contract ['kɑːntrækt] n 契约
potential [pə'tenʃl] a 潜在的；可能的
speak to phr 对……说
handle ['hændl] v 处理
case [keɪs] n 案件
bill [bɪl] n 账单

Situation 6
有特别的人物到来

The government will send an inspector next month. We need to be up to par to be able to keep our license.
政府将在下个月派遣一位督察员。我们必须达到标准以保住我们的执照。

inspector [ɪn'spektər] n 督察员
par [pɑːr] n 平均；标准
license ['laɪsns] n 执照

Situation 7
股票的问题

All the shareholders have been waiting for ⑧ you in the meeting room.
所有的股东已经在会议室等你了。

Grammar-8
"wait for"有"等候"的意思，和其相同的短语为"watch for（等待）"。

shareholder ['ʃerhoʊldər] n【英】股东
meeting room phr 会议室

老外不会教你的小秘密

★ 公司如果有开会通知，公文中通常会写上"Please be on time.（请准时出席。）"；我们也可以替换成"Please be punctual.（请准时出席。）"。

Chapter 8 教你财源滚滚来

Unit 3 行行出状元
Master it

 原来老外这样记单词 / 老外从小到大学习单词的方法，就是看到什么就学什么！

cleaner [ˈkliːnər]
n 清洁工

librarian [laɪˈbrerɪən]
n 图书馆员

attorney [əˈtɜːrni]
n 【美】律师

interior designer
phr 室内设计师

nurse [nɜːrs]
n 护理师

其他衍生单词：

lawyer [ˈlɔːjər] n 律师
vet [vet] n 兽医

farmer [ˈfɑːrmər] n 农夫
lecturer [ˈlektʃərər] n 讲师

author [ˈɔːθər] n 作家
accountant [əˈkaʊntənt] n 会计师

老外最常用的单词
连这些单词都不会，你还敢说你学过英语吗？

书念得多的人 ★★

judge [dʒʌdʒ] n 法官

- **zoologist** [zʊˈɑːlədʒɪst] n 动物学家
- **economist** [ɪˈkɑːnəmɪst] n 经济学者
- **interpreter** [ɪnˈtɜːrprɪtər] n 口译员
- **translator** [trænsˈleɪtər] n 译者
- **columnist** [ˈkɑːləmnɪst] n 专栏作家
- **chairman** [ˈtʃermən] n 主席；（大学的）系主任
- **meteorologist** [ˌmiːtɪəˈrɑːlədʒɪst] n 气象学家

燃烧生命牺牲奉献的人 ★★

priest [priːst] n 牧师

- **fire fighter** phr 【美】救火队员
- **police officer** phr 警察
- **statesman** [ˈsteɪtsmən] n 政治家
- **journalist** [ˈdʒɜːrnəlɪst] n 新闻记者
- **fisherman** [ˈfɪʃərmən] n 渔夫
- **miner** [ˈmaɪnər] n 矿工
- **proofreader** [ˈpruːfriːdər] n 校对者
- **engineer** [ˌendʒɪˈnɪr] n 工程师
- **tutor** [ˈtjuːtər] n 家教

不同的工作 ★★

astronaut [ˈæstrənɔːt] n 宇航员

- **pilot** [ˈpaɪlət] n 飞行员
- **sailor** [ˈseɪlər] n 水手
- **novelist** [ˈnɑːvəlɪst] n 小说家
- **carpenter** [ˈkɑːrpəntər] n 木匠
- **housewife** [ˈhaʊswaɪf] n 家庭主妇
- **anchor** [ˈæŋkər] n 【美】（电台／电视台）新闻节目主播

Chapter 8 教你财源滚滚来

用英语聊天，原来这么简单
老外每天说的英语，其实就是这几句。

So, how's your work going?
Brown

Pretty nice. How about you?
Perry

布朗：怎么样？工作如何？　佩里：还不错啊。你呢？

Situation 1
职业不分贵贱

All jobs are equal. You cannot look down on ❶ any jobs!
职业不分贵贱。你不能轻视任何一个工作！

equal ['iːkwəl] a 相等的；平等的 同 even ['iːvn] a 一致的；均等的

Grammar-1
"look down on"的意思为"轻视"，和其相同的短语为"look down one's nose at（瞧不起）"。

Situation 2
公司的制度

Many companies hold video conferences ❷ to save costs on traffic fares.
很多公司举行视频会议来节省交通费上的开销。

company ['kʌmpəni] n 公司

video conference phr 视频会议

Grammar-2
"conference"当名词时，意思为"会议"，其用法相当于"meeting（会议；集会）"与"council（会议；议事）"。

Situation 3
公务员的工作

Crime scene investigators will arrive ❸ in a few minutes.
犯罪现场调查人员将会在几分钟后抵达。

Grammar-3
"arrive"当动词时，有"抵达"之意，其用法相当于"come（到达）"与"reach（抵达；到达）"。

Grammar-4
"well-ordered"当形容词时，意思为"井然有序"，其用法相当于"well-arranged"一词。

A prison warden has to manage the whole jail and keep it well-ordered ❹.
典狱长必须管理整座监狱并将监狱维持得井然有序。

Unit 3 行行出狀元

Grammar-5
"sue" 當動詞時，有"起訴"的意思，其用法相當於 "litigate（訴訟）" 一詞。

Grammar-6
"disqualify" 當動詞時，有"取消資格"之意，其反義詞為 "qualify" 與 "entitle"，其意為"使有資格"。

The prosecutor decided to **sue** the person who embezzled public money.
檢察官決定起訴那位盜用公款的人。

The candidate was **disqualified** after his scandal was uncovered.
候選人的醜聞被揭露後被解除資格。

An ambassador enjoys diplomatic immunity.
大使享有外交豁免權。

- investigator [ɪnˈvɛstɪɡeɪtər] n 調查者
- manage [ˈmænɪdʒ] v 管理；經營
- prosecutor [ˈprɑːsɪkjuːtər] n 檢察官
- embezzle [ɪmˈbɛzl] v 盜用；侵占
- public [ˈpʌblɪk] a 公用的；公共的
- candidate [ˈkændɪdət] n 候選人
- scandal [ˈskændl] n 醜聞；弊案
- uncover [ʌnˈkʌvər] v 揭露；揭發 ≒ reveal [rɪˈviːl] v 揭示；揭露
- ambassador [æmˈbæsədər] n 大使；使節
- diplomatic immunity phr 外交豁免權

Situation 4 千奇百怪的工作

There are always many street artists **gathering** around train stations.
有很多街頭藝人聚集在火車站附近。

Grammar-8
"fortuneteller" 為名詞，其意思為"算命師"，用法相當於 "soothsayer（預言者；算命者）"。

Grammar-7
"gather" 當動詞時，有"聚集"之意，其用法相當於 "assemble（集合；聚集）"與 "cluster（群；組）"。

I don't believe what **fortunetellers** say; I believe that the future is in my hand, not others.
我不相信算命師說的話；我相信未來在我手上，而不是別人。

Fire fighters tried their best to save the baby who got stuck in the burning house.
消防隊員盡全力搶救被困在火場裡的嬰兒。

After years of working as a funeral worker, he got a different outlook on life.
在擔任墓園工作者幾年後，他對生命有不同的領悟。

Grammar-9
"disclose" 當動詞時，意思為"揭穿；公開"，其用法與 "unveil（揭露；使公之於世）" 相同。

The paparazzi stayed out of that actress' house to see if there was anything that could be **disclosed**.
狗仔隊守在女演員的家門口，看看有什麼可以爆料的。

Chapter **8** 教你財源滾滾來

Archaeologists dug out some fossils from prehistoric times.
考古学家挖出一些史前时代的化石。

Grammar-10
"shake hands with"的意思为"和……握手"，后面通常会接上人称。

The pet trainer is going to train that husky to **shake hands with** ⑩ her.
宠物训练师即将训练哈士奇和她握手。

Those models are all too skinny. Have they eaten anything today?
那些模特儿也太瘦了吧。她们今天吃东西了吗？

Grammar-11
"so...that..."有"太……以至于"的意思。

The novice newscaster was **so** nervous **that** ⑪ she got tongue-tied.
新主播太紧张，所以说不出话。

Grammar-12
"be determined to"有"下定决心"的意思，后接动词原形。

David **is determined to** ⑫ become a trapeze artist as he grows up.
大卫立志长大后要成为空中飞人。

Darren wanted to be a clown since he was a child.
达伦从小就想当个小丑。

Grammar-13
"suggest to sb."的意思为"建议某人做某事"，后面需要接上动词原形。

The Feng Shui specialist **suggested to me** ⑬ that reorganize the living room.
风水师建议我重新布置客厅。

street artist [phr] 街头艺人　　save [seɪv] [v] 挽救

burning [ˈbɜːrnɪŋ] [a] 燃烧的；着火的

funeral [ˈfjuːnərəl] [n] 葬礼

archaeologist [ˌɑːrkɪˈɑːlədʒɪst] [n] 考古学家　　dig out [phr] 挖掘；发现

prehistoric [ˌpriːhɪˈstɔːrɪk] [a] 史前的

train [treɪn] [v] 训练；培养　　husky [ˈhʌski] [n] 哈士奇

novice [ˈnɑːvɪs] [n] 新手 [反] veteran [ˈvetərən] [n] 老手；老兵

newscaster [ˈnuːzkæstər] [n] 新闻主播

tongue-tied [ˈtʌŋˌtaɪd] [a] （因胆怯等）说不出话的

become [bɪˈkʌm] [v] 变成；成为　　grow up [phr] （指人或动物）长大；成熟

Feng Shui [phr] 风水　　reorganize [rɪˈɔːrɡənaɪz] [v] 整顿；改组

Chapter 9 科技，始终来自人性

Technology comes from humanity

现今的社会，已经进展到人手至少一机。
身处在这样的时代，
还不快来用最 International 的方式学会科技语言！

Unit 1
光速的时代

Unit 2
生活中无所不在

Unit 3
现代人的生命线

Unit 1 光速的时代
Internet generation

原来老外这样记单词 / 老外从小到大学习单词的方法，就是看到什么就学什么！

inventor [ɪnˈventər] n 发明家

screwdriver [ˈskruːdraɪvər] n 螺丝刀

notebook [ˈnəʊtbʊk] n 笔记本

wire [ˈwaɪər] n 电线

robotic arm phr 机器手臂

其他衍生单词：

lever [ˈlevər] n 杠杆
invent [ɪnˈvent] v 发明
robotics [rəʊˈbɑːtɪks] n 机器人学
motor [ˈməʊtər] n 马达
AI = Artificial Intelligence phr 人工智能
high-end a 高档的；高层次的

老外最常用的单词 / 连这些单词都不会，你还敢说你学过英语吗？

没有这些发明就没有现代社会

phonograph ['fəʊnəɡræf]
n 【美】留声机

generator ['dʒenəreɪtər] n 发电机
negative ['neɡətɪv] n 底片
microscope ['maɪkrəskəʊp] n 显微镜
planetarium [ˌplænɪ'terɪəm] n 星象仪
steam engine phr 蒸汽机
hybrid electric vehicle
phr 油电混合动力车

没有这些人和事物就没有发明

laboratory ['læbrətɔːri] n 实验室

innovative ['ɪnəvɪtɪv] a 创新的
research [rɪ'sɜːtʃ] n （学术）研究
scientist ['saɪəntɪst] n 科学家
high-tech millionaires phr 高科技
white room
phr （医院的）无菌室；无尘室
computer programmer phr 电脑工程师
Nobel Prize phr 诺贝尔奖

不接触这些就表示落伍了

solar car phr 太阳能车

nanotechnology n 纳米科技
wafer ['weɪfər] n 晶片
semiconductor [ˌsemɪkən'dʌktər]
n 半导体
wind power generator
phr 风力发电机
digital signboard phr 数码电子看板
tablet ['tæblət] n 平板

用英语聊天，原来这么简单 / 老外每天说的英语，其实就是这几句。

斯芬克斯：我们想制造一个能够飞上月球的飞行器。　茱莉亚：听起来很棒。

Situation 1
早期的发明，就用这几句来唤起你的记忆

Turn down the volume ❶ on the radio. I can't clear my thoughts.
收音机的音量调小一点，我无法整理我自己的思绪。

This old record player is so outdated ❷ that only my grandfather knows how it works.
这台电唱机是如此的老旧，只有我爷爷才知道如何操作。

I surely ❸ don't want to do without my music player.
我确定不丢掉我的音乐播放机了。

When I reformatted my music player, all my songs got deleted, even my favorite ones.
当我格式化我的音乐播放机时，我所有的歌曲都被删除了，甚至连我最喜欢的音乐也是。

The Video cassette recorder has gradually ❹ vanished.
录像机已经逐渐消失。

Grammar-1
"turn down the volume" 的意思为 "转低音量；降低音量"，和其意思相反的短语为 "turn up the volume"。

Grammar-2
句中的 "outdated" 为形容词，有 "旧式的、过时的" 之意，和其用法相当的词汇有 "old-fashioned（过时的；老派的）"。

Grammar-3
"surely" 当副词使用，有 "一定；确实" 的意思，和其相同用法的词汇还 "certainly（必定；确实）" 和 "definitely（明确地；当然）"。

Grammar-4
"gradually" 为副词，有 "逐渐地；渐渐地" 的意思，也可以用短语 "by degrees" 来替换。

clear [klɪr] v 清除；收拾
record player phr 电唱机
do without phr 摒弃；戒绝
player ['pleɪər] n （不能录音的）随身听；单放机
thought [θɔːt] n 思维；思考
work [wɜːrk] v （机器等）运转；活动

Unit 1 光速的时代

reformat [rɪˈfɔrmæt] v 重新格式化   delete [dɪˈliːt] v 删除

even [ˈiːvn] ad （加强语气）甚至；连

video cassette recorder phr 录放影机

vanish [ˈvænɪʃ] v 消失；突然不见 ≡ disappear [ˌdɪsəˈpɪr] v 消失；不见

Situation 2
想要和你的朋友网络聊天吗？

After school, I'll download a new **program** ⁵ to make movies, send a few e-mails and chat with my friends on Facebook.
放学后，我要下载一个新程序来制作电影、发一些电子邮件并和朋友在"脸书"上聊天。

This web page is well-designed and user-friendly.
这个网页设计良好且容易操作。

Grammar-5
"program" 当名词时，为美式用法的词汇，意思为"程式；节目"的意思，和英式"programme"相同。

LAN ⁶ stands for Local Area Network.
LAN 代表局域网络。

Grammar-6
"LAN" 是 "Local Area Network" 的缩写形式，其意思为"局域网络"；而 wireless network 则为"无线网络"的意思。

I will also **log on** ⁷ to my favorite band's website.
我也会登入我最喜欢的乐团网站。

Grammar-7
此句中的 "log on" 有 "【电脑】注册；登记" 的意思，为固定短语。

James is **trying to** ⁸ iron out all the problems on his new website.
詹姆斯正在试着解决新网站的所有问题。

Grammar-8
句型 "try to ＋ V..." 有 "试图……" 的意思，后接动词原形。

We may encroach on someone's intelligence right without awareness. Be careful when you write something on the Internet.
我们可能在无意识的情况下侵犯别人的知识产权，所以在网络上发表文章时要格外小心。

Grammar-9
"frequently" 当副词时，意思为"频繁地；屡次地"，和其用法相同的词汇有 "constantly（不断地；时常地）"。

I set Google as my home page because I use it **frequently** ⁹.
我把 Google 设成我的首页，因为我经常使用它。

This website's **click through rate** ¹⁰ was not as high as predicted.
这网站的点击率不如预期中的高。

Grammar-10
"click through rate" 有"点击率"的意思，其缩写形式为 "CTR"。

Grammar-11
用以表示"从过去到现在持续在做某事"的句型为 "have / has been...for many years"，为现在完成时。

Linda **has been** a blogger **for many years** ¹¹. She always shares her life experience on her web blog.
琳达已经当博主好几年了。她总是在博客分享她的生活经验。

Chapter **9** 科技，始终来自人性

169

Grammar-12
"be fed up with"有"厌烦；受够了"的意思，可以替换成"be tired of"或"be sick of"。

Grammar-13
句型"A is faster than B"用以表示"A比B快"，其中A与B的词性须为一致。

Grammar-14
"hyperlink"当名词时，有"超链接"的意思，其中"hyper-"又有"超越、非常"之意。

Grammar-15
"after"当介词时，其后所接的动词需以Ving来呈现，但因为在本句中"被黑客入侵"是属"被动语态"，所以省略主语和be V，仅留过去分词当被动。

I am fed up with ⑫ receiving endless spam e-mails!
我受够了无尽的垃圾邮件！

A broadband network is faster than ⑬ a dial-up connection.
宽带网络的速度比拨号连线快。

Click the hyperlink ⑭ and you can have an overview of the government website.
点击超链接，你便可以浏览政府的网站。

Our website was paralyzed after ⑮ being intruded by hackers.
网站在被黑客入侵后就瘫痪了。

- download [ˌdaʊnˈlɔd] v 下载
- web page phr 网页
- well-designed [ˈwel dɪˈzaɪnd] a 设计良好的
- user-friendly [ˈjuːzər ˈfrendlɪ] a 容易使用的
- stand for phr 代表
- iron out phr 消除；解决
- awareness [əˈwernəs] n 察觉；体认
- predict [prɪˈdɪkt] v 预料
- blogger n 博主（即写网络日志的人）
- endless [ˈendləs] a 无尽的；无止境的 ≒ infinite [ˈɪnfɪnət] a 无限的；无边的
- broadband network phr 宽带网络
- dial-up connection phr 拨号连线
- overview [ˈəʊvərvjuː] n 【美】概观；概要；综述
- paralyze [ˈpærəlaɪz] v 使瘫痪；麻痹
- intrude [ɪnˈtruːd] v 侵入；闯入
- hacker [ˈhækər] n 【电脑】黑客

Situation 3 拥有好配备

Grammar-16
"state-of-the-art"作形容词时，有"先进的"之意，也可以用"advanced"来替换。

Our company is equipped with state-of-the-art ⑯ equipment, so we have confidence in ⑰ producing the best product.
我们公司拥有最先进的设备，所以我们有信心能制造出最好的产品。

Grammar-17
"have confidence in"的意思为"对……有信心"，与其相同的短语有"have faith in"。

- company [ˈkʌmpəni] n 公司
- produce [prəˈduːs] v 生产；制造
- product [ˈprɑːdʌkt] n 产品；结果；作品

Unit 2 生活中无所不在
Everywhere in our lives

原来老外这样记单词 / 老外从小到大学习单词的方法，就是看到什么就学什么！

cable television phr 有线电视

smoke detector phr 烟雾探测器

vacuum cleaner phr （真空）吸尘器

anti-theft sensor phr 防盗感应器

其他衍生单词：

LCD TV (= Liquid Crystal Display TV) phr 液晶电视
plasma display phr 电子显示器
remote control phr 遥控器

dehumidify [ˌdiːˈhjuːmɪdəˌfaɪ] v 除去湿气
water filter phr 滤水器
telephone [ˈtelɪfəʊn] n 电话

老外最常用的单词 / 连这些单词都不会，你还敢说你学过英语吗？

每个家庭都要有这些

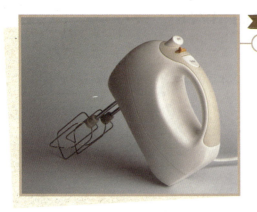

egg beater `phr` 打蛋器
digital camera `n` 数码相机
air purifier `phr` 空气净化器
fire sprinkler system `phr` 自动淋水系统
water dispenser `phr` 饮水机
exhaust fan `phr` 抽风机
water heater `phr` 热水器
extractor hood `phr` 抽油烟机
rice cooker `phr` 电饭锅
ionic hairdryer `phr` 负离子吹风机

每家公司都要有这些

webcam `n` 视频系统

calculator [ˈkælkjʊleɪtər] `n` 计算器
microphone [ˈmaɪkrəfəʊn] `n` 麦克风
shredder [ˈʃredər] `n` 碎纸机
scanner [ˈskænər] `n` 扫描仪
pen recorder `phr` 录音笔
laser printer `phr` 激光打印机
fax machine `phr` 传真机
monitor [ˈmɑːnɪtər] `n` 监视器
intercom [ˈɪntərkɑːm] `n` 对讲机
extinguisher [ɪkˈstɪŋɡwɪʃər] `n` 灭火器

别忘了还有这么多好发明

vehicle video recorder `phr` 行车记录仪

projector [prəˈdʒektər] `n` 放映机
blender [ˈblendər] `n` 搅拌机
thermometer [θərˈmɑːmɪtər] `n` 温度计
high voltage `phr` 高压电
body fat scale `phr` 身体脂肪计量器
convenience food `phr` 便利食品
waffle maker `phr` 松饼机
SRS `abbr` 安全气囊 (=Supplementary Restraint System)

用英语聊天，原来这么简单 / 老外每天说的英语，其实就是这几句。

Steven: Dear, I would like to buy a dish washer for you. Do you like the idea?

Angela: Oh, darling. You're so sweet.

史蒂文：亲爱的，我想买台洗碗机给你，你觉得呢？　安吉拉：噢，亲爱的，你太贴心了。

Situation 1
生活中的好发明

I can cook a delicious dinner for my family in ❶ 15 minutes when I use the microwave.
当我使用微波炉时，我可以在 15 分钟内为家人做好一顿美味的晚餐。

Grammar-1
"in + 时间"，意思为"在时间之内"，通常会用于现在时或将来时。

Mom washed our uniforms in the washing machine and then she dried them in the dryer. Finally she ironed them with her iron.
妈妈用洗衣机洗我们的制服，然后用烘衣机烘干它们，最后再用熨斗烫平。

Grammar-2
句中"freezer"为名词，有"冷冻室"的意思，与其相同的词汇为"cooler"和"compartment"。

Most refrigerators have a freezer ❷ where we can make ice.
大多数的冰箱都有冷冻室让我们可以制作冰块。

Grammar-4
"love"后面可以衔接不定式"to + V"或用"Ving"来呈现，两者都解释为"喜爱做……"的意思。

It is nice to ❸ use the air conditioner in this hot weather.
在这样酷热的天气里，使用空调真好。

Grammar-3
"It's nice to + V..."为固定句型，其意思为"做某件事真好"。

Dora used icemakers in the refrigerator to make ice cubes.
朵拉利用冰箱里的制冰器来制作冰块。

Grammar-5
"aroma"当名词时，有"咖啡的香气"的意思，不同于"fragrance"的用法，因为后者是指"芬芳的花香"。

I love ❹ using a coffee grinder to make coffee because the aroma ❺ of the beans will be preserved.
我喜欢用咖啡研磨机煮咖啡，因为咖啡豆的香气会被保留。

Grammar-6
"various"当形容词，意思为"多种的"，和其相同的词汇有"diverse（不同的；多变化的）"。

Grammar-7
此句中的"provide A with B"意思为"把B提供给A"。

A rice cooker has <mark>various</mark> ❻ functions, so <u>almost</u> each family has one.
电饭锅有很多功能，所以几乎每个家庭都有一台。

A home theater system <mark>provides</mark> people <mark>with</mark> ❼ hearing enjoyment.
家庭影院提供人们听觉上的享受。

microwave ['maɪkrəweɪv] n 微波炉

washing machine phr 洗衣机   dryer ['draɪər] n 烘干机

iron ['aɪərn] n 熨斗 v 烫平；熨衣

refrigerator [rɪ'frɪdʒəreɪtər] n 冰箱 同 fridge [frɪdʒ] n 电冰箱

ice cube phr 冰块   coffee grinder phr 咖啡豆研磨机 (= coffee mill)

bean [biːn] n （可作食物或饮料的）豆

preserve [prɪ'zɜːrv] v 保存；维持   function ['fʌŋkʃn] n 功能；作用

almost ['ɔːlməʊst] ad 几乎；差不多   hearing ['hɪrɪŋ] n 听觉

enjoyment [ɪn'dʒɔɪmənt] n 乐趣；享受

Situation 2
生活中随处可见的材料

Which <u>bookcase</u> do you prefer, the heavier <u>wood</u> one or the lighter <u>plastic</u> one?
你比较喜欢哪个书架，是较重木制的还是较轻塑料制的呢？

Daniel has learned that <u>leather</u> <u>jackets</u> <u>require</u> lots of care <mark>even though</mark> ❽ they look <u>nice</u>.
丹尼尔学到皮革的夹克是需要保养的，虽然它们很好看。

Grammar-8
句中"even though"与"although"、"though"的意思相同，为"即使；虽然"之意。

This <u>glass</u> table is more <mark>fragile</mark> ❾ than that <u>metal</u> one.
这个玻璃桌比那个金属桌更容易碎。

Grammar-9
"fragile"当形容词时，有"易碎的"的意思，也可以使用"delicate（脆的；易碎的）"来替换。

bookcase ['bʊkkeɪs] n 书架；书橱   wood [wʊd] a 木制的

plastic ['plæstɪk] a 塑料的；塑料制的   leather ['leðər] a 皮革的

jacket ['dʒækɪt] n 夹克   require [rɪ'kwaɪər] v 需要

nice [naɪs] a 好的；细致的   glass [glæs] n 玻璃

metal ['metl] n 金属；金属制品

Situation 3
认识更有用的发明

Grammar-10
"protect A against B" 为短语，其有"保护A免受B的伤害"的意思，其中A与B的词性要一致。

Grammar-12
句中的"laugh at"后面通常会接上名词，意思为"嘲笑；因……而发笑"。

Most stores use surveillance cameras to protect themselves against ⑩ thieves.
大多数的商店会使用监视器来防止小偷盗窃。

This green house is very efficient in retaining energy.
温室在能量维持方面有很高的效率。

Grammar-11
"be useful to + V" 有"对……很有帮助"的意思，其后面要接动词原形。

Robots could be useful to ⑪ do housework.
机器人对做家务很有帮助。

Hitch earphones cause less pressure to the ears.
耳挂式耳机对耳朵所造成的压力比较小。

My brother and I stand before the magic mirror and laugh at ⑫ the funny images.
哥哥和我站在哈哈镜前面，然后对着镜中好笑的自己大笑。

- surveillance [sɜːrˈveɪləns] n 监视；监督
- thief [θiːf] n 小偷 复数 thieves
- efficient [ɪˈfɪʃnt] a 效率高的
- retain [rɪˈteɪn] v 保留；拦住
- energy [ˈenərdʒi] n 【物】能量
- robot [ˈrəʊbɑːt] n 机器人
- housework [ˈhaʊswɜːrk] n 家事
- hitch earphones phr 耳挂式耳机
- cause [cause] v 导致；引起
- pressure [ˈpreʃər] n 压力；压迫
- funny [ˈfʌni] a 有趣的；滑稽可笑的
- image [ˈɪmɪdʒ] n 影像；图像

不怕你学不会

1. The washing machine is useful _____ do the laundry.
2. The father tried his best to protect his daughter _____ some bad information.
3. Glasses are very delicate. Please hold them carefully.
   = Glasses are very _____. Please hold them carefully.
4. My brother always laughs _____ my old jacket.

答案：1. to 2. against 3. fragile 4. at

Unit 3 现代人的生命线
Modern people's lifeblood

原来老外这样记单词 老外从小到大学习单词的方法，就是看到什么就学什么！

- **software** [ˈsɔːftwer] n 软件
- **social networking website** phr 社交网站
- **USB flash drive** phr 内存盘
- **CPU** abbr 中央处理器 (= Central Processing Unit)
- **laptop** [ˈlæptɑːp] n 笔记本电脑

其他衍生单词：

- **stylus** [ˈstaɪləs] n 触控笔
- **network** [ˈnetwɜːrk] n 电脑网络
- **hand-held** [ˈhændˌheld] a 手提式的
- **PDA** n 个人数字助理 (= Personal Digital Assitant)
- **memory card** phr 记忆卡
- **ISP** abbr 网际网络服务提供商 (= Internet Service Provider)

老外最常用的单词
连这些单词都不会，你还敢说你学过英语吗？

只是近在指间的距离

bluetooth earphone phr 蓝牙耳机

- **mobile phone** n 手机；移动电话
- **cell phone** n 手机
- **smartphone** n 智能手机
- **touch screen** phr 触控屏幕
- **text message** phr 短信
- **mass text** phr 群组信息

奇妙的宇宙科技

rocket ['rɑːkɪt] n 火箭

- **radar** ['reɪdɑːr] n 雷达
- **radiator** ['reɪdieɪtər] n 散热器
- **space shuttle** phr 航天飞机
- **communications satellite** phr 通信卫星
- **meteorological satellite** phr 气象卫星
- **cooling system** phr （机内）冷却系统
- **GNSS** abbr 全球导航卫星系统
  (=Global Navigation Satellite System)
- **GPS** abbr 全球定位系统
  (=Global Positioning System)

有了这些没烦恼

developer [dɪ'veləpər] n 显影剂

- **electroplate** [ɪ'lektrəpleɪt] v 电镀
- **thermostat** ['θɜːrməstæt] n 恒温器
- **compressor** [kəm'presər] n 压缩机
- **condenser** [kən'densər] n 冷凝器
- **reverse osmosis** phr 逆渗透技术
- **money detector** phr 验钞机
- **pinhole camera** phr 针孔摄影机
- **energy saving system** phr 节能装置
- **electronic tagging** phr 电子脚镣

用英语聊天，原来这么简单
老外每天说的英语，其实就是这几句。

鲍勃：这是比伯的歌！　帕特里克：我不是很喜欢。　詹尼弗：我也是。

Situation 1
离不开手机的生活

Grammar-1
"remind sb. to + v"
有"提醒某人做某事"的意思，也可以替换成"remind sb. of + n / ving"的句型。

Grammar-2
"forget to + v"为一句型用法，有"忘记做某事"的意思，但若句型为"forget + ving"时，则解释为"忘记已经做过某事"。

The teacher **reminded** the students **to** ① put their phones away because some students were sending text messages during class.
老师提醒学生们收起他们的手机，因为有些学生在课堂上发短信。

I **forgot to** ② recharge the battery of my cell phone so now I cannot receive any calls.
我忘记给手机电池充电了，所以我现在无法接听任何电话。

Why don't you ③ buy a smartphone? Get with the show!
你为何不买个智能手机呢？别落伍了！

Grammar-3
"Why don't you + v...?"的句型，意思为"你为何不……？"，其用法相当于"Why not...?"的句型，但两者后面皆需以动词原形来呈现。

text message phr 文字短信

recharge [ˌriːˈtʃɑːrdʒ] v 充电　　receive [rɪˈsiːv] v 接到；收到

Situation 2
改变人类生活的高科技

Maybe ④ my grandchildren will be able to play with androids.
或许我的孙子们可以和机器人一起玩耍。

Grammar-4
"maybe"当副词时，意思为"可能；大概；或许"，和其用法相同的词汇有"probably（很有可能；大概）"与"perhaps（或许；大概）"。

Unit 3 现代人的生命线

Grammar-5
"microchip" 当名词时，有"微晶片"的意思。

Many of our electric appliances have microchips ❺ installed in them.
我们很多的电器设备里都安装了微晶片。

Our high-tech lifestyles are more comfortable and convenient than our grandparents.
我们高科技的生活方式比我们祖父母的生活模式更加舒适和方便。

grandchild [ˈɡræntʃaɪld] n 孙子；孙女

android [ˈændrɔɪd] n 机器人

electric [ɪˈlektrɪk] a 电的   appliance [əˈplaɪəns] n 设备；装置

install [ɪnˈstɔːl] v 设置；安装   high-tech [haɪ tek] a 高科技的

lifestyle [ˈlaɪfstaɪl] n 生活方式   comfortable [ˈkʌmftəbl] a 舒适的

Situation 3
有了电脑好帮手

Should I do a right-click or a left-click?
我应该按鼠标右键还是左键呢？

My computer might ❻ have a virus, so I must update any anti-virus program.
我的电脑可能中毒了，所以我必须要更新我的杀毒软件。

Grammar-6
"might" 的原型为"may"，即"可能"的意思，与其用法相当的词汇有"probably（大概；或许）"。

Amber set her browser to refuse cookies ❼.
安布尔设定好她的浏览器以拒绝第三方存取她的资料。

Grammar-7
"cookies" 是一种能够让网站服务器把少量数据储存到客户端的硬盘或从客户端的硬盘读取数据的技术。

Grammar-8
"had + 过去分词" 为"过去完成时"的用法。

I had forgotten ❽ to turn on my computer, and therefore I thought it was broken.
我忘了打开我的电脑，因此我以为它应该是坏掉了。

Grammar-9
"suggest" 后面所接的 that 从句中，其主语后面的助动词 should 可以省略，但不要忘了动词需以原形呈现！

I suggest ❾ that you make a back up of your essay.
我建议你要把你的论文备份。

My computer crashed when I was doing my final report.
我的电脑在我做期末报告的时候死机了。

My brother created a shortcut on the desktop after installing Photoshop.
我哥哥安装完图片处理软件后，在桌面设置了一个快捷菜单。

Grammar-10
"get accustomed to + N / Ving" 意思为"适应；习惯于"，和其相同用法的短语为"get used to"。

It's hard for me to get accustomed to ❿ the new operating system.
适应一个新的操作系统对我来说是一件很困难的事。

Chapter 9 科技，始终来自人性

Grammar-11

"as a result" 有"因此"的意思，和其用法相同的短语有"in consequence"。

The video card on my computer has broken down. **As a result**, the screen could not receive the message signals from the computer.

电脑的显示卡坏掉了，所以屏幕无法从主机接收信号。

right-click n 鼠标右键　　left-click n 鼠标左键

virus ['vaɪrəs] n 病毒　　update [ˌʌp'deɪt] v 更新

program ['prəʊɡræm] n 程序　　set [set] v 设定

browser ['braʊzər] n 浏览器

refuse [rɪ'fjuːz] v 拒绝 同 reject [rɪ'dʒekt] v 拒绝；否决

turn on phr 开机 反 turn off phr 关掉　　broken ['brəʊkən] a 损坏的；中断的

back up phr 备份　　crash [kræʃ] v 死机

shortcut ['ʃɔːrtkʌt] n 捷径；快捷方式　　desktop ['desktɑːp] n 桌面

operating system phr 操作系统　　video card phr 视频卡

screen [skriːn] n 屏幕　　message ['mesɪdʒ] n 信息；通讯

 老外不会教你的小秘密

★ 开关电器的英语短语应该很熟悉吧！比方说要打开电脑时，我们可以用"*Turn on the computer.*（电脑开机。）"或"*Switch on the computer.*（电脑关机。）"来表达，现在我们来学习另一种的表达方式：
  ✦ *Power up the computer.* 电脑开机。
  ✦ *Boot up the computer.* 电脑开机。

★ 对于一个需要电脑来辅助完成工作的人来说，最怕遇到的问题就是电脑死机了。我们来学习各种的表达句子吧！例如：
  ✦ *The server is down.* 服务器死机了。
  ✦ *My computer crashed.* 我的电脑死机了。
  ✦ *My computer froze up.* 我的电脑死机了。
  上面的句子中，最后一句最为传神，电脑"冻"住了，又怎么作业呢？所以，为了避免上述情况发生，最好还是要有"*Make a backup.*（做备份。）"喔！

Chapter 10 环游世界 8分钟

Travel around the world

国外旅游、商务出差、游学打工……
除了与人交流之外,最重要的莫过于交通了!
这些要如何开口表达呢?赶快一起来学学看吧!

| **Unit 1** 起飞了! 请系好安全带 | **Unit 2** 出门逛逛 | **Unit 3** 需要休息一下 | **Unit 4** 平平安安回家 |

Unit 1 起飞！请系好安全带
Fasten your seatbelt

原来老外这样记单词 / 老外从小到大学习单词的方法，就是看到什么就学什么！

check-in counter
phr 登记柜台

visitor ['vɪzɪtər]
n 旅客

international flight
phr 国际航线

departure lobby
phr 出境大厅

suitcase ['suːtkeɪs]
n 手提箱

其他衍生单词：

arrival lobby phr 入境大厅
flat panel display phr 平板显示屏
electronic ticket phr 电子机票
boarding pass phr 登机牌
boarding gate phr 登机口
passport ['pæspɔːrt] n 护照

老外最常用的单词
连这些单词都不会，你还敢说你学过英语吗？

机票上都写这些词 ★★

passport ID `phr` 护照号码

surname [ˈsɜːrneɪm] `n` 姓
given name `phr` 名
airfare [ˈerfer] `n` 机票费
endorsement [ɪnˈdɔːrsmənt] `n` 机票限制
class [klæs] `n` 座舱等级
annotation [ˌænəˈteɪʃn] `n` 注解
Sched-Time `phr` 预定起飞时间
(=scheduled-time)
EST-Time `phr` 实际起飞时间
(=established-time)

过海关时请注意这些 ★★

metal detector `phr` 金属探测器

quarantine [ˈkwɔːrəntiːn] `n` 检疫所；隔离区
carry-on [ˈkærɪ ɑːn] `a` 可随身携带的
limit [ˈlɪmɪt] `n` 限制
liquid [ˈlɪkwɪd] `n` 液体
x-ray `n` X光检查 `v` X光检查
customs declaration form `phr` 海关申报单
luggage inspection `phr` 行李检查

飞机上也要孜孜不倦 ★★

inflight meal `phr` 机上餐点

airline [ˈerlaɪn] `n` 航空公司；航线
crew [kruː] `n` 全体机组员
cockpit [ˈkɑːkpɪt] `n` 驾驶舱
pilot [ˈpaɪlət] `n` 机长
layover [ˈleɪəʊvər] `n` 中途候机；短暂停留
flight attendant `phr` 空乘员
overhead compartment `phr` 舱顶置物柜
domestic flight `phr` 国内航线
oxygen mask `phr` 氧气罩

用英语聊天，原来这么简单 / 老外每天说的英语，其实就是这几句。

空乘员：我来帮您，小姐。　海伦娜：感谢！

Situation 1
订机票

Grammar-1
"Here + be + S."
为一倒装句型，其动词置前，主语为后。

I would like a direct flight with no stopover.
我想要没有短暂停留的直飞航班。

Please reconfirm your flight 72 hours before departure.
请在出发前 72 小时再次确认您的航班。

Here is ❶ your itinerary for your e-ticket.
这是你的电子机票行程路线。

direct flight phr 直飞航班　　stopover [ˈstɑːpəuvər] n 中途停留

reconfirm [ˌriːkənˈfɜːrm] v 再确认；再确实　反 double-check v 仔细检查

departure [dɪˈpɑːrtʃər] n 离开；起程；出发　反 arrival [əˈraɪvl] n 到达

Situation 2
登机柜台

Here are my e-ticket confirmation and my passport.
这是我的电子机票确认单和护照。

I would like to sit with my mother. Is it possible to ❷ switch seats?
我想要和妈妈坐在一起。有可能换位置吗？

Grammar-2
"It is possible to + v" 为固定用法，解释为"有……的可能"，其中 "to" 为不定词，后面应接动词原形。

Do you have anything to declare?
你有要申报的物品吗？

184

Unit 1 起飞！请系好安全带

Grammar-3
"place" 在这里当动词使用，有"放置"的意思；当名词时，为"地方"的意思。

Could you **place** ❸ your check-in luggage on the scale, please?
可以请您把托运行李放到磅秤上吗？

Is it overweight? I don't want to pay the **fee** ❹.
行李超重了吗？我不想支付费用。

Grammar-4
"fee" 为名词，意思为"服务费；酬金"，多用在专业服务费用或罚款上。和其相同解释的单词有"fare"及"bill"。然而，"fare"多用在搭乘交通工具上，"bill"则是用在账单上。

Grammar-5
"at least" 解释为"至少；最少"。和其相反的用法为"at most"，有"至多；最多"的意思。

Here is your boarding pass. Be at the boarding gate **at least** ❺ 30 minutes before the departure time.
这是您的登机牌。请在起飞前 30 分钟到登机口。

Grammar-6
"between" 当介词，解释为"在……之间"，用来指两端距离、空间或时间，所以常会和"and"一起连用。

The shuttle bus **between** ❻ the terminals leaves every 10 minutes.
航站之间的摆渡车每 10 分钟一班。

Did you bring any fruits, vegetables, or animal products?
你有携带任何水果、蔬菜或动物制品吗？

Grammar-7
"custom" 当名词时，解释为"海关；习俗"；当形容词时，意思则为"订制的"。

The contraband she brought was confiscated by the **customs** ❼.
她带的违禁品被海关没收了。

e-ticket `phr` 电子机票　　confirmation [ˌkɑːnfərˈmeɪʃn] `n` 确认；批准

switch [swɪtʃ] `v` 调换；更换　　declare [dɪˈkler] `v` 申报（纳税品等）

luggage [ˈlʌɡɪdʒ] `n`【英】行李　baggage [ˈbæɡɪdʒ] `n`【美】行李

scale [skeɪl] `n` 天平；秤盘

shuttle [ˈʃʌtl] `n` 火车站或是机场的摆渡车

terminal [ˈtɜːrmɪnl] `n` 航站楼　　bring [brɪŋ] `v` 携带

contraband [ˈkɑːntrəbænd] `n` 违禁品

confiscate [ˈkɑːnfɪskeɪt] `v` 没收、充公

Situation 3
上飞机后你会用到的句子

We will **take off** ❽ in a few minutes. Please fasten your seatbelt. Bon voyage!
我们即将在几分钟后起飞。请系上您的安全带。祝您旅途愉快！

Grammar-8
"take off" 为"起飞"的意思，此短语还有其他的用法，如"take one day off"意为"请一天假"的意思；"take off your coat"则为"脱掉外套"的意思。

Grammar-9
"blanket" 当名词时，有"毛毯；覆盖物"之意；当动词时，为"覆盖、裹以毛毯"的意思。

Jason asked the flight attendant for a **blanket** ❾ because he felt cold.
杰森向空乘人员要了一条毯子，因为他觉得冷。

fasten [ˈfæsn] `v` 扎牢；系紧　　Bon voyage! `phr`【法】一路平安

Chapter **10**
环游世界 8 分钟

Situation 4
下飞机后出海关前

- People have to fill out disembarkation forms and immigration forms when they go abroad.
  人们在出国的时候必须填出境登记和入境表格。

What is the purpose of your visit?
你来访的目的是什么呢？

How long ⑩ do you plan on staying?
您打算待多久呢？

Grammar-10
"How long...?"为"多久……？"之意，为询问"时间"上的疑问副词，因此，必须以时间的长短来回应。

I fly out on August 7th.
我 8 月 7 号离开。

Grammar-11
"enjoy one's stay"有"好好享受……的时光"的意思，我们也可以将"stay"改为"trip"的来替换。

You are good to go. Enjoy your stay ⑪.
你可以走了。好好享受你在这里的时光。

disembarkation form phr 出境登记表　　immigration form phr 入境表格

go abroad phr 出国　　purpose ['pɜːrpəs] n 目的；意图

plan on phr 打算 同 intend to phr 想要；打算　　fly out phr 飞离

 老外不会教你的小秘密

★ 当我们在订机票的时候，一定都会遇到客满的状况；但在开票前，航空公司也都会有提供候补的机会，就是怕有旅客会没有在规定的时间内进行"check in"的手续过程。因此，候补的英语为"*standby*"，为名词。我们便可以用"*be on standby*"这个短语，即："*I'm on standby for economy seat.*（我正在候补经济舱的座位。）"；或是用"*put on standby*"这个短语，即："*I put on standby for economy seat.*（我在候补经济舱的座位。）"。

Unit 2 出门逛逛
Fooling around

 原来老外这样记单词 / 老外从小到大学习单词的方法，就是看到什么就学什么！

free travel phr 自由行

backpacker [ˈbækpækər] n 背包客

destination [ˌdestɪˈneɪʃn] n 目的地；终点

single-lens reflex camera phr 单反相机

其他衍生单词：

digital camera phr 数码相机
binoculars [bɪˈnɑːkjələrz] n 双筒望远镜
compass [ˈkʌmpəs] n 指南针

trench coat phr 军用雨衣
battery [ˈbætri] n 电池
flashlight [ˈflæʃlaɪt] n 手电筒

老外最常用的单词 / 连这些单词都不会，你还敢说你学过英语吗？

规划完美行程就靠它们

safari [səˈfɑːri] n 狩猎旅行

itinerary [aɪˈtɪnəreri] n 行程计划；旅程
agency [ˈeɪdʒənsi] n 中介
budget [ˈbʌdʒɪt] n 预算
insurance [ɪnˈʃʊrəns] n 保险
recommendation [ˌrekəmenˈdeɪʃn] n 推荐
homestay [ˈhəʊmsteɪ] n （在国外的访问者）在当地居民家居住的时期
incentive trip phr 员工旅游

要去哪玩都帮你想好了

river tour phr 河岸游览

attraction [əˈtrækʃn] n 旅游景点
resort [rɪˈzɔːrt] n 旅游胜地
brochure [brəʊˈʃʊr] n 小册子
guidebook [ˈɡaɪdbʊk] n 旅游指南
height [haɪt] n 高度；海拔
sightseeing [ˈsaɪtsiːɪŋ] n 观光；游览
hot spring phr 温泉
aurora [ɔːˈrɔːrə] n 极光
sunset [ˈsʌnset] n 日落

游客们的那些小事

tourist information center phr 旅客服务中心

visit [ˈvɪzɪt] v 参观；拜访
passenger [ˈpæsɪndʒər] n 旅客
guest [ɡest] n 客人
nationality [ˌnæʃəˈnæləti] n 国籍
expiration date phr 签证到期日
tourist [ˈtʊrɪst] n 观光客
sightseeing [ˈsaɪtsiːɪŋ] n 观光、游览 ad 观光的

用英语聊天，原来这么简单 / 老外每天说的英语，其实就是这几句。

琼森：看！这个网站说附近有一些有名的餐厅，我们去试试看吧！　埃尔娃：酷！那就把它排进我们的行程吧！

Situation 1
你有想去的地方吗？

We're going to go sightseeing in Japan.
我们要去日本旅游。

My college classmates backpacked across Canada.
我的大学同学背着背包去加拿大玩。

Grammar-1
"such as" 为 "例如；像是……" 的意思，其后需要接名词。和其相同的用法有 "for example（譬如）"和 "for instance（例如）"。

I would like to see the major attractions in Chicago, such as ❶ Wallys Tower, Navy Pier, Magnificent Mile and The Field Museum.
我想去看芝加哥的主要景点，像是沃利塔、海军码头、壮丽大道和菲尔德自然历史博物馆。

Grammar-2
"no longer" 为短语，有 "不再……" 的意思，和其相同用法的短语为 "not...any longer"。

Traveling to the Moon is no longer ❷ an unachievable ❸ dream.
到月球旅行不再是一个遥不可及的梦想。

Grammar-3
"unachievable" 为形容词，为 "无法达成的" 之意，反义词为 "achievable"，意思为 "可达成的"。

major ['meɪdʒər] a 主要的；重要的

attraction [ə'trækʃn] n 景点；喜闻乐见的事物

pier [pɪr] n 码头；防波堤

magnificent [mæg'nɪfɪsnt] a 壮丽的；宏伟的

Situation 2
钱包紧巴巴又想出国

Let's travel to Canada on a budget.
我们去穷游加拿大吧。

Grammar-4
"tip"当名词时，为"小费"的意思；当动词时，则有"给……小费"之意。"要不要给……小费"的英语可以用"To tip or not to tip?"来表达。

Grammar-7
"a few"为单位量词，为"一些；几个"的意思，用来修饰可数名词。

Grammar-8
"save a buck"有"省下一分一毫"之意。"buck"当名词使用，解释为"元"，且为美式俚语。另有"雄鹿；公羊；牝兔"的意思。

Tips ⁴ for local guides are not included.
这不包含给当地导游的小费。

Grammar-5
"steal"可作动词或名词，原意都有"偷窃"的意思，在本句中当名词使用，且引申为"优惠的事物"之意。

The price of the tour package is really a steal ⁵.
这个旅游套餐的费用真的是太便宜了。

It's cheaper to travel during the off-season.
去旅游的话淡季会比较便宜。

Grammar-6
"a self-guided tour"解释为"自助旅行"的意思，其中"self-guided"为形容词，有"自导的；自动导向的"之意。

I think a self-guided tour ⁶ would be the best for my budget.
我想自助游最符合我的预算。

The cheapest flights will have a few ⁷ layovers but it will save a buck ⁸.
最便宜的航班需要转几次机，但可以省下一些钱。

budget [ˈbʌdʒɪt] n 预算；经费
local [ˈləʊkl] a 当地的；本地的
guide [gaɪd] n 导游
tour [tʊr] n 旅行；游览
flight [flaɪt] n 班次

Situation 3
旅游就是为了享受

We met crocodiles and piranhas in the trip to the Amazon River. It was a thrilling and unforgettable ⁹ experience.
我们在亚马孙河之旅遇到了鳄鱼和食人鱼。这是一次刺激且难忘的经历。

I am looking forward to ⁱ⁰ taking a sauna bath.
我很期待洗桑拿。

Grammar-10
"look forward to..."为固定短语，即"期待"的意思，后面接"动名词（Ving）"。

Grammar-9
"unforgettable"当形容词时解释为"难以忘怀的；难忘的"之意，和其相同用法的词汇为"memorable（难忘的；显著的）"。

Capsule hotels originated from ¹¹ Japan. They are cheaper than in general hotels.
胶囊旅馆起源于日本，它比一般的旅馆便宜。

Grammar-11
"originated from"为固定搭配，即"起源于"的意思，和其相同用法的短语为"derived from"。

We went diving in the Great Barrier Reef last year.
我们去年去了大堡礁潜水。

piranha [pɪˈrɑːnə] n 食人鱼
sauna [ˈsɔːnə] n 桑拿；芬兰浴
capsule hotel phr 胶囊旅馆
in general [ˈdʒenrəl] phr 一般地

Situation 4
称赞美丽的景点

How ¹² scenic the coast is!
多么风景秀丽的海岸啊！

Grammar-12
"How + adj. + S + be !"意为"多么……啊！"，此为感叹句的用法；和其用法相同的还有由"What + a / an + adj. !"的句型。

I rode on the hot air balloon to have a bird's-eye view of the valley's beautiful scenery.
我搭乘热气球鸟瞰山谷的美丽风景。

scenic ['si:nɪk] a 风景秀丽的　　coast [kəust] n 海岸；沿海地区

hot air balloon phr 热气球　　bird's-eye a 鸟瞰的

valley ['væli] n 山谷；溪谷　　scenery ['si:nəri] n 风景；景色

Situation 5
需要拍照吗？

Can you take a photo of ⑧ me?
可以帮我照张相吗？

Grammar-13
"take a photo of..."有"拍张……的相片"的意思。我们也可以将短语中的"photo"替换成"picture"。

Let's take a group photo!
我们一起合照吧!

group [gru:p] n 团体

老外不会教你的小秘密

★ 多种旅行方式，您究竟喜欢哪一种呢？是"*backpacking*（背包旅行）"还是"*budget traveling*（穷游）"？是"*group tour*（旅行团旅行）"还是"*cruise*（邮轮旅游）"？此时，我们可以用"*I'm going on a budget travel.*（我想要来一趟穷游。）""*I'm joining a group tour.*（我要参加旅行团旅游。）"或是"*I want to do a cruise.*（我想要搭邮轮旅游。）"

不怕你学不会

1. Traveling to the Moon is no longer an unachievable dream.

    = Traveling to the Moon is _____ an unachievable dream _____ _____ .

2. The experience of scuba diving was really unforgettable.

    = The experience of scuba diving was really _____ .

3. The Olympics is derived from Athens.

    = The Olympics _____ from Athens.

答案：1. not, any, longer　2. memorable　3. originated

Unit 3 需要休息一下
Take a rest

原来老外这样记单词 / 老外从小到大学习单词的方法，就是看到什么就学什么！

- **deluxe** [ˌdə'lʌks] a 豪华的
- **bellhop** ['belhɑːp] n 侍者
- **reception** [rɪ'sepʃn] n 接待处
- **lobby** ['lɑːbi] n 大厅
- **trunk** [trʌŋk] n 大皮箱

其他衍生单词：

- **registration form** phr 登记住宿表
- **concierge** [kɔːn'sjerʒ] n 服务台人员
- **staircase** ['sterkeɪs] n 楼梯
- **janitor** ['dʒænɪtər] n 门警、看门人
- **front desk** phr 服务台
- **corridor** ['kɔːrɪdɔːr] n 走廊、回廊

老外最常用的单词 / 连这些单词都不会,你还敢说你学过英语吗?

记得先确定住所再出发

hotel porter phr 饭店行李员

accommodation [əˌkɑːməˈdeɪʃn] n 住宿
suite [swiːt] n 套房
trolley [ˈtrɑːli] n 行李推车
checkroom [ˈtʃekruːm] n(车站/旅馆等的)行李寄放处
twin room phr 双人房
single room phr 单人房
deluxe room phr 豪华套房

你的重要物品也请注意

overweight [ˌəʊvərˈweɪt] a 超重的

drag [dræɡ] v 拖;拉
fragile item phr 易碎物品
excess baggage phr 超重行李
conveyor belt phr 行李输送带
luggage rack phr 行李架
baggage tag phr 行李吊牌
baggage claim phr 行李领取处
baggage delivery phr 行李托运处

在饭店房间放松一下

bathrobe [ˈbæθrəʊb] n 浴袍

bedspread [ˈbedspred] n 床罩
storage [ˈstɔːrɪdʒ] n 置物柜
blind [blaɪnd] n 窗帘
equipment [ɪˈkwɪpmənt] n 器材;设备
housekeeping [ˈhaʊskiːpɪŋ] n 总务部;客房整理服务
guestbook n 访客留言簿
room service phr 客房服务

用英语聊天，原来这么简单 / 老外每天说的英语，其实就是这几句。

Sir, here is your reservation information. Please confirm it.

接待员：先生，这边是您的预订信息。请确认。

Situation 1
向饭店预订床位

Could I have a room with a hot spring?
我可以要一间有温泉的房间吗？

We'd like **the room for 7 nights** ❶, please.
我们想要一间可以住 7 个晚上的房间。

Grammar-1
"a room for...nights"就是"要住……天"的意思，所以我们在这里仅需用数字来代表需要住宿的天数即可。

We want to upgrade our room.
我们想要升级房间。

Situation 2
入住时说这几句就够了

My reservation was made through a travel agency.
我是通过旅行社预订的。

Please sign your name here, and then here is your **key card**.
请在这里签名，然后这是您的房卡。

Grammar-2
"help sb. with sth."解释为"帮……做……"的意思。

Grammar-3
"facility"为名词，其意为"工具；设施；设备"，和其相同的词汇有"equipment（设备）"，但前者为可数名词，后者为不可数名词。

Our bellboy will **help** you **with** ❷ your bags.
我们的服务生会帮你拿行李。

Can I ask you about the hotel **facilities** ❸ ?
我可以询问一下关于旅馆设施的问题吗？

Unit 3 需要休息一下

Grammar-4
"help someone v / to v" 为固定短语，即"帮助某人做某事"的意思。

Could we have some more quilts?
我们可以多拿几条被子吗？

Can you help me put ❹ my luggage on the luggage cart?
你能帮我把行李放到行李推车上吗？

This is your key card and your room number is 666.
这是您的房卡，您的房号是 666。

You can press the call button if you need anything.
如果您有任何需要可以按服务铃。

If you need any help, please call the front desk.
如果您需要任何帮助，请打电话至前台。

Please give me a wake-up call at seven o'clock tomorrow morning.
请给我一个明早 7 点的晨唤。

Excuse me. There is a problem with the heater.
不好意思，房间的暖气有问题。

key card **phr** 房卡　　bellboy ['belbɔɪ] **n** 旅馆大厅的服务生

room number **phr** 房号　　press [pres] **v** 按；压；挤

call button **phr** 服务铃

wake-up call **phr** 晨唤（通常指饭店叫房客起床的服务）

Situation 3
别忘了入住时要说的这几句

What time is the latest I can check-out?
我最晚可以几点退房？

Could you please have somebody bring down my luggage?
请问可以派人将我的行李拿下楼吗？

Situation 4
记得准备地图

The route map indicates that the final destination station is the science museum.
路线图显示终点站是科学博物馆。

Chapter **10** 环游世界 8 分钟

195

Grammar-5
"ask sb. for sth...." 为固定搭配，即"向某人要求某物"的意思。

You can **ask** the locals **for** ❺ direction when you **get lost** ❻ during the trip.
你在旅游途中迷路的时候，可以向当地人询问方向。

Grammar-6
"get lost" 即为"迷路"的意思，和其相同的短语用法为"lose one's way"。

route map phr 路线图　　　destination n 目的地

science museum phr 科学博物馆

direction [dəˈrekʃn] n 方向；方位

老外不会教你的小秘密

★ 房间的类型选择性很多，如：*single room*（单人房）、*double room*（双人房）、*deluxe room*（豪华房）、*business suite*（商务套房）、*executive suite*（高级行政套房）和 *presidential suite*（总统套房）。床铺的类型也有多种选择，如：*single bed*（单人床）、*double bed*（双人床）、*queen-size bed*（大号尺寸床）和 *king-size bed*（特大号床）。将这些相关词牢记，就可以自行替换至短句当中，衍生出不同的说法！

★ 旅行中，除了饮食之外，睡眠更是不可以马虎的。要如何和柜台人员预订房间呢？我们可以用最简单的句子说："*I need a single room.*（我需要一间单人房。）"或"*Please give us a room with a queen-size bed.*（请给我一间大床房。）"，也可以说"*I'd like a room with two double beds.*（我要一间有两张双人床的房间。）"。

不怕你学不会

1. Excuse me. I need a deluxe room _____ four nights, please.
2. Could you please help me _____ the luggage?
3. Asking people _____ help is not an embarrassing thing.
4. I got lost on the first day going my new job.
   = I _____ on the first day going my new job.

答案：1. for 2. with 3. for 4. lost my way

Unit 4 平平安安回家
Come back safe and sound

原来老外这样记单词 / 老外从小到大学习单词的方法，就是看到什么就学什么！

traditional clothes
phr 传统服饰

knock-off
phr 名牌仿制品

stand [stænd]
n 摊位

souvenir [ˌsuːvəˈnɪr]
n 纪念品

其他衍生单词：

traveler's check n 旅行支票　　**memorable** [ˈmemərəbl] a 值得怀念的
duty-free shop phr 免税商店　　**occupied** [ˈɑːkjupaɪd] a （洗手间）有人使用的
exchange [ɪksˈtʃeɪndʒ] n 交易所　　**vacant** [ˈveɪkənt] a （洗手间）无人使用的

197

老外最常用的单词 / 连这些单词都不会，你还敢说你学过英语吗？

出现这些单词时要提高注意力

payphone [ˈpeɪfəʊn] n 公共电话
Centigrade [ˈsentɪɡreɪd] n 摄氏温度
Fahrenheit [ˈfærənhaɪt] n 华氏温度
information desk phr 服务台
lost and found phr 失物招领处
pit stop phr 旅行休息站
OTA abbr 旅游警示制度 (=Outbound Travel Alert System)

好用又方便的旅游小单词

concourse [ˈkɑːŋkɔːrs] n （机场／车站等）中央大厅

coach [kəʊtʃ] n 巴士
international driving permit phr 国际驾照
console [kənˈsəʊl] n 操作台
window seat phr 靠窗座位
aisle seat phr 走道座位
round-trip ticket phr 往返票
emergency exit phr 安全门
Easy card phr 一卡通
waiting room phr 候车室

用眼睛带走最美的风景

instant camera phr 拍立得相机

picture [ˈpɪktʃər] n 画面 v 拍摄
lens [lenz] n 透镜；相机镜头 v 拍摄影片
focus [ˈfəʊkəs] n 焦距 v 使聚焦
strap [stræp] n 背带
self portrait phr 自拍照
memory card phr 记忆卡

Unit 4 平平安安回家

用英语聊天，原来这么简单
老外每天说的英语，其实就是这几句。

Say cheese, baby.

Edward

爱德华：笑一个，宝贝！

Situation 1
出门在外要小心

Whitewater rafting is an exciting but <u>dangerous</u> ❶ activity. <u>Be careful</u> ❷ when you do it.

Grammar-1
"dangerous"为形容词，有"危险的"之意，其同义词为"hazardous（冒险的）"和"risky（危险的；大胆的）"。

泛舟是刺激但危险的活动，所以在从事此活动的时候要小心一点。

whitewater rafting phr 泛舟　　activity [æk'tɪvəti] n 活动

Grammar-2
"be careful of..."为固定短语，即"小心；注意"的意思，和其相同的短语为"watch out for..."。

Situation 2
旅游必需品

Bug spray is a <u>necessity</u> for those who take a trip to the <u>outskirts</u>.

防虫喷雾是到郊外旅游时的必需品。

bug spray phr 防虫喷雾　　necessity [nə'sesəti] n 必需品
outskirts ['aʊtskɜːrts] n 郊区；边境

Situation 3
发现钱不够了

Where is the money exchange? May I exchange my traveler's checks for dollars?

请问兑换外币的柜台在哪儿？我可以把旅行支票换成美元吗？

Please break these100-dollar bills into small bills for me.

请帮我把 100 元钞票换成小钞。

Chapter **10** 环游世界 8 分钟

🎧 199

There is no commission charge when you exchange money here.
在这里换钱不用手续费。

Situation 4
旅行时遇到的不适

It took me a long time to adjust to the jet lag.
调整时差花了我好长一段时间。

Grammar-3 "jet lag"为固定短语,为"时差"之意,和其相同用法的短语为"time lag"。

My ears plug up when the plane takes off every time.
飞机每次起飞我都会耳鸣。

Most travelers are very nervous when they encounter turbulence during the flight.
大部分的旅客在搭飞机遇到乱流时都会很紧张。

adjust [ə'dʒʌst] v 调整；适应   turbulence ['tɜːrbjələns] n 乱流

Grammar-4 "encounter"当名词时,解释为"邂逅；偶遇"之意；当动词时,则有"遭遇"的意思,其用法相当于"confront（面临；遭遇）"或"face（正视；面临）"等词汇。

Situation 5
有东西遗失了

I couldn't find my luggage. What should I do?
我找不到我的行李,我该怎么办？

Where should I report my missing bag?
行李遗失要在哪里报失呢？

Situation 6
不走不行的状况

My visa is going to expire, so I have to leave here as soon as possible.
我的签证快过期了,所以我要尽快离开。

Grammar-6 "as soon as possible"为固定短语,即"尽快"的意思,其缩写形式为"ASAP"。

I spent all my money in 5 days. I guess we should go back home right now.
我这5天花了所有的钱,我想我们应该立刻回家。

expire [ɪk'spaɪər] v 过期；吐气；熄灭

Grammar-5 "visa"当动词时,解释为"给予签证"之意；当名词时,则有"签证"的意思。

Situation 7
准备回程

Time flies! The trip has come to an end.
时光飞逝！旅行已经结束了。

The longer we stay here, the happier we will be.
我们待得越久,就会越开心。

Let's go to Angkor Wat in Cambodia next time!
我们下次去柬埔寨时要去吴哥窟。

Grammar-7 "The + 比较级 + S + V, the + 比较级 + S + V."为比较级的倒装句型,有"越……,就越……。"的意思。

Unit 4 平平安安回家

Grammar-8
"long for" 为固定短语，意为 "渴望"，和其相同的短语有 "be eager for" "yearn for"，皆有 "渴望；期盼" 的意思。

I'm longing for a chance to go on a trip to Australia.
我期待下一次到澳大利亚旅行的机会。

Many tourists were stuck at the airport because the flights were all canceled due to the bad weather.
大部分的旅客都被困在机场，因为所有航班都因为天气不佳而取消。

chance [tʃæns] n 机会；良机   airport [ˈerpɔːrt] n 机场

weather [ˈweðər] n 天气；气候

 不怕你学不会

1. I'm yearning for a chance to go to Japan.
   = I'm _____ for a chance to go to Japan.

2. I need somebody to help me with my lost luggage. Please come here _____ soon _____ possible.

3. It took me a long time to adjust to the jet lag.
   = It took me a long time to adjust to the _____ lag.

4. We are afraid of facing typhoons. They will totally spoil our plan.
   = We are afraid of _____ typhoons. They will totally spoil our plan.

5. The _____ (high) the mountain is, the _____ (low) temperature would be.

答案：1. longing 2. as, as 3. time 4. confronting / encountering 5. higher, lower

Chapter 10 环游世界 8 分钟

看看老外怎么学
请将选项填到表中适当的位置

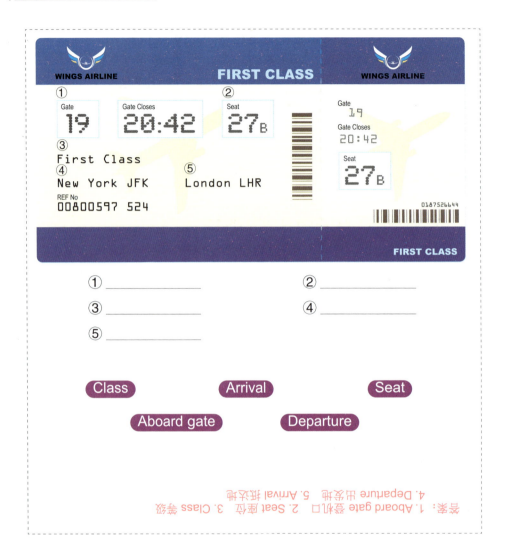

① _____ ② _____
③ _____ ④ _____
⑤ _____

Class   Arrival   Seat

Aboard gate   Departure

答案：1. Aboard gate 登机口 2. Seat 座位 3. Class 等级 4. Departure 出发地 5. Arrival 抵达地

Chapter 11 生活中的必要之美

No music no life

音乐，是生命中不可或缺的重要元素！不管你喜欢西方音乐或东方音乐、古典音乐或流行音乐，都一起来学学它们的英语该怎么说！

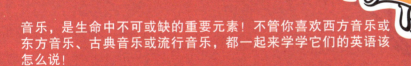

Unit 1 进入音符的世界

Unit 2 聚光灯下

Unit 3 倾听最美的声音

Unit 4 跟我一起大声唱

Unit 1 进入音符的世界
Enter the world of music

原来老外这样记单词 / 老外从小到大学习单词的方法，就是看到什么就学什么！

bar [bɑːr]
n 小节

staff [stæf]
n 五线谱（复数为 staves）

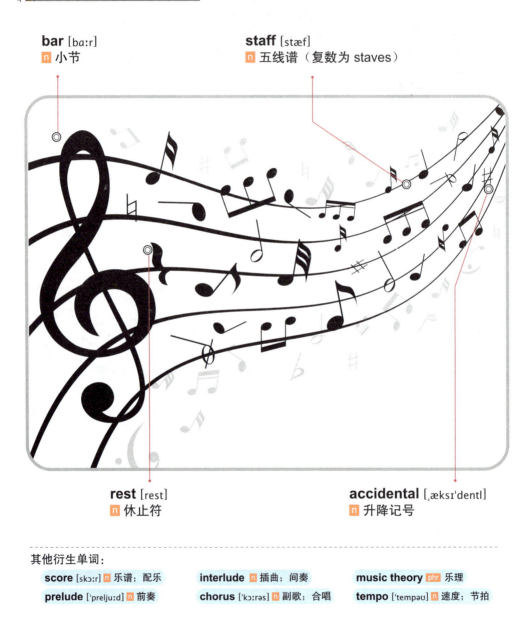

rest [rest]
n 休止符

accidental [ˌæksɪˈdentl]
n 升降记号

其他衍生单词：

score [skɔːr] n 乐谱；配乐　　**interlude** n 插曲；间奏　　**music theory** phr 乐理

prelude [ˈpreljuːd] n 前奏　　**chorus** [ˈkɔːrəs] n 副歌；合唱　　**tempo** [ˈtempəʊ] n 速度；节拍

老外最常用的单词 / 连这些单词都不会,你还敢说你学过英语吗?

老外都听这些

heavy metal music
`phr` 重金属音乐

reggae [ˈregeɪ] `n` 雷盖音乐
rock and roll `phr` 摇滚乐
upbeat [ˈʌpbiːt] `a` 节拍活泼的
melodic [məˈlɑːdɪk] `a` 音调优美的
soothing [ˈsuːðɪŋ]
`a` 慰藉的;令人宽心的;镇静的
disco music `phr` 迪斯科音乐
R&B (=rhythm and blues) `abbr` 节奏蓝调

来听听有深度的

gospel music 福音音乐

sonata [səˈnɑːtə] `n` 奏鸣曲
concerto [kənˈtʃɜːrtəʊ] `n` 协奏曲
spiritual music `phr` 心灵音乐
contemporary music `phr` 现代音乐
crystal music `phr` 水晶音乐
classical music `phr` 古典音乐
blues [bluːz] `n` 蓝调
folk [fəʊk] `n` 民谣
jazz [dʒæz] `n` 爵士乐
symphony [ˈsɪmfəni] `n` 交响乐

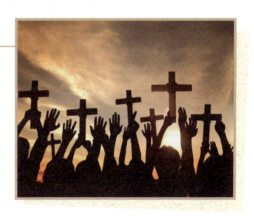

懂这些,才能跟上老外脚步

jukebox [ˈdʒuːkbɑːks] `n`
(投币式)自动唱机

karaoke [ˌkærɪˈəʊki] `n` 卡拉 OK
billboard [ˈbɪlbɔːrd] `n` 排行榜
fan [fæn]
`n` (运动/音乐/电影等)粉丝;迷
DJ (= disc jockey)
`abbr` 流行音乐播音员
VJ (= video jockey) `abbr` 音乐节目主持人
MV (= movie video) `abbr` 音乐录影带

用英语聊天，原来这么简单 / 老外每天说的英语，其实就是这几句。

迪伦：来听些音乐吧。 艾伦：好哇！你想听哪张专辑？

Situation 1
讨论音乐类型

Do you like chinese traditional music?
你喜欢中国传统音乐吗？

Do you prefer country music ❶ or ❷ jazz?
你喜欢乡村音乐还是爵士乐呢？

Grammar-2
"or"为选择性连词，前后需连接一致性的词性、短语或是句子；回答时亦须在选项中择其一。

Grammar-1
"country music"解释为"乡村音乐"。

I like Japanese pop music. It gives me a lot of inspiration.
我很喜欢听日本流行音乐，它给我很多启发。

I prefer jazz because of ❸ its rhythms and its soothing beat.
我喜欢爵士乐，是因为它的节奏和令人放松的节拍。

Grammar-3
"because of"解释为"因为；由于"的意思，其用法和"because"相同，只是前者后面加上 N；后者要接完整从句。

Kate is crazy about ❹ disco music because she likes to dance to the beat.
凯特对迪斯科音乐非常狂热，因为她喜欢随着节拍跳舞。

Grammar-4
"be crazy about"为固定搭配，是"为……而疯狂"的意思，也可以使用"be wild about"来替换。和其相反的用法还有"be indifferent to"，为"对……冷淡的"之意。

I have been fascinated with R&B for many years.
我已经对节奏蓝调着迷好几年了。

Jason always says that rock and roll is his life.
杰森总是说摇滚乐是他的生命。

Unit 1 进入音符的世界

Grammar-5
"anxious" 当形容词时,为"焦虑的"之意,其用法相当于"disturbed(心乱的)"和"troubled(不安的;忧虑的)"等词汇。

Music can smooth people's anxious ❺ spirits.
音乐可以抚平人们焦虑的灵魂。

traditional [trə'dɪʃnəl] a 传统的

rhythm ['rɪðəm] n 节奏;韵律;节拍

smooth [smuːð] v 使平静;使缓和

spirit ['spɪrɪt] n 精神;灵魂

Situation 2
了解音乐的历史

In the mid-1950s, rock and roll emerged as ❻ a new genre ❼ of music with such performers as Elvis Presley and Jerry Lee Lewis.
在 20 世纪 50 年代中期,摇滚乐以新的音乐类型出现,这类的表演者有埃尔维斯·普雷斯利和杰瑞·李·路易斯。

Grammar-6
"emerge as" 为固定短语,解释为"以……姿态出现"的意思,也可以用"appear as" 来替换。

Grammar-7
"genre" 当名词时,为"类型"的意思,其用法和"category"相同。

Do you know the Woodstock Music Festival?
你知道伍德斯托克音乐节吗?

Grammar-8
"dislike" 当动词使用,解释为"不喜欢;厌恶"的意思,其后需要接上 Ving 形式。

Situation 3
也不是每种音乐都那么悦耳时

My dad dislikes ❽ listening to heavy metal music; he just can't stand ❾ it.
我父亲不喜欢听重金属音乐,他就是无法忍受。

Grammar-9
"can't stand" 中的 "stand" 不解释为"站立",而是"忍受"的意思 也可以用"bear"、"tolerate"来替换。

Classical music makes me sleepy.
我听古典音乐会想睡觉。

Situation 4
当你发现充斥在生活中的音乐时

I am deeply moved by the main theme of this song.
我被这首歌的主旋律深深打动。

When I go to record shops, I always listen carefully to the music they play.
我每次去唱片行时,都会仔细聆听播放的音乐。

My grandfather likes to tap his fingers while listening to music.
我祖父喜欢在听音乐时用手指打拍子。

My sister played music very loudly in her room. It is really annoying.
我妹妹在房间放音乐放得很大声,吵死人了。

Chapter **11**
生活中的必要之美

🎧 207

Grammar-11
"easy listening music" 为固定搭配, 为"轻音乐"的意思, 其音乐类型和 "elevator music" 相同。在美国电梯里通常会放些柔和音乐, 但似乎不受年轻人的喜爱。

Easy listening music ⑩ is often played in the elevator of our office building.
轻音乐通常在我们办公大楼的电梯里播放。

be deeply moved by `phr` 被……深深感动

main theme `phr` 主旋律   tap one's fingers `phr` 用手指打节拍

 老外不会教你的小秘密

★ 音乐类型很多种, 如果你想询问其他人对于音乐的喜好, 就可以用 "*Do you like pop music?*" (你喜欢流行音乐吗?) 的句子, 我们也可以用 "*Are you into rap music?*" (你热衷说唱音乐吗?) 来代换。

 不怕你学不会

1. She just can't tolerate rock and roll. She thinks it noisy.

    = She just can't _____ rock and roll. She thinks it noisy.

2. Amber loves disco music because she can dance to the beat.

    = Amber loves disco music _____ its upbeat rhythm.

3. My brother is crazy about heavy metal music, but other members of my family think it is very noisy.

    = My brother is _____ about heavy metal music, but other members of my family think it is very noisy.

答案: 1. stand/bear 2. because of 3. wild

Unit 2 聚光灯下
Under the spotlight

 原来老外这样记单词 / 老外从小到大学习单词的方法，就是看到什么就学什么！

guitarist [gɪ'tɑːrɪst] n 吉他手

stage [steɪdʒ] n 舞台

spotlight ['spɑːtlaɪt] n 聚光灯

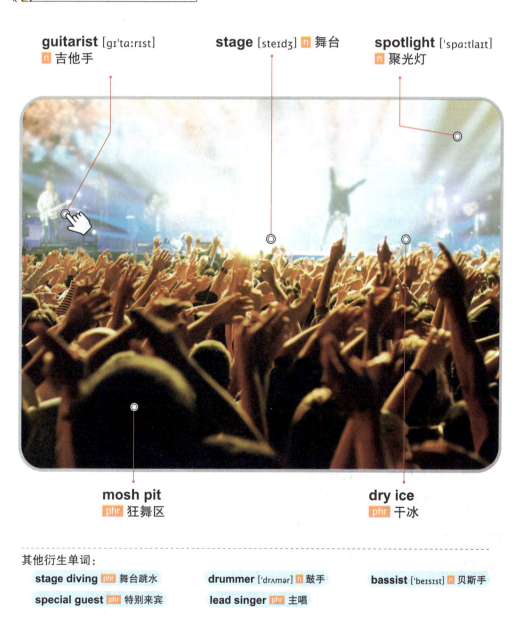

mosh pit phr 狂舞区

dry ice phr 干冰

其他衍生单词：

stage diving phr 舞台跳水

drummer ['drʌmər] n 鼓手

bassist ['beɪsɪst] n 贝斯手

special guest phr 特别来宾

lead singer phr 主唱

老外最常用的单词
连这些单词都不会,你还敢说你学过英语吗?

老外疯追星

entrance ticket `phr` 门票

balcony [ˈbælkəni] `n` 包厢
spectator [ˈspekteɪtər] `n` 观众
improvisation [ɪmˌprɑːvəˈzeɪʃn] `n` 即兴演奏
light stick `phr` 荧光棒
charm on stage `phr` 舞台魅力
nosebleed seats `phr` 离舞台最远的座位

他们都是音乐 PRO

conductor [kənˈdʌktər]
`n` (合唱团／音乐会等)指挥

musician [mjuˈzɪʃn] `n` 音乐家;乐师
performer [pərˈfɔːrmər] `n` 演出者;表演者
artist [ˈɑːrtɪst] `n` 歌手;艺术家
composer [kəmˈpoʊzər] `n` 作曲家;词作者
scout [skaʊt] `n` 星探
amateur [ˈæmətər] `n` (艺术等)业余从事者

那些你不该做的

pirate [ˈpaɪrət] `v` 盗版;剽窃

bootleg [ˈbuːtleg] `a` 非法的
unoriginal [ˌʌnəˈrɪdʒənəl] `a` 模仿的;非原创的
purloin [pɜːrˈlɔɪn] `v` 盗取
critic [ˈkrɪtɪk] `n` 评论家
depreciate [dɪˈpriːʃieɪt] `v` 轻视,贬低
cut in a line `phr` 插队
scalper ticket `phr` 黄牛票

Unit 2 聚光灯下

用英语聊天，原来这么简单
老外每天说的英语，其实就是这几句。

One day, I will be a guitar star……
William

威廉：有一天，我将会成为吉他之星……

Situation 1
想成为一个音乐才子

The singer listened to the demo before recording the song.
歌手在录制这首歌之前先听样本唱片。

Our performance day is coming soon, so I need to practice harder and harder.
我们表演的日子就快到了，所以我必须加紧练习。

Jeremy arranged the old song and put in modern elements.
杰瑞米把老歌重新编曲并加入现代元素。

Simplified notations are easier for beginners ❶.
简谱对初学者来说比较简单。

She practices ❷ playing the electric guitar in band practice room every Friday ❸.
她每周五都在练习室里练习电吉他。

A composer must ❹ work hard ❺ to write new songs.
一个作曲家必须努力地创作新歌曲。

Grammar-2
"practice" 当动词时，为"练习；实行；经营"的意思，且其后接动词需以 Ving 的形式来呈现。

Grammar-3
"every Friday" 为固定用法，即"每个星期五"的意思，和其相同的短语为"on Fridays"；前者后面需要接单数名词，后者需要接复数名词。

Grammar-4
"must" 为助词，为"必须"的意思，其后需接动词原形；可以用"have to"替换。

Grammar-1
"beginner" 当名词时，为"初学者"之意，其用法相当于"novice（新手；初学者）"和"neophyte（生手）"等词汇。

Grammar-5
"hard" 当形容词时，解释为"硬的；辛苦的；努力的；困难的"，用以修饰名词；当副词时，则为"努力地；艰苦地；困难地"之意，用来修饰动词。

Chapter **11** 生活中的必要之美

demo [ˈdeməʊ] n 样本唱片　　arrange [əˈreɪndʒ] v 改编（音乐/剧本等）

modern [ˈmɑːdərn] a 现代的　contemporary [kənˈtempəreri] a 当代的

simplified notations phr 简谱　　electric guitar phr 电吉他

Situation 2
音乐天才

The judges were stunned by the child's musical talent.
评审对于这个小孩的音乐才能感到惊叹。

Elsa has played the piano since she was three years old.
艾莎从 3 岁开始弹钢琴。

Yvonne has cultivated ❻ her appreciation of art since ❼ her childhood.
伊芳从小就培养艺术的鉴赏能力。

Grammar-6
"cultivate"为动词时，为"培养"之意，其用法相当于"develop（发展；进化）"或是"train（训练；培养）"等词汇。

Grammar-7
"since + 一段时间"为"自从……"之意，语法上习惯用现在完成时来表示。

Although she didn't practice for the piano test, she can still pass it easily.
她就算不练习钢琴，一样能轻松通过考试。

judge [dʒʌdʒ] n 裁判员

be stunned by phr 对……感到惊叹　be mesmerized by phr 被……迷惑

talent [ˈtælənt] n 才能　　appreciation [əˌpriːʃɪˈeɪʃn] n 鉴赏能力

childhood [ˈtʃaɪldhʊd] n 童年时期

Situation 3
和朋友讨论音乐名人

Selena Gomez will tour Asia to promote her new album.
赛琳娜•戈麦兹将要巡回到亚洲来宣传她的新唱片。

You can come to my place to see my album collections.
你可以来我家看看我的唱片收藏。

My uncle collects records of classical music.
我叔叔收集了古典音乐的唱片。

Grammar-8
"for"在这里当介词使用，解释为"为了……"的意思，其后需接 N 或是 Ving 的形态。

John Lennon and Paul McCartney authored many songs for ❽ the Beatles.
约翰•列侬和保罗•麦卡特尼帮披头士编写了很多歌曲。

Grammar-9
"for"在此为表示时间的介词，其后需要接"一段时间"。

PSY's song "Gangnam Style" had been on the top-ten for ❾ many weeks.
PSY 的歌曲《江南风格》已经好几个星期排在前 10 名了。

Unit 2 聚光灯下

Grammar-10
"most" 当形容词，为"最多的"之意，其为形容词的最高级形式，前面需要有定冠词"the"或"所有格"做引导。

Beethoven's <mark>most</mark> ⑩ popular composition is "For Elise".
贝多芬最受欢迎的乐曲是《致爱丽丝》。

promote [prəˈmoʊt] v. 宣传；推销　　album [ˈælbəm] n. 唱片；录音带

author [ˈɔːθər] v. 编写；著作　　top-ten n. 前十名

composition [ˌkɑːmpəˈzɪʃn] n. 写作；作曲；（大型）乐曲

老外不会教你的小秘密

★ 歌手发行第一张唱片，我们可以说"*debut album*"；如果是第二张唱片就说"*follow-up album*"；金唱片就可以说"*gold album*"；白金唱片可以用"*platinum album*"来表达；现场实况专辑是"*live album*"！

★ 演唱会进行到高潮时，歌迷们都会对着舞台大喊"安可"，我们可以大声呐喊出"*Encore!*（安可！）"或是"*Bravo!*（太棒了！）"的词汇。

不怕你学不会

1. She practices _____ (sing) almost every day because she wants to perform her best on the formal competition.

2. You shouldn't ask a beginner to reach such a high level.
   = You shouldn't ask a _____ to reach such a high level.

3. The recording room only available on Sundays.
   = The recording room only available _____ Sunday.

4. After playing the violins _____ ten years, he finally became a violin master.

5. Being a musician is _____ myself, not _____ any other people.

答案：1. singing　2. novice / neophyte　3. every　4. for　5. for, for

Chapter 11 生活中的必要之美

Unit 3 倾听最美的声音
The sound of music

 原来老外这样记单词 / 老外从小到大学习单词的方法，就是看到什么就学什么！

xylophone [ˈzaɪləfəun]
n 木琴

timpani [ˈtɪmpəni]
n 定音鼓

saxophone [ˈsæksəfəun]
n 萨克斯

oboe [ˈəubəu]
n 双簧管

music stand
phr 乐谱架

其他衍生单词：

pluck [plʌk] v 拨弦　　**tambourine** [ˌtæmbəˈriːn] n 铃鼓　　**gong** [ɡɑːŋ] n 锣；铜锣

pick [pɪk] n 拨吉他的弹片　　**percussion instrument** phr 打击乐器　　**cymbal** [ˈsɪmbl] n 铙钹

老外最常用的单词
连这些单词都不会,你还敢说你学过英语吗?

各式各样可以吹的

piccolo [ˈpɪkələʊ] n 短笛;吹笛手

harmonica [hɑːrˈmɑːnɪkə] n 口琴
French horn phr 法国号
tuba [ˈtuːbə] n 低音号
wind instrument phr 管乐器;吹奏乐器
trumpet [ˈtrʌmpɪt] n 喇叭;小号
flute [fluːt] n 长笛;横笛

各式各样可以拉或弹的

harp [hɑːrp] n 竖琴

accordion [əˈkɔːrdɪən] n 手风琴
organ [ˈɔːrɡən] n 管风琴
piano [pɪˈænəʊ] n 钢琴
viola [vɪˈəʊlə] n 中提琴
cello [ˈtʃeləʊ] n 大提琴
violin [ˌvaɪəˈlɪn] n 小提琴
ukulele [ˌjuːkəˈleɪli] n 尤克里里;四弦琴
string instrument phr 弦乐器
double bass phr 低音提琴

各式各样的重要配备

mixing console phr 混音台

mixer [ˈmɪksər] n 混音器
amplifier [ˈæmplɪfaɪər] n 扩音器
compressor [kəmˈpresər] n 效果器
equalizer [ˈiːkwəlaɪzər] n 均衡器
kiosk [ˈkiːɑːsk] n 试听机
speaker [ˈspiːkər] n 扬声器
sound box phr 音箱;共鸣器
stage illumination phr 舞台灯光设备
band practice room phr 乐队排练室

用英语聊天，原来这么简单 / 老外每天说的英语，其实就是这几句。

艾莉森：好精彩的表演！ 布拉德：是啊！我到现在还是觉得很陶醉。

Situation 1
乐器介绍

Drums are probably the first musical instrument ever used.
鼓可能是最先使用的乐器。

The mandolin, the ukulele and the guitar are string instruments while the clarinet, the horn and the trumpet are wind instruments.
曼陀林、尤克里里和吉他是弦乐器，而竖笛、小号和喇叭是管乐器。

Grammar-1
"after"为表示"时间"的连词，其后需接时间副词从句。也可作为介词用，但要注意其后需接 Ving 形式。

After ❶ working long hours on this old piano, the piano tuner made it sound beautiful again.
修理这架老旧的钢琴一段时间之后，这位钢琴调音师再次让琴声变得优美了。

Grammar-2
"the smallest"为"small"的最高级形容词，为"最小的"之意。

The piccolo is the smallest ❷ instrument in the orchestra; it can fit in the musician's pocket.
短笛在管弦乐队里是最小的乐器，它可以放在音乐家的口袋里。

Grammar-3
"among"为介词，即"（三者以上）在……之间"的意思；"between"则是指"（两者）在……之间"的意思。

Bagpipes are a musical instrument that is popular among ❸ many places among Europe.
苏格兰风笛是在欧洲许多地方都很流行的乐器。

Unit 3 倾听最美的声音

Grammar-4
"be suitable for" 为固定短语,即"合适的"的意思,和其相同用法的短语为"be appropriate for"。

The timbre of the tuba is majestic and solemn, so it **is suitable for** a composition like *Slavonic March*.
低音号的音色雄伟而庄严,因此它很适合演奏像《斯拉夫进行曲》这样的曲子。

Grammar-5
"combine" 当动词时,为"结合"之意,其用法相当于词汇"merge(合并;同化)"和"associate(使联合;使结合)"。

Dulcimer **combines** features of percussion instruments with those of stringed instruments.
扬琴结合了打击乐器和弦乐器的特性。

Grammar-6
"common" 当形容词时,为"常见的"之意,其用法相当于"general(一般的;普遍的)"或"ordinary(普通的;平凡的)"等词汇。

Triangle and castanets are **common** instruments in schoolchildren's music class.
三角铁和响板是学童的音乐课中常见的乐器。

drum [drʌm] n 鼓;鼓声   musical instrument phr 乐器
mandolin [ˈmændəlɪn] n 曼陀林
tuner [ˈtuːnər] n 调音师;定弦者   bagpipe [ˈbæɡpaɪp] n 苏格兰风琴
popular [ˈpɑːpjələr] a 受欢迎的;流行的
timbre [ˈtæmbər] n 音色;音质
majestic [məˈdʒestɪk] a 雄伟的;崇高的
dulcimer [ˈdʌlsɪmər] n 扬琴   feature [ˈfiːtʃər] n 特征;特色
triangle [ˈtraɪˌæŋɡəl] n (打击乐器)三角铁
castanet [ˌkæstəˈnet] n (常为复数)响板

Situation 2 音乐会

The city is building a new concert hall for the symphony orchestra.
这个城市正在为交响乐团建造一座新的音乐厅。

The talented maestro conducts the orchestra.
这位才华横溢的著名指挥家指挥这支管弦乐团。

Grammar-7
"every" 和 "each" 后面需要接上单数名词和单数动词。

Every member of the orchestra tunes their instrument before a concert.
管弦乐团的每一位成员在音乐会开始前调整乐器的音调。

Grammar-8
"have much leeway to..." 为短语用法,即"有很大的空间去做……"的意思。

Chamber music doesn't need conductors. As a result, performers **have much leeway to** display their skills.
室内乐不需要指挥。所以表演者有更多的空间来展示他们的技巧。

Chapter 11 生活中的必要之美

concert hall `phr` 音乐厅   symphony orchestra `phr` 交响乐团

maestro ['maɪstrəʊ] `n` 大音乐家；名指挥家

conduct [kən'dʌkt] `v` 指挥   orchestra ['ɔːrkɪstrə] `n` 管弦乐团

tune [tuːn] `v` 为……调音   chamber music `phr` 室内乐

 老外不会教你的小秘密

★ 对于音乐的正面评价，除了可以用 *This is my favorite song.*（这是我最喜欢的歌曲。）之外，也可以用 *This song rocks.*（这首歌太棒了。）或是 *This song is tight.*（这首歌太酷了。）来表达；相反地，负面评价除了可以用 *This music is terrible.*（这音乐真差。）之外，还可以用 *This music sucks.*（这音乐真烂。）或是 *This music is lousy.*（这音乐真差劲。）来表达。

 不怕你学不会

1. Every member of the band _____ (focus) on their performance.

2. Triangle and castanets are general instruments in schoolchildren's music class.

    = Triangle and castanets are _____ instruments in schoolchildren's music class.

3. Dulcimer combines features of percussion instruments with those of stringed instruments.

    = Dulcimer _____ features of percussion instruments with those of stringed instruments.

4. After _____ (listen) to this great concert, I felt totally relaxed.

5. Classical music is suitable for kids.

    = Classical music is _____ for kids.

答案：1. focused 2. common / ordinary 3. merges / associates 4. listening 5. appropriate

Unit 4 跟我一起大声唱
Sing out loud

原来老外这样记单词 / 老外从小到大学习单词的方法，就是看到什么就学什么！

headset ['hedset]
n 头戴式耳机

voice actor
phr 配音员

soundproof equipment
phr 隔音设备

lip-sync ['lɪp sɪŋk]
n 对嘴配音 v 对口型

microphone ['maɪkrəfəʊn]
n 麦克风

其他衍生单词：

recording studio phr 录音室
record ['rekərd] n 唱片 v 录音；录影
artist ['ɑːrtɪst] n 艺人
editor ['edɪtər] n 剪辑者
release [rɪ'liːs] v （专辑）发行；发表
manager ['mænɪdʒər] n 经纪人

老外最常用的单词 连这些单词都不会，你还敢说你学过英语吗？

 老外爱合唱

choir ['kwaɪər] n 唱诗班

ensemble [ɑːn'sɑːmbl] n 合奏；合唱
hymn [hɪm] n 赞美诗，圣歌
harmony ['hɑːrməni] n 和声
opera ['ɑːprə] n 歌剧
trio ['triːəʊ] n 三重唱
musical ['mjuːzɪkl] n 歌舞剧
ballad ['bæləd] n 民谣，民歌
nursery rhyme phr 童谣；儿歌

 老外也爱 SOLO

vocalist ['vəʊkəlɪst] n 主唱

accompaniment [ə'kʌmpənɪmənt] n 伴奏；伴唱
tenor ['tenər] n 男高音
bass [beɪs] n 男低音
soprano [sə'prɑːnəʊ] n 女高音
alto ['æltəʊ] n 女低音
vocal music phr 声乐
sounds of nature phr 天籁

 会写歌的单词最帅气

metronome ['metrənəʊm] n 节拍器

inspiration [ˌɪnspə'reɪʃn] n 灵感；创作灵感
decibel ['desɪbel] n 分贝
chord [kɔːrd] n 和弦
pitch [pɪtʃ] n 音高
melody ['melədi] n 旋律；主调
theme [θiːm] n 主旋律
beat [biːt] n 拍子，节奏

用英语聊天，原来这么简单
老外每天说的英语，其实就是这几句。

We wish you a merry Christmas and a happy new year!
Singers

歌手：祝你有个快乐的圣诞节，新年快乐！

Situation 1
准备上台表演

Jason will sing a duo, but Paul will play in a quartet.
杰森要唱二重奏，但保罗要表演四重奏。

Before the presentation, the conductor asked David in what key he wanted to sing.
在表演之前，指挥询问大卫他想要唱哪一个音调。

Peter downloaded the lyrics of a love song because ❶ he wanted to sing it for his sister's wedding.
彼得下载情歌的歌词，因为他想要在他姐姐的婚礼上演唱。

He told the band leader that he wanted to sing in G key ❷.
他向乐队指挥表示想唱 G 调。

Gina's sweet voice caught everybody's attention ❸ in the singing contest.
吉娜甜美的嗓音在歌唱比赛中引起了大家的注意。

Grammar-1
"because" 当连词，表示"理由；原因"的意思。常置于主句之后，但无须加"逗号"。

Grammar-2
"sing in G key" 为固定用法，即"唱 G 调"的意思。

Grammar-3
"catch one's attention" 为固定用法，即"吸引某人的注意"的意思。

duo [ˈduːəʊ] n 二重唱；二重奏   quartet [kwɔːrˈtet] n 四重奏

presentation [ˌpriːzenˈteɪʃn] n 上演；演出

lyric [ˈlɪrɪk] n 歌词；抒情歌词   band leader phr 乐队指挥

voice [vɔɪs] n 声音；嗓子   singing contest phr 歌唱比赛

Chapter **11** 生活中的必要之美

Situation 2
唱歌的技巧

Gary has great range; he can reach very low notes and high notes.
盖瑞的音域很广，他可以唱非常低的音和非常高的音。

Judy is an alto in the chorus of her school. She always practices her singing skill at home.
朱迪在学校的合唱团担任女低音。她常常在家里练习她的歌唱技巧。

Julie is a soprano; that means she can hit high notes.
茱莉是女高音，也就是说她可以飙高音。

My mother went to the concert of 3 world tenors. She was impressed by their splendid voice.
我妈妈去了世界三大男高音的演唱会，她对他们美妙的声音印象深刻。

Jason is a bass, he can sing very low notes ❹.
杰森是男低音歌手，他可以唱非常低的音。

Grammar-4
"sing low note" 为固定短语，即"唱低音"的意思。

We shouldn't invite Pan to our karaoke party. His voice is horrible.
我们不应该找潘来参加卡拉OK派对的。他的声音很可怕。

I cannot carry a tune with a bucket.
我五音不全。

range [reɪndʒ] n 范围；幅度；区域   note [nəʊt] n 调子；音符

hit high notes phr 达到高音；飙高音   carry a tune phr 唱歌

bucket ['bʌkɪt] n 水桶

Situation 3
喜欢哼哼唱唱的你

Although I love singing so much, I still won't go to the singing competition.
我虽然很爱唱歌，但我是不会去参加歌唱比赛的。

My sister often hums a tune while doing the dishes.
我姐姐通常会在洗碗时哼着歌曲。

Let's perform some new year songs at the year-end party!
我们在年末派对上表演一些新年歌曲吧！

Many nuns sing Christmas carols in the church on Christmas Eve.
许多修女于圣诞节前夕在教堂里唱圣诞歌曲。

Unit 4 跟我一起大声唱

The young children soon fell asleep when their mother sang them a lullaby.
当妈妈哼唱摇篮曲给小孩子们听时，他们很快就入睡了。

hum a tune `phr` 哼歌　　　nun [nʌn] `n` 修女；尼姑

Christmas carol `phr` 圣诞歌曲　　lullaby [ˈlʌləbaɪ] `n` 催眠曲；摇篮曲

 老外不会教你的小秘密

★ 有没有听过歌手在现场演唱时却走调的状况呢？这个时候，我们可以用 *She is singing a little bit off key.*（她有一点走音了。）或是 *She is singing out of key.*（她唱走音了。）来形容。也可以委婉地说 *Your pitch isn't quite right for this song.*（你的音域不适合唱这首歌。）

 不怕你学不会

1. He told the band leader that he wanted to sing _____ G key.
2. The young children soon fell asleep when their mother sang them a lullaby.
   = The young children soon fell asleep when their mother sang lullaby _____ them.
3. I cannot c_____y a tune with a bucket.
4. Gospel music is suitable for the occasion like this.
   = Gospel music is _____ for the occasion like this.
5. Maya _____ learned piano since she was three years old.

答案：1. in　2. to　3. carry　4. appropriate　5. has

Chapter **11** 生活中的必要之美

看看老外怎么学

你常去听音乐会吗？一起来看看以下这些名词你认识哪些？

① _____   ② _____
③ _____   ④ _____
⑤ _____

- audience
- balcony
- VIP seats
- nosebleed seats
- stage

答案：1. stage 舞台 2. audience 观众 3. nosebleed seats 剧院只看起远处的座位 4. VIP seats 贵宾席 5. balcony 包厢

Chapter 12 一场视听享受

What a movie!

现代的生活多彩多姿！这当然少不了看电影休闲了！一起来学学老外聊电影的方法！

| **Unit 1**
看电影去 | **Unit 2**
开拍啦！ | **Unit 3**
你也可以是电影名嘴 |

Unit 1 看电影去
Go to See a Movie

原来老外这样记单词 / 老外从小到大学习单词的方法，就是看到什么就学什么！

moviegoer [ˈmuːvɪɡəʊər]
n 常看电影的人

3D glasses
phr 3D 眼镜

junkie [ˈdʒʌŋki]
n 影迷

soft drink
n 不含酒精的饮料（汽水类）

popcorn [ˈpɒpkɔːn]
n 爆米花

其他衍生单词：

ticket stub phr 票根
queue up phr 排队
concession stand phr 售卖部

kettle corn phr 水壶爆米花
expletive [ˈeksplətɪv] n 感叹词
hot dog phr 热狗

Unit 1 看电影去

老外最常用的单词
连这些单词都不会，你还敢说你学过英语吗？

老外这样看电影

combo deal phr （电影）套票

cast [kæst] n 演员阵容；班底
cameo [ˈkæmɪəʊ] n 客串演出
line [laɪn] n 台词
review [rɪˈvjuː] n 评论
rate [reɪt] n 等级；费用 v 定……的费率
feature [ˈfiːtʃər]
n （电影等）正片；故事片
matinee [ˌmætnˈeɪ]
n 午后的演出；（电影）日场

老外看哪些电影

kung fu movie phr 功夫电影

tragedy [ˈtrædʒədi] n 悲剧
costume piece phr 古装剧
fairy tale phr 神话故事；童话
drama film phr 剧情片
epic film phr 史诗电影
detective film phr 侦探片
jidai-geki films phr 日本时代剧
propaganda film phr 宣传片

老外看电影都配这些

pretzel [ˈpretel] n 椒盐脆饼

gum [gʌm] n 口香糖
chips [tʃɪps] n 炸薯条
mustard [ˈmʌstərd] n 芥末
ketchup [ˈketʃəp] n 番茄酱
hot dog phr 热狗
chicken nugget phr 鸡块
caramel popcorn phr 焦糖爆米花

Chapter **12** 一场视听享受

用英语聊天，原来这么简单 / 老外每天说的英语，其实就是这几句。

米歇儿：人可真多！　乔希：当然，这可是首映会！　曼迪：我等不及了！

Situation 1
新片上映时

- Star Trek – Into the Darkness is a new release. It came out this year.
  《星际争霸：暗黑无界》是一部新发行的电影，它今年上映。

Grammar-1
"sb. can't wait to…"为常见的短语，用以表示"等不及"的意思，其后面需要接动词原形。

- The release date of Les Misérables is on February 8th. I can't wait to ❶ see it.
  《悲惨世界》的上映日期是2月8日。我已经等不及要看了。

Grammar-2
"be set in…"为固定短语，其意思为"场景设在……"。

- This newly released film is set in ❷ Europe in the late 1800s.
  这部新电影的场景是在19世纪后期的欧洲。

`release` [rɪ'liːs] **n** 发行的电影 **v** 发行；出版

`come out` **phr** 出版；发表　　`newly` ['njuːli] **ad** 新近；再次

Situation 2
和朋友一起看电影

- The Cinema is a new art form.
  这个电影院是一种新艺术形态。

Grammar-4
指"科幻电影"。其缩写为"sci-fi"。

Grammar-3
"should"为助动词，放在句首形成疑问句时，为问答句的句型。因此需以"Yes"或"No"来应答。

- Should ❸ we watch a thriller or a science fiction ❹ movie?
  我们应该看惊悚片还是科幻片呢？

- Let's purchase the tickets online first.
  我们先在网上订票吧。

Unit 1 看电影去

Grammar-5
"understand" 为动词，有"了解；知道"的意思，其可替换成"comprehend"或"know"等词汇。

Does this movie have the Chinese subtitles? I need them because I cannot **understand** ⑤ the plot very well.
这部电影有中文字幕吗？我需要它们，因为我不太了解剧情。

Why do you still want to see that movie?
为什么你一定要看那部电影？

Grammar-6
"munch on" 为固定短语，解释为"吱吱作响地嚼"，也可以替换成"crunch on（嘎吱作响地咀嚼）"的用法。

I always **munch on** ⑥ popcorn when I go to see a movie.
当我去看电影的时候，我总是喜欢吃爆米花。

Grammar-7
"more and more" 即为"越来越多的"的意思，和其相反意思的为"less and less（越来越少的）"。

More and more ⑦ movie theaters provide online booking services, which enables moviegoers to buy tickets more easily.
越来越多的电影院提供线上订票的服务，如此一来电影迷就能轻松订票了。

I always have a nightmare after watching horror movies.
我总是在看完恐怖电影后做噩梦。

Grammar-8
"have to" 有"必须"的意思，后面接动词原形，表示客观不得不做的事。

We **have to** ⑧ wear 3D glasses when we watch 3D films.
看 3D 电影的时候要带 3D 眼镜。

cinema ['sɪnəmə] n 电影院 movie theater phr 电影院

form [fɔːrm] n 外形；类型   thriller ['θrɪlər] n 惊悚电影；惊悚片

subtitle ['sʌbtaɪtl] n 对白的字幕；副标题

provide [prə'vaɪd] v 提供；供给   service ['sɜːrvɪs] n 服务

Situation 3
国外的电影分级

I am not allowed to watch a horror movie without parental guidance.
没有家长陪同，我不能看恐怖片。

Grammar-9
"censor" 当动词解释时，为"审查；检查"的意思；我们也可以用"examine（检查；审问）"或"inspect（检阅；审查）"等词汇来替换。若当名词时，则意为"审查员；检查员"。

Some violent scenes in this film were **censored** ⑨.
这部电影里因有些暴力场景而被审查。

When my little sister **is around** ⑩, we only watch family movies.
当我妹妹在旁边时，我们只能观赏家庭电影。

Grammar-10
"be around" 为固定短语，有"在附近；在周围"的意思。

allow [ə'laʊ] v 允许；准许   horror movie phr 恐怖片

parental [pə'rentl] a 父母亲的   violent ['vaɪələnt] a 暴力的；凶暴的

scene [siːn] n 一个镜头；场景

Chapter **12** 一场视听享受

229

Situation 4
电影的历史

My great-grandmother used to ⓫ watch silent films. That is before the synchronized sound was invented.
我曾祖母以前习惯看默剧,也就是在同步音效发明之前的默片。

The invention of the first movie camera in the late 1880s ⓬ was the start of motion pictures.
19世纪80年代后期,第一台电影摄影机的发明促使电影的诞生。

Grammar-11
"used to"为固定用法,为"习惯……",但这属于"过去的习惯",且"to"为不定词,其后所接的动词需以原形呈现。要注意的是,"be used to"的意思也为"习惯……",但却属于"现在的习惯",且"to"为介词,后面接Ving。

Grammar-12
"in the late 1880s"是指19世纪八十年代后期,年代是"一段长时间",需用时间介词"in"。

- silent film phr 默片;无声电影
- synchronize [ˈsɪŋkrənaɪz] v 画面和声音一致
- invent [ɪnˈvent] v 发明;创造
- invention [ɪnˈvenʃn] n 发明;创造
- movie camera phr 电影摄影机
- motion picture phr 电影

老外不会教你的小秘密

★ 你知道电影分哪些等级吗?在美国,电影被分为 5 个等级,依序如下:

- ✦ G (= General),是所有人都可以观看的,也就是我们说的老少咸宜"普通级"。
- ✦ PG (= Parental Guidence),是一些内容不适合孩子观看的,属于警告级,由家长决定孩子是否可以观赏的影片。
- ✦ PG-13 (= Parents Strong Cautioned),是 13 岁以上青少年需辅导观看,13 岁以下孩子不适合观看的影片。
- ✦ R (= Restricted),为 17 岁以下青少年需父母陪同观看的影片。
- ✦ NC-17 (= No One 17 and Under Admitted 17),是 17 岁以下青少年禁止观看之影片。

因此,当有人问你说:"What is this movie rated?(这部电影分为哪一级呢?)"时,你便可以用上述电影等级来回应,如:"It's rated G.(是普通级。)"。

Unit 2 开拍啦! Action!

原来老外这样记单词 / 老外从小到大学习单词的方法，就是看到什么就学什么！

cosmetician [ˌkɒzməˈtɪʃən]
n 化妆师；美容师

actress [ˈæktrəs]
n 女演员

video camera
phr 摄影机

cameraman [ˈkæmrəmæn]
n 摄影师

director [dəˈrektər]
n 导演

其他衍生单词：

- **stage manager** phr 舞台监督
- **light technician** phr 灯光师
- **boom man** phr 录音师
- **assistant director** phr 副导演
- **promoter** [prəˈməʊtər] n 场记
- **producer** [prəˈdjuːsər] n 制作人

老外最常用的单词
连这些单词都不会,你还敢说你学过英语吗?

拍电影好伙伴

double ['dʌbl] n 替身演员;特技替身

actor ['æktər] n 男演员
aside [ə'saɪd] n 旁白
choreographer [ˌkɔːri'ɑːgrəfər] n 舞蹈指导
extra ['ekstrə] n 临时演员
substitute actor phr 替身演员
language director phr 语言指导
executive producer phr 执行监制
publicity manager phr 公关
art editor phr 美术编辑

如何制作一部电影

shooting script
phr (电影)拍摄用的剧本

script [skrɪpt] n (戏剧/广播等的)脚本;底稿
mimicry ['mɪmɪkri] n 模仿;模拟
footage ['fʊtɪdʒ] n (影片的)连续镜头
plagiarize ['pleɪdʒəraɪz] v 剽窃;抄袭
copyright ['kɑːpɪraɪt] n 版权;著作权
episode ['epɪsəʊd] n 连续剧的一片段(或一集)
persistence of vision phr 视觉暂留
post-production phr 后期制作

如何行销一部电影

coming attraction phr 预告片

soundtrack ['saʊndtræk] n 原声带
sequel ['siːkwəl] n 续集
preview ['priːvjuː] n (电影/电视等的)预告片;预告
trailer ['treɪlər] n 电影预告片;预告节目
product placement phr 植入式广告
original work phr 原作

用英语聊天，原来这么简单 / 老外每天说的英语，其实就是这几句。

梅根：我们来拍恐怖片吧！　布莱特：好！我们也可以加点爱情元素。

Situation 1
拍摄电影

Many of Andersen's masterpieces were adapted into movies.
许多安徒生的杰作被改编成电影。

Avatar is a movie that integrates ❶ elements of art and technology.
《阿凡达》是一部结合艺术和科技元素的电影。

The screenwriter created the script in ❷ two years, and then the producer hired the actors.
这位编剧在 2 年内编写出剧本，然后制作人再雇演员。

Grammar-1
"integrate"当形容词时，解释为"完整的；综合的"；当动词时，则有"结合"的意思，其用法相当于"combine（结合；联合）"。

Grammar-2
"in"为时间介词，其后需要使用"一段长时间"的时间副词。

Andersen [ˈændəsən] n 安徒生

masterpiece [ˈmæstərpiːs] n 杰作；名作 同 masterwork n 杰作

adapt [əˈdæpt] v 改编；改写

element [ˈelɪmənt] n 元素；要素；成分

technology [tekˈnɑːlədʒi] n 技术

screenwriter [ˈskriːnraɪtər] n 剧本作家；编剧家

create [krɪˈeɪt] v 创作；设计

Situation 2
杀青！电影要上映了

I saw my brother's name on the end roll of the hit movie. I'm so proud of him.
我看见我哥哥的名字出现在这部热门电影的工作人员名单中。我以他为荣。

The Finnish film was dubbed into ❸ English so that more people can understand it.
这部芬兰电影用英语配音，所以有更多人能够理解它。

This director has his unique style. He always asks ❹ actors and actresses to improvise.
这位导演有他独特的风格。他总是要求演员们即兴演出。

All casts and crew will take part in the wrap party to celebrate the completion of the movie.
所有的演员和工作人员都会参加杀青派对庆祝电影的完成。

Actors have to memorize ❺ the words of the script.
演员们必须要记住剧本中的台词。

The blocking of this movie is not well-arranged ❻. The two actors almost bumped into each other.
这部电影的演员走位没有安排好。那两位演员差点就撞在一起了。

Grammar-3
"be dubbed into language" 为固定短语，即"配音成某种语言"的意思。

Grammar-4
"ask sb. to V" 为常用的短语，意思为"要求某人做某事"，后面加上动词原形。

Grammar-5
"memorize" 当动词时，为"记住；背熟"的意思，其用法和"remember（记得；记住）"相当，而反义词则为"forget（忘记；忽略）"。

Grammar-6
"well-arranged" 为形容词，为"安排妥当的"之意，其用法相当于"well-organized"。

- end roll phr 工作人员名单
- hit movie phr 热门的电影
- be proud of sb. phr 以……为荣
- Finnish ['fɪnɪʃ] a 芬兰的 n 芬兰语
- dub [dʌb] v 配音
- unique [jʊ'ni:k] a 独特的；唯一的
- improvise ['ɪmprəvaɪz] v 即兴表演（或朗诵等）
- take part in phr 参加
- wrap party phr 杀青派对
- completion [kəm'pli:ʃn] n 圆满；结束
- have to phr 必须
- word [wɜ:rd] n 谈话；歌词
- blocking [blɑ:kɪŋ] n 【戏】舞台调度；演员走位
- bump into phr 碰撞上……

Situation 3
电影

You can hire Mark to do the voice-over for your commercial.
你可以雇马克来给你的商业广告念旁白。

Actors and actresses like to attend red carpet events, such as ❼ the premiere of their films.
男演员和女演员喜欢出席红地毯活动，像他们的电影首映礼。

Grammar-7
"such as" 为固定短语，其意思为"如此……的；像……那样的"。

Unit 2 开拍啦！

Grammar-9
"reporter"为名词时，为"记者"之意，其用法相当于"journalist（新闻记者）"。

The film festival is held once a year ⑨.
电影节一年举办一次。

Grammar-8
"once a year"为固定短语，即"一年一次"的意思。

Many reporters ⑨ were invited to attend *Spiderman*'s press conference.
很多记者应邀出席《蜘蛛人》的记者招待会。

hire [haɪr] v 雇用　　voice-over phr 旁白

commercial [kəˈmɜːrʃl] n 商业广告

festival [ˈfestɪvl] n （定期举行的）音乐节；戏剧节

press conference phr 记者招待会

Situation 4
讨论知名演员们

Who is the main actor? Who are the supporting actors?
谁是男主角呢？谁又是男配角呢？

Jackie Chan and Owen Wilson starred ⑩ in *Shanghai Knights*.
成龙和欧文·威尔逊主演《皇家威龙》。

Grammar-10
"star"当名词时，解释为"星星"的意思，但在此句中是动词，有"使成明星；主演"之意。若要表达主演哪部电影时，在后面使用介词"in"即可。

The female lead role charges high remuneration because of her high popularity.
由于女主角的人气高，所以她的片酬高。

Because Jackie Chan did not use stunt men in the movies, he often got hurt ⑪.
因为成龙在电影里不用替身，所以他经常受伤。

Grammar-11
"get hurt"为固定短语，解释为"受伤"的意思，和其相同用法的短语有"be injured"和"be wounded"等。

supporting actor phr 男配角 对 supporting actress phr 女配角

female lead role phr 女主角 对 male lead role phr 男主角

remuneration [rɪˌmjuːnəˈreɪʃn] n 酬劳；薪资

popularity [ˌpɑːpjuˈlærəti] n 讨人喜欢的特点；声望

stunt man phr 特技演员；替身演员 同 substitute actor phr 替身

Chapter **12**
一场视听享受

235

Unit 3 你也可以是电影名嘴
Be a movie critic

原来老外这样记单词 / 老外从小到大学习单词的方法,就是看到什么就学什么!

costume [ˈkɑːstuːm]
n 戏服;装束

stage props phr 道具

villain [ˈvɪlən]
n (戏剧/小说中的)反派角色

character [ˈkærəktər]
n (小说/戏剧等的)人物;角色

scene [siːn]
n (电影/电视的)一个镜头

其他衍生单词:

key figure phr 核心人物　　**castle** [ˈkæsl] n 城堡　　**superman** [ˈsuːpərmæn] n 超人

zombie [ˈzɑːmbi] n 僵尸　　**space capsule** phr 太空船　　**vampire** [ˈvæmpaɪər] n 吸血鬼

Unit 3 你也可以是电影名嘴

老外最常用的单词
连这些单词都不会，你还敢说你学过英语吗？

电影都在演这些 ★★

tension ['tenʃn]
n 紧张局势；张力

crisis ['kraɪsɪs] n 紧要关头；危机
ending ['endɪŋ] n （故事等的）结尾；结局
metaphor ['metəfər]
n 象征；隐喻（一种修辞法）
gamble ['gæmbl] n v 赌博；打赌
surrealism [sə'riːəlɪzəm] n 超现实主义
horrible ['hɔːrəbl] a
可怕的；令人毛骨悚然的
overact [ˌəʊvər'ækt] v 表演过火；行为过火

电影人梦寐以求的单词 ★★

paparazzi [ˌpæpə'rætsəʊ] n 狗仔队

nominate ['nɑːmɪneɪt] v 推荐；提名
nominee [ˌnɑːmɪ'niː] n 被提名的人
presenter [prɪ'zentər] n 节目主持人
Oscar Academy Awards
phr 奥斯卡金像奖
box office phr 售票处；票房
the Oscar statuette phr 奥斯卡小金人

电视也会播的单词 ★★

remote control phr 遥控器

mellow ['meləʊ] n 极好的、令人愉快的
cable channel phr 有线频道
pay-per-view phr （电视节目）收费的
prime time phr 黄金时段
DVD player phr DVD 播放器
fast forward phr 快进
slow motion phr 慢动作

Chapter 12 一场视听享受

用英语聊天，原来这么简单 / 老外每天说的英语，其实就是这几句。

> What do you think about the movie we have just watched?
>
> I am a little confused. Let's check out what the film critics will say.

康纳：你觉得刚刚那部电影怎么样？　埃琳娜：我有点看不懂。来看看影评怎么说。

Situation 1
介绍自己看电影的习惯

I don't like low-budget movies, especially when the casting or the director is not good enough.
我不喜欢低预算的电影，尤其是当演员阵容和导演都不怎么厉害的时候。

I love going to second-run cinemas because tickets cost less.
我喜欢去二轮剧院，因为票比较便宜。

Grammar-1
"like to..." 为短语，意思为"喜欢……"，后面需要接动词原形。

My grandfather likes to ❶ watch musicals like *Singing in the rain*.
我爷爷喜欢看像是《雨中曲》那样的歌舞剧。

Mike likes to rent a DVD or Blue Ray, but Susan prefers to download movies from the Internet.
迈克喜欢租借 DVD 或蓝光光碟，但是苏珊比较喜欢从网上下载电影。

Grammar-2
"on the weekends" 为固定短语，为"在周末"的意思，因为"weekend"为特定时间，故时间介词要用"on"；也可以替换成"every weekend"，有"每个周末"之意，要记住"every"后面所接的名词须为"单数"。

I like to watch documentaries on the weekends ❷.
我喜欢在周末时观赏纪录片。

low-budget a 低预算的 （反）high-budget a 高预算的

casting [ˈkæstɪŋ] n 演员阵容　　second-run cinema phr 二轮戏院

cost [kɔːst] n 花费　　musical [ˈmjuːzɪkl] n 歌舞片；音乐剧

documentary [ˌdɑːkjuˈmentri] n 纪录片

Unit 3 你也可以是电影名嘴

Situation 2
发表你的独到见解

Let's ❸ read the movie reviews!
我们来看影评吧！

Grammar-3: "let's" 有 "邀请；建议" 的意思在，后面的动词一律采 "动词原形" 的形式。

The Incredibles is a blockbuster.
《超人特攻队》是一部卖座的电影。

Some movie critics have given the movie *Man of Steel* the thumbs up, but my friends have given it the thumbs down ❹.
有些影评给予《钢铁侠》肯定，但我的朋友们却不看好这部影片。

Grammar-4: "thumbs up" 为固定短语，为 "赞誉；肯定" 的意思，而其相反用法则为 "thumbs down"，有 "否定；贬低" 之意。

This film had great camera work and fantastic visual effects.
这部电影有高超的摄影技巧和超棒的视觉效果。

The sequel of that popular film disappointed me because it was not as exciting as expected.
那部热门电影的续集让我感到失望，因为它没有想象中精彩。

The special effects of this movie impress ❺ me the most.
这部电影的特效让我印象最为深刻。

Grammar-5: "be impressed by" 为固定短语，即 "对……印象深刻" 的意思。

The background music is a good match for the storyline.
背景音乐非常符合故事情节。

incredible [ɪnˈkrɛdəbl] a 惊人的

blockbuster [ˈblɑːkbʌstər] n 卖座电影

movie critics phr 影评   fantastic [fænˈtæstɪk] a 极好的；了不起的

visual [ˈvɪʒuəl] a 视觉的

effect [ɪˈfɛkt] n （色彩／声音等的）印象；效果

disappointed [ˌdɪsəˈpɔɪntɪd] a 失望的；沮丧的

as expected phr 正如所料   background [ˈbækɡraʊnd] n 背景音乐

match [mætʃ] v 和……相配   storyline [ˈstɔːrɪlaɪn] n 故事情节

Situation 3
剧透

The plot is about ❻ a former CIA agent who chases a killer.
这个剧情是关于前美国中央情报局的人追捕杀人犯。

An interesting action movie may also contain a few good romantic scenes.
一部有趣的动作片可能也会包含一些浪漫的场景。

Grammar-6: "about" 为介词，其后可接 N 或 Ving。

Chapter 12 一场视听享受

🎧 239

Grammar-7
"by the same name" 有 "以相同的名字来……" 的意思，其中的 "by" 还有 "通过；借由" 的意味在。

Grammar-8
"who" 为关系代词，用来修饰先行词 "hero" 和 "heroine"；而在关系从句里，"who" 为主格，当作形容词从句中的主语。

Grammar-9
"turn into" 为固定短语，即 "变成" 的意思，后面通常会接上一 "名词"。

Toy Story is a great computer animated comedy movie produced by Pixar Animation Studios.
《玩具总动员》是由皮克斯动画工作室所制作的一部很棒的电脑动画喜剧电影。

The movie *The Hobbit* is an adaptation of the novel <mark>by the same name</mark> ❼ written in 1937, by J.R.R. Tolkien.
《霍比特人》电影是改编自约翰·罗纳德·瑞尔·托尔金撰写于1937年的同名小说。

Adventure movies involve a hero or a heroine <mark>who</mark> ❽ tries to save a situation for the good of everyone.
冒险电影包含了英雄或女英雄想要为了每个人转危为安的情节。

In *Twilight*, werewolves would <mark>turn into</mark> ❾ wolf-forms during the full moon.
在《暮光之城》中，狼人会在月圆时现出原形。

Western films' characteristics include easy conversations and clear moral values.
西部片的特色包含浅显易懂的对白和鲜明的道德观。

former [ˈfɔːrmər] a 前任的 反 present [ˈpreznt] a 现任的

CIA (Central Intelligence Agency) abbr 美国中央情报局

agent [ˈeɪdʒənt] n 代理人；政府代表

chase [tʃeɪs] v 追逐 同 run after phr 追逐；追求

interesting [ˈɪntrəstɪŋ] a 有趣的

action movie phr 动作片   romantic [roʊˈmæntɪk] a 多情的；浪漫的

animated [ˈænɪmeɪtɪd] a 卡通（片）的；动画的

comedy [ˈkɑːmədi] n 喜剧   produce [prəˈduːs] v 制作

animation studio phr 动画工作室   adaptation [ˌædæpˈteɪʃn] n 改编

novel [ˈnɑːvl] n （长篇）小说   hero [ˈhɪroʊ] n 英雄

heroine [ˈheroʊɪn] n 女英雄   for the good of sb. phr 为了某人好

werewolf [ˈwerwʊlf] n 狼人   full moon phr 满月

characteristic [ˌkærəktəˈrɪstɪk] n 特性；特征

conversation [ˌkɑːnvərˈseɪʃn] n 谈吐；会话

clear [klɪr] a 清晰的；明显的

Chapter 13

爱与和平 救地球

Love & Peace

想要处理好人际关系,来场浪漫的异国之恋,
有哪些单词、句子可以让你完成梦想呢?
千万别错过这个章节!

Unit 1	Unit 2	Unit 3	Unit 4
关于爱	关于家庭	关于差异	关于恨

Unit 1 关于爱 About love

原来老外这样记单词 / 老外从小到大学习单词的方法，就是看到什么就学什么！

boyfriend [ˈbɔɪˌfrend]
n 男朋友

lover [ˈlʌvər]
n 情人

tie a knot
phr 结为连理

girlfriend [ˈɡɜːrlfrend]
n 女朋友

其他衍生单词：

kiss [kɪs] v 亲吻
court [kɔːrt] v 追求；向……献殷勤
couple [ˈkʌpəl] n 夫妇；未婚夫妻

anniversary [ˌænɪˈvɜːrsəri] n 结婚周年纪念
accost [əˈkɔːst] v 引诱；勾引
date [deɪt] n 约会

Unit 1 关于爱

老外最常用的单词 / 连这些单词都不会，你还敢说你学过英语吗？

初次见面的怦然心动

hostility [hɑːˈstɪləti] n 敌意

déjà vu phr 【法】似曾相识的感觉
stereotype [ˈsteriətaɪp] n 刻板印象
bias [ˈbaɪəs] n 偏见
empathy [ˈempəθi] n 移情作用
vigilance [ˈvɪdʒɪləns] n 警戒；警惕（性）
impression [ɪmˈpreʃn] n 印象
stage fright phr （初上舞台的）怯场

相恋时的甜甜蜜蜜

third wheel
phr 【美】电灯泡；多余的人

fiancée n 未婚妻
fiancé n 未婚夫
hug [hʌg] v 拥抱
matchmaker [ˈmætʃmeɪkər] n 媒人
romantic [rəʊˈmæntɪk] a 浪漫的
sense of belonging phr 归属感
sweetheart [ˈswiːthɑːrt] n 甜心

步入礼堂共创幸福

wedding cake phr 结婚蛋糕

bridesmaid [ˈbraɪdzmeɪd] n 伴娘
best man phr 伴郎
honeymoon [ˈhʌnɪmuːn] n 蜜月
mistress [ˈmɪstrəs] n 情妇
marriage vows
phr 婚礼宣誓；结婚誓言
wedding invitation phr 喜帖
wedding anniversary phr 结婚纪念日

Chapter **13** 爱与和平救地球

用英语聊天，原来这么简单 / 老外每天说的英语，其实就是这几句。

约翰尼：甜心，你为何那么可爱？ 伊娃：噢，强尼宝贝！

Situation 1
恋爱中的甜言蜜语

I'm in love! I met the most wonderful girl and it was love at first sight for both of us.
我恋爱了！我遇见了最完美的女孩，而且我们是一见钟情。

Felix is seeing someone.
菲力克斯正在和某人谈恋爱。

Grammar-1
"迷恋某人"可以使用"have a crush on sb."的短语来表达。

Olivia has a big crush on ❶ one of her classmates.
奥莉薇亚迷恋她班上的一个同学。

William is attracted to Cindy, and she likes him too. They might soon go steady.
辛迪对威廉很有吸引力，而辛迪也很喜欢他。他们可能很快就会稳定交往。

Peter is always so thoughtful that I can't stop myself falling in love with him.
彼得总是那么贴心以至于我无法不爱上他。

Since James moved to the capital city, I love him more than ever. Absence makes the heart grow fonder ❷.
自从詹姆斯搬到首都市区后，我比以往更加爱他。真是小别胜新婚。

Grammar-2
"Absence makes the heart grow fonder."
此为谚语，其意思为"小别胜新婚"。

Unit 1 关于爱

Alex only met Emily last week, but he is already head over heels for her.
艾力克斯上星期才遇见艾米丽，但他已经完完全全地为她疯狂了。

be in love [phr] 恋爱　　wonderful ['wʌndərfl] [a] 极好的

love at first sight [phr] 一见钟情　　attract [ə'trækt] [v] 吸引；引起……的注意

soon [suːn] [ad] 不久；很快地　　steady ['stedi] [a] 稳定的；平稳的

capital ['kæpɪtl] [n] 首都 [a] 首位的　　already [ɔːl'redi] [ad] 已经

Situation 2
勇敢追求爱

You are my other half! You have a special place in my heart.
你是我的另一半！你在我心中占有特殊的地位。

Be my girl, please.
请当我女朋友。

Grammar-3
用以表达"使某人着迷"的短语为"get sb. hooked"。

You are my permanent love. You've got me hooked ❸.
你是我永恒的爱。你已经使我深深着迷了。

special ['speʃl] [a] 特别的；特殊的　　place [pleɪs] [n] 位置；身份

permanent ['pɜːrmənənt] [a] 永恒的；永远的

Situation 3
永远的承诺

Jeremy promises ❹ his girlfriend that he will take care of her forever.
杰瑞米向她的女友承诺会永远照顾她。

Grammar-4
"promise"当名词时，有"诺言；约定"的意思；当动词时，则为"保证"之意，用法相当于"assure（担保；确保）"和"guarantee（保证；担保）"等词汇。

Will you love, honor, comfort and cherish her for as long as you both shall live?
你愿意在你的有生之年都爱着她、尊敬她、安慰她、关爱她吗？

take care of [phr] 照顾；留意　　forever [fər'evər] [ad] 永远

Situation 4
幸福的求婚

I want to spend the rest of my life with you ❺. Would you marry me?
我想要和你共度余生。你愿意嫁给我吗？

Grammar-5
在婚礼中的誓词，若要表达"和某人共度余生"，可用"spend the rest of one's life with sb."的短语。

We made a surprising proposal for the couple yesterday.
昨天我们替一对情侣举办了一场惊喜的求婚仪式。

Chapter **13** 爱与和平救地球

Grammar-6
"向……求婚"，英语的表达为"propose to"。

Grammar-7
"give sb. the hand of one's daughter" 意思为"把某人女儿的手交到某人手中"，进而引申为"同意嫁娶"。

Ian **proposed to** Mary last night and she accepted.
伊恩昨晚向玛丽求婚，而她答应了。

Mr. Martin, would you **give me the hand of your daughter** in marriage?
马丁先生，您愿意将女儿嫁给我吗？

marry ['mæri] Ⓥ 和……结婚 ㊙ divorce [dɪ'vɔːrs] Ⓥ 离婚

accept [ək'sept] Ⓥ 接受；答应 ㊙ refuse [rɪ'fjuːz] Ⓥ 拒绝；不愿

marriage ['mærɪdʒ] ⓝ 结婚；婚姻

 不怕你学不会！

1. That girl totally _____ Jimmy hooked. He chased after her almost every day.

2. I want to propose _____ Mary, but I don't know what I should prepare.

3. Jeremy promises her girlfriend that he will take care of her forever.
= Jeremy _____ her girlfriend that he will take care of her forever.

4. I had a crush _____ the girl who is the prettiest girl in our school.

答案：1. got 2. to 3. assures / guarantees 4. on

Unit 2 关于家庭 About family

原来老外这样记单词 / 老外从小到大学习单词的方法，就是看到什么就学什么！

uncle [ˈʌŋkl]
n 舅舅；伯父；叔叔

father-in-law [ˈfɑðərɪnˌlɒ]
n 公公

clan [klæn]
n 家族；部落

mother-in-law [ˈmʌðərɪnˌlɒ]
n 婆婆

aunt [ænt]
n 舅妈；婶婶；阿姨

daughter-in-law [ˈdɔtərɪnˌlɒ]
n 媳妇

其他衍生单词：

son-in-law [ˈsʌnɪnˌlɒ] n 女婿
genealogy n 族谱
direct blood relative phr 直系血亲

relative [ˈrelətɪv] n 亲戚，亲属
reunion [ˌriˈjunɪən] n 团聚
great-grandfather [ˌgreɪtˈgrændˌfɑːðə] n 曾祖父

老外最常用的单词
连这些单词都不会，你还敢说你学过英语吗？

我们这一家

triplet ['trɪplət] n 三胞胎

stepmother ['stepmʌðər] n 继母；后母
orphan ['ɔːrfn] n 孤儿
inherit [ɪn'herɪt]
v 继承（传统/遗产等）；遗传
blood relationship phr 血统
child bride phr 童养媳
Retaining Order phr 保护令
child custody phr 监护权

左邻右舍也来参加

neighbor ['neɪbər] n 邻居

classmate ['klæsmeɪt] n 同学
roommate ['ruːmmeɪt] n 室友
teammate ['tiːmmeɪt] n 队友
peer [pɪr] n 同龄；同辈
buddy ['bʌdi] n 好朋友，伙伴
brother ['brʌðər]
n （用于称呼）老兄，朋友
mate [meɪt] n 同伴，伙伴
company ['kʌmpəni]
n 伴侣(们)；同伴(们)；朋友(们)

关系良好的人们

fair-weather friend phr 酒肉朋友

benefactor ['benɪfæktər] n 恩人
acquaintance [ə'kweɪntəns]
n 相识的人
intimate ['ɪntɪmət] a 亲密的
pen pal phr 笔友
soul mate phr 心灵伴侣
hold hands phr 牵手
nodding acquaintance phr 点头之交

Unit 2 关于家庭

用英语聊天，原来这么简单
老外每天说的英语，其实就是这几句。

爷爷：来吧！大家多吃一点！　儿子：大家能齐聚一堂真的很棒。

Situation 1
亲戚之间打招呼

Most of my relatives live in the U.S.A. We don't see each other very often.
我的大部分亲戚都住在美国，我们不常见面。

I call my mother's aunt "great-aunt". She is a great person.
我称呼我妈妈的姑姑为"姑姥姥"，她是一个很棒的人。

Grammar-1
短语"look like"的意思为"看起来像……（一样）"，后面通常接名词。

My nephew and niece look like ❶ me because they are my brother's children.
我的侄子和侄女长得像我，是因为他们是我哥哥的小孩。

In this picture we can see my extended family. Everyone is there: my parents, siblings, my grandparents and cousins.
在这张照片中，可以看到我的大家庭。大家都在里面；我的父母亲、兄弟姐妹及我的祖父母和堂/表兄弟姐妹。

Who is the black sheep ❷ in your family?
你家的败家子是谁呢？

Grammar-2
此句中的"black sheep"有"败类；害群之马"的意思；与之用法相似的谚语为"rotten apple in the barrel"。

Grammar-3
此句中的"family tree"有"家谱（图）"的意思，为短语用法。

Our family tree ❸ goes back many generations.
我们家的族谱追溯到好几代人。

Chapter 13 爱与和平救地球

call [kɔːl] v 称呼；把……叫

great-aunt [ˈɡreɪtˈɑːnt] n 伯祖母；姑姥姥

nephew [ˈnefjuː] n 侄儿；外甥

niece [niːs] n 侄女；外甥女

extended family phr 大家庭

cousin [ˈkʌzn] n 堂（或表）兄弟姐妹

family [ˈfæməli] n 家庭；家族

go back phr 追溯

generation [ˌdʒenəˈreɪʃn] n 世代

Situation 2
介绍你的家庭成员

Since my mother remarried, her husband has become my stepfather. I also have a stepsister.
因为我妈妈再嫁，她先生就是我的继父。
我也有一个继姐。

Grammar-4
"since" 当连接词使用，有"因为"的意思，用法相当于"because（因为）"、"due to（由于；因为）"和"owing to（由于；因为）"。

My family consists of my parents, my younger sister, and me.
我的家庭成员有我、父母和妹妹。

Ethan drives his wife to his parents-in-law's house every Sunday so that she can visit her parents.
伊森每周日都会开车载着太太回岳父母家，以便让她可以看看她的父母亲。

Grammar-5
"so that" 有 "以便；为了" 的意思，也可以用 "in order that" 的短语来替换。

remarry [ˌriːˈmæri] v （使）再婚

stepfather [ˈstepfɑːðər] n 继父

stepsister [ˈstepsɪstər] n 继父/母与前妻所生的女儿；异父/母的姐妹

wife [waɪf] n 妻子；太太

parent-in-law n 配偶的父亲或母亲

Situation 3
谈论爸妈

Debby is grateful to her adoptive parents for choosing her to be their daughter.
黛比很感激她的养父母选择她成为他们的女儿。

Do you still visit your parents often?
你常回去看你爸妈吗？

Grammar-6
"give birth to" 后面接上名词，表示"生产"，后面接上具体物，指"生小孩"。

Did you hear of the woman who gave birth to quadruplets?
你听说过一名妇女生了四胞胎吗？

grateful [ˈɡreɪtfl] a 感激的

adoptive parents phr 养父母

choose [tʃuːz] v 选择；挑选

quadruplet [ˈkwɑːdrʊplət] n 四胞胎

Unit 2 关于家庭

Situation 4
兄弟姐妹间的感情

Grammar-7
"soon" 为副词用法，意思为"不久；很快地"，用法相当于"before long（不久以后）"，但"before long"只能单独使用，后面不接从句。

Grammar-8
"teenager"用以指称"青少年"，其年纪介于13至18岁。

Grammar-8
"not only...but..." 为常用的短语，其有"不仅……而且……"的意思。

Soon I will have a half-brother.
不久之后，我将会有个同父异母的弟弟。

My little sister is only two years old, and she is a toddler.
我妹妹只有两岁，她还是个学步中的小孩。

My older brother is sixteen years old, and he is a teenager.
我哥哥十六岁，他是一个少年。

Not only does my twin brother look exactly like me, but we also think the same.
我的双胞胎弟弟不只长得像我，而且我们的想法也一样。

Nancy is jealous of her sister's beauty.
南希忌妒她妹妹的美貌。

When I came home from school, my siblings were waiting for me to play with them.
当我放学回到家时，我的兄弟姐妹们正在门口等我和他们一起玩耍。

half-brother [hæf ˈbrʌðɚ] n 同父异母（或同母异父）的兄弟

toddler [ˈtɑːdlɚ] n 学步的小孩　　exactly [ɪɡˈzæktli] ad 完全地

beauty [ˈbjuːti] n 美貌　prettiness [ˈprɪtɪnəs] n 漂亮；可爱

sibling [ˈsɪblɪŋ] n 兄弟姐妹（手足）　　play with phr 和……一起玩

 老外不会教你的小秘密

★ 到亲朋好友家做客时，一定离不开孩子长得像谁的话题。而我们要表达长得像爸爸或是妈妈的英语是什么呢？其实很简单，你可以说"*I look like my mom.*（我长得像我妈妈。）"或者是"*I take after my mom.*（我长得像我妈妈。）"；如果有人说你的眼睛像妈妈时，我们就会说"*I have my mother's eyes.*（我的眼睛像妈妈。）"，当然，你也可以用"*my dad*"来替换！

Chapter **13** 爱与和平救地球

Unit 3 关于差异
About the difference

原来老外这样记单词 / 老外从小到大学习单词的方法，就是看到什么就学什么！

social manners
phr 社交礼仪

social skills
phr 社交技巧

shake hands
phr 握手

smile [smaɪl]
v 微笑

其他衍生单词：

interaction [ˌɪntərˈækʃn] n 互动
etiquette [ˈetɪket] n 礼仪；礼节
table manners phr 餐桌礼仪

socialization [ˌsəʊʃələˈzeɪʃn] n 社会化
communicate [kəˈmjuːnɪkeɪt] v 传达；沟通
polite [pəˈlaɪt] a 有礼貌的，客气的

Unit 3 关于差异

老外最常用的单词
连这些单词都不会，你还敢说你学过英语吗？

与人相处一点都不难 ★★★

bribe [braɪb] n 贿赂 v 行贿

personality [ˌpɜːrsəˈnæləti] n 人格
cooperation [koʊˌɑːpəˈreɪʃn] n 合作
characteristic [ˌkærəktəˈrɪstɪk]
n 特性，特征
make up phr 和解
play the field phr 骑驴找马
interpersonal relationship
phr 人际关系

人人平等 ★★

gay [geɪ] n 同性恋者

immigration [ˌɪmɪˈgreɪʃn]
n （外来的）移民
hostage [ˈhɑːstɪdʒ] n 人质
emigrate [ˈemɪgreɪt] v 移居外国
lesbian [ˈlezbɪən] n 女同性恋
intermarriage [ˌɪntəˈmærɪdʒ]
n 近亲结婚
homosexuality [ˌhəʊməˌsekʃuˈæləti]
n 同性恋关系

不擅长处理人际关系 ★★

unsociable [ʌnˈsəʊʃəbl]
a 不爱交际的

generation gap phr 代沟
social phobia phr 社交恐惧症
Oedipus complex phr 恋母情结
Electra complex phr 恋父情结
Stockholm syndrome phr 斯德哥尔摩综合征（被劫持人质对劫持者产生好感并同情、宽容他）

Chapter 13 爱与和平救地球

用英语聊天，原来这么简单 / 老外每天说的英语，其实就是这几句。

米奇：我想我们可以合作愉快。 菲利斯：一定可以的！

Situation 1
与人相处

My boyfriend isn't rich. We usually go Dutch ❶ when eating out.
因为我的男朋友不是很有钱，在外面吃饭，我们通常都各付各的。

These four young people were soon seen on a double date ❷.
这四个年轻人很快就两两成对约会了。

Grammar-1
此句中的"go Dutch"为一常用且常见的短语，意思为"各自付账；平摊费用"。

Grammar-2
短语"double date"用以表示"两对男女一起的约会（或出游）"。

Sorry, you cannot go out with my boyfriend and me. Two's company, three's none ❸.
对不起，你不可以和我跟我男朋友一起出游。你不可以当电灯泡。

Grammar-3
谚语"Two's company, three's none."，的意思为"两人结伴，三人不欢"，引申为"不喜欢第三者当电灯泡"之意。

Last night, I had the most wonderful date with Roger. We had a candle-lit dinner ❹.
昨晚，我和罗杰有一个最棒的约会。我们享用了烛光晚餐。

Ethan and Joyce are now together because of Sophia's matchmaking. She set them up.
因为索菲亚的做媒，伊森和乔伊丝现在在一起了。她将他们撮合在一起。

Grammar-4
"a candle-lit dinner"表示"烛光晚餐"。

Eva is playing hard to get with Ben, even though ❺ she really likes him.
伊娃假装对本不感兴趣，即使她真的很喜欢他。

Grammar-5
"even though"的意思为"即使；纵然"，也可以用"although"来替换。

young [jʌŋ] a 年轻的 同 juvenile ['dʒuːvənl] a 少年的 反 old [əʊld] a 老的；上了年纪的

go out phr 外出   matchmaking ['mætʃmeɪkɪŋ] n 做媒

set up phr 设置；安排

Situation 2
想邀约别人

Our family is going on a picnic this weekend. Would you like to join us?
我们家这个周末要去野餐。要一起来吗？

Grammar-6
"take sb. on a date"
的意思为"带某人去约会"。

May I take you on a date? We could go watch a movie, or go to a concert if you wish.
我可以和你去约会吗？如果你愿意的话，我们可以去看电影或是听音乐会。

Come on! Let's go mountain hiking tomorrow morning.
走吧！我们明天早上去爬山。

Jay had a date with Emma, but she stood him up.
杰和艾玛有约，但是艾玛失约了。

Taking a sunbath is really comforting. Would you like to go with me?
做日光浴真的很舒服。你想和我一起去吗？

I'd be happy to go out with you. Could we go dancing together?
我很开心能和你出游。我们可以去跳舞吗？

I want to have a barbecue in my house. Do I have the honor of having you as my guest?
我在我家要办一个烤肉聚会。请问有荣幸邀请你当我的来宾吗？

How about going to a movie later?
等下要去看电影吗？

together [tə'geðər] ad 一起；共同

Situation 3
尝试征婚或相亲

Lucy and Jacob met on a blind date a few years ago. They will get engaged next month.
露西和雅各布几年前在相亲中认识。他们下个月要订婚了。

Grammar-7
"arranged marriage" 意思为"父母之命（或媒妁之言）的婚姻"，此为短语。

Grammar-8
"dating service" 有"婚介所"的意思，也可以使用 "dating agency" 来替换。

My grandmother had an <mark>arranged marriage</mark> ❼. Her father found a husband for her.
我外婆有个媒妁之言。她的父亲帮她挑选了丈夫。

Some people use online <mark>dating services</mark> ❽ to meet people of the other sex; however, some think it is not safe.
有些人会使用网络上的婚介所来寻找另一半；然而有些人却认为这并不安全。

blind date [phr] 相亲　　engage [ɪnˈgeɪdʒ] [v] 使订婚

husband [ˈhʌzbənd] [n] 丈夫　　online [ˌɑːnˈlaɪn] [a] 线上的

safe [seɪf] [a] 安全的；平安的

 不怕你学不会

1. Do you want to take me _____ a date? I am free this weekend.

2. Would you like to use dating agency to find your future wife?
   = Would you like to use dating _____ to find your future wife?

3. Eva is playing hard to get with Ben even though she really likes him.
   = Eva is playing hard to get with Ben _____ she really likes him.

4. Have you ever heard "Two's _____ , three's none."?

答案：1. on　2. services　3. although　4. company

Unit 4 关于恨
About hatred

原来老外这样记单词 / 老外从小到大学习单词的方法，就是看到什么就学什么！

negotiate [nɪˈgəʊʃieɪt]
v 谈判；协商

concentrate [ˈkɑːnsntreɪt]
v 全神贯注

consult [kənˈsʌlt]
v 商议

body language
phr 肢体语言

其他衍生单词：

discuss [dɪˈskʌs] v 讨论；商谈
compromise [ˈkɑːmprəmaɪz] v 妥协；让步
fight [faɪt] v 争吵

snort [snɔːrt] v 轻蔑（或愤怒）地哼哼
silent treatment phr 冷战
isolation [ˌaɪsəˈleɪʃn] n 孤立

老外最常用的单词 / 连这些单词都不会，你还敢说你学过英语吗？

 有点火药味出现 ★★

stranger ['streɪndʒər] n 陌生人

enemy ['enəmi] n 敌人
discrimination [dɪˌskrɪmɪ'neɪʃn] n 歧视
separate ['seprət] v （夫妻）分居
bully ['bʊli] n 恶霸 v 欺侮；胁迫
backbite ['bækbaɪt] v 背后中伤
attack [ə'tæk] v 抨击，责难

 这是什么态度 ★★

aggressive [ə'gresɪv]
a 好斗的，挑衅的

malicious [mə'lɪʃəs] a 恶意的
alienated ['eɪlɪəneɪt] a 不合群的
sophisticated [sə'fɪstɪkeɪtɪd] a 世故的
eloquent ['eləkwənt] a 雄辩的
mean [miːn] a 卑鄙的；吝啬的
picky ['pɪki] a 吹毛求疵的；挑剔的
find fault with phr 挑剔；抱怨

 君子动口不动手 ★★

debate [dɪ'beɪt] n. v 辩论

argue ['ɑːrgjuː] v 争论
apologize [ə'pɑːlədʒaɪz] v 道歉；认错
retort [rɪ'tɔːrt] v 反驳；顶嘴
confrontation [ˌkɑːnfrən'teɪʃn] n 对质
misunderstanding [ˌmɪsʌndər'stændɪŋ] n 误解；不和
break the ice phr 打破僵局

Unit 4 关于恨

 用英语聊天，原来这么简单 / 老外每天说的英语，其实就是这几句。

尼尔森：别离开我，宝贝。　莉莉：我们已经结束了，别再来纠缠我！

Situation 1
被最爱的人背叛

Mrs. Fisher asked for ❶ a divorce when she discovered that her husband and his secretary had an affair.
当费雪太太发现她丈夫和他的秘书有外遇时，她要求离婚。

How dare you betray me! You said you would love me forever.
你竟敢背叛我！你说过会爱我一辈子的。

discover [dɪˈskʌvər] v 发现　　secretary [ˈsekrəteri] n 秘书

Grammar-1
"ask for"后面若接某人，表示"找某人或要见某人"，后面若接某物，表示"征求/要求某物"。

Situation 2
关系走到尽头

Did you hear that Joseph and Lisa broke up ❷? She was totally crushed.
你听说约瑟夫和丽莎分手了吗？丽莎彻底崩溃了。

They haven't talked to each other ❸ since they terminated the relationship.
他们自从绝交后就没说过话了。

totally [ˈtoʊtəli] ad 完全　　crush [krʌʃ] v 压垮；摧毁

terminate [ˈtɜːrmɪneɪt] v 终止；结束

relationship [rɪˈleɪʃnʃɪp] n 关系；人际关系

Grammar-2
"break up"有"（婚姻或男女朋友）终止关系"，可为及物动词与不及物动词，副词"up"和有关动词搭配，表示"结束;完成"之意。

Grammar-3
"each other"与"one another"都表示相互，"each other"一般用于两者之间的关系；"one another"用于三者以上的关系。

Chapter 13 爱与和平救地球

Situation 3
生离死别

The widow [4] was very sad about losing her husband.
这名寡妇对于失去丈夫感到非常难过。

Grammar-4
"widow"当名词时，有"寡妇；鳏夫"之意，当动词时，则有"使丧偶"的意思；"grass widow"为"守活寡的先生或太太"的意思。

My grandfather passed away last week. I was too sad to do anything.
我爷爷上周过世了。我难过得无法任何事。

lose [luːz] v 丧失

Situation 4
人的个性

Linda enjoys flirting with men.
琳达喜欢和男人调情。

I just can't stand my roommate any longer. She is too annoying.
我已经再也受不了我的室友了。她太烦人了。

Grammar-5
"while"为连词，意思为"然而"，用法相当于"however（然而；可是）"与"nevertheless（仍然；不过）"。

Some people think cohabitation is acceptable while [5] others think it is not.
有些人认为同居是可以被接受的；然而有些人并不这么认为。

I always talk straight [6]; I hate beating around the bush.
我总是实话实说，我讨厌拐弯抹角地说话。

Grammar-6
"talk straight"有"实话实说"的意思，反义短语为"talk in a roundabout way"，即"拐弯抹角地说话"。

flirt with phr 与……调情   cohabitation [ˌkəʊhæbɪˈteɪʃn] n 同居

acceptable [əkˈseptəbl] a 可以接受的 反 disagreeable [ˌdɪsəˈɡriːəbl] a 不合意的

Situation 5
特殊的行为举止

My uncle is zealous [7] for public affairs.
我舅舅热衷于公共事务。

Grammar-7
"zealous"当形容词时，意思为"热心的"，同义词为"ardent（热切的；热心的）"和"enthusiastic（热情的；热烈的）"。

As the old saying goes [8], familiarity breeds contempt [9].
俗话说，亲密产生轻视。

Grammar-9
用以表示"亲密产生轻视"的谚语为"Familiarity breeds contempt."，原意为"亲不敬，熟生蔑。"

Grammar-8
"as the old saying goes"有"俗话说"的意思，同义短语为"as a proverb goes"。

I have no comment on your suggestion.
我对于你的提议不予置评。

My father always wears only one underwear at home.
我爸爸在家总是只穿一条内裤。

Unit 4 关于恨

public affairs phr 公共事务　　no comment phr 不予置评；无可奉告

suggestion [sə'dʒestʃən] n 建议；提议 同 advice [əd'vaɪs] n 劝告；忠告

Situation 6
人生若只如初见

People exchange their name cards when meeting for the first time ⑩.
人们在初次见面的时候交换名片。

Grammar-10
此句中的"for the first time"有"第一次"的意思。

There's someone I'd like you to meet.
有一个人我想让你们见见面。

I want to meet your family. When do they have time?
我想认识你的家人。他们何时有空？

Could you introduce me to your co-worker?
可以把我介绍给你同事吗？

exchange [ɪks'tʃeɪndʒ] v 交换　　name card phr 名片

不怕你学不会

1. Could you please give me some useful suggestions?
   = Could you please give me some useful ＿＿＿＿ ?

2. My grandmother is enthusiastic for public affairs.
   = My grandmother is ＿＿＿＿ for public affairs.

3. Hello, I would like to ask ＿＿＿＿ Shelly.

4. I had a group of friends in my college, but we haven't met ＿＿＿＿ another since our graduation.

答案：1. advice　2. ardent / zealous　3. for　4. one

Chapter **13** 爱与和平救地球

看看老外怎么学 / 请将选项填到表中适当的位置

Family Tree

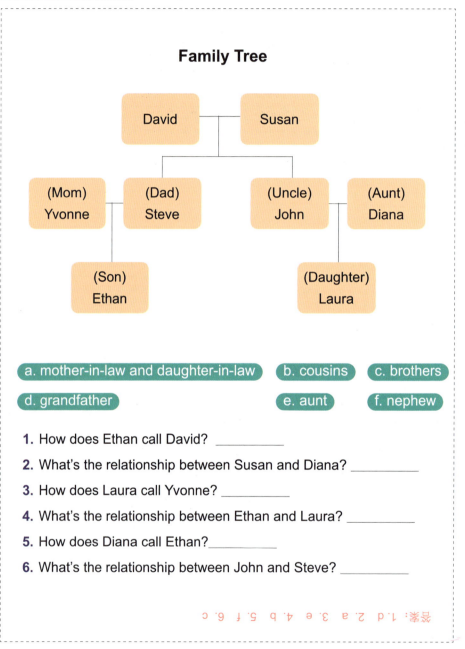

- a. mother-in-law and daughter-in-law
- b. cousins
- c. brothers
- d. grandfather
- e. aunt
- f. nephew

1. How does Ethan call David? _____
2. What's the relationship between Susan and Diana? _____
3. How does Laura call Yvonne? _____
4. What's the relationship between Ethan and Laura? _____
5. How does Diana call Ethan? _____
6. What's the relationship between John and Steve? _____

答案：1.d 2.a 3.e 4.b 5.f 6.c

Chapter 14 喜怒哀乐爱恶欲

Mood swings

快乐、忧愁、愤怒、厌恶、惊讶，
不知该用哪句话才能正确表达情绪吗？
快来用老外的方式学一学！

| **Unit 1** 天天都有好心情 | **Unit 2** 天空蓝蓝的 | **Unit 3** 午后雷阵雨 | **Unit 4** 复杂的心情天气图 |

Unit 1 天天都有好心情
Happy every day

 原来老外这样记单词 / 老外从小到大学习单词的方法，就是看到什么就学什么！

frightened [ˈfraɪtnd]
a 害怕的

surprised [sərˈpraɪzd]
a 感到惊讶的

joyful [ˈdʒɔɪfl]
a 高兴的，充满喜悦的

emotion [ɪˈmoʊʃn]
n 感情，情感

其他衍生单词：

pleasurable [ˈpleʒərəbl] a 使人快乐的

rosy [ˈroʊzi] a 乐观的；美好的

mood [muːd] n 心情

cheerful [ˈtʃɪrfl] a 兴高采烈的

buoyant [ˈbɔɪənt] a 活泼的；心情愉快的

affectionate [əˈfekʃənət] a 充满深情的

老外最常用的单词
连这些单词都不会，你还敢说你学过英语吗？

看到单词都振奋了起来

feverish ['fiːvərɪʃ] a 狂热的；兴奋的

exultant [ɪɡ'zʌltənt] a 欢欣鼓舞的
stirring ['stɜːrɪŋ] a 激动人心的
stimulate ['stɪmjʊleɪt] v 刺激；激励
hearten ['hɑːrtn] v 鼓舞；激励
overwhelming [ˌəʊvər'welmɪŋ] a 势不可挡的
excited [ɪk'saɪtɪd] a 兴奋的；激动的

神经也紧绷了起来

jealous ['dʒeləs] a 妒忌的；吃醋的

possessive [pə'zesɪv] a 占有欲强的
green-eyed [ɡriːn'aɪd] a 嫉妒的
hostility [hɑː'stɪləti] n 敌意
abhorrence [əb'hɔːrəns] n 厌恶；憎恨
isolated ['aɪsəleɪtɪd] a （被）孤立的；（被）隔离的
sick [sɪk] a 对……厌烦的
dislike [dɪs'laɪk] v 厌恶；讨厌

懂这些，才能跟上老外脚步

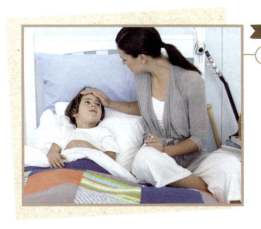

considerate [kən'sɪdərət] a 体贴的

solicitous [sə'lɪsɪtəs] a 挂念的；热心的
heartfelt ['hɑːrtfelt] a 真诚的；衷心的
attentive [ə'tentɪv] a 留意的；注意的
grateful ['ɡreɪtfl] a 感激的
gracious ['ɡreɪʃəs] a 亲切的；仁慈的
good-natured [ɡʊd'netʃəd] a 和蔼的

用英语聊天，原来这么简单
老外每天说的英语，其实就是这几句。

约瑟芬：哦，我的天！我们赢了！太棒了！　泰德：太赞了！

Situation 1
高兴的事

Thank you very much for inviting me to your home party. I will be there on time.
谢谢你邀请我参加你家的派对，我一定会准时到。

George was glad to run into ❶ his old friend on the street.
乔治很高兴能在街上遇到老朋友。

Grammar-1
"run into" 表示"偶然碰到"，后面一般接某人。

There is joyful news to tell you. My wife is pregnant!
有个好消息要告诉你。我太太怀孕了！

I am delighted to have lunch with you.
我很高兴能与你共进午餐。

It is so happy to have a talk with you.
和你谈话真是太开心了。

Do I have the pleasure of inviting you to my promotion party?
我有这个荣幸邀请您参加我的升职派对吗？

glad [glæd] a 高兴的；乐意的

delighted [dɪˈlaɪtɪd] a 高兴的；快乐的

Situation 2
兴奋得不能自己

The baby gets very excited whenever it sees balloons.
每当婴儿看到气球的时候都很兴奋。

All the students are looking forward to the summer vacation.
所有学生都在期待着暑假。

Grammar-2
"jump on" 表示"对某人生气"。

The English teacher **jumped on** ❷ us for being dishonest.
英语老师对我们大发脾气因为我们不诚实。

I can't wait to see that concert!
我等不及去看那场演唱会了！

Situation 3
与人相处

Jessica was green with envy when she knew one of her colleagues was going to marry a rich man.
当杰西卡得知她的一位同事将要嫁给有钱人后，感到忌妒。

Don't be so rude to me. I'm not your enemy.
别对我这么粗鲁，我又不是你的敌人。

Grammar-3
stand 意思为"忍受"，同义词有"tolerate"。

I can't **stand** ❸ her arrogance anymore.
我再也无法忍受她的傲慢了。

My brother is hostile to strangers. As a result, he refuses to talk to them.
我弟弟对陌生人有敌意，因此他拒绝与陌生人交谈。

You should respect your teacher more.
你应该更尊重你的老师。

Grammar-4
"care about" 表示"关心"，后面接名词或名词从句。

Mark is indifferent toward his classmates; he doesn't **care about** ❹ what happens to them.
马克对同学漠不关心，他完全不在乎他们发生什么事。

I am very grateful for your help. I don't know how I can repay your kindness.
我非常感谢你的帮助。我不知道该如何回报你的好意。

Grammar-5
"without（没有；假如没有）"为介词，可以引导假设句，用以表示条件。

I hurt Ken's feeling **without** ❺ meaning it. I didn't mean to criticize his parents.
我不小心伤害了肯恩的感情。我不是故意要批评他父母的。

colleague [ˈkɑːliːɡ] n 同事；同僚

arrogance [ˈærəɡəns] n 傲慢；自大 反 modesty [ˈmɑːdəsti] n 谦逊；虚心

hostile [ˈhɑstl] a 怀敌意的；不友善的   refuse [rɪˈfjuːz] v 拒绝

indifferent [ɪnˈdɪfrənt] a 不关心的；冷淡的

happen [ˈhæpən] v 发生   grateful [ˈɡreɪtfl] a 感谢的；感激的

repay [rɪˈpeɪ] v 报答；回报   kindness [ˈkaɪndnəs] n 好意；仁慈

criticize [ˈkrɪtɪsaɪz] v 批评；批判 同 condemn [kənˈdem] v 谴责；责难

老外不会教你的小秘密

★ 幻想是人的天性，有人想要嫁入豪门，成为贵妇；有人想要中彩票，一夜暴富。面对这些微乎其微的可能性与情况，可以这样回应：
- *In your dreams!* 做梦吧！
- *Dream on!* 继续做梦吧！
- *You wish!* 想得美！

如果平时与人交情不好、不得人缘却想借钱或求人帮忙，对方应该会说：
- *Over my dead body!* 做梦吧！
- *Not in a million years!* 再过一百年吧！

★ 运气人人都有，只是好坏不同而已。今天幸运女神眷顾了你，你可以用下列的句子来表达：
- *I'm so lucky!* 我好幸运啊！
- *I feel so blessed to win the lottery.* 我觉得好幸运，中了彩票。
- *I luck out by staying home. It's pouring now.* 我运气不错，待在家里，因为现在下大雨了。

以上这些短句，都能用来表明当时幸运的状态呢！

Unit 2 天空蓝蓝的
The sky is blue

原来老外这样记单词 / 老外从小到大学习单词的方法，就是看到什么就学什么！

sadness [ˈsædnəs]
n 悲哀；悲伤

comfort [ˈkʌmfərt]
v 安慰；慰问

sob [sɑːb]
v 啜泣；呜咽

sympathy [ˈsɪmpəθi]
n 同情心

其他衍生单词：

gloomy [ˈgluːmi] a 阴沉的；忧郁的
woe [wəʊ] n 悲痛；不幸
yammer [ˈjæmə] v 叹息，哭泣；抱怨；吼叫

painful [ˈpeɪnfl] a 痛苦的
unfortunately [ʌnˈfɔːrtʃənətli] ad 不幸地
tragedy [ˈtrædʒədi] n 悲剧

老外最常用的单词 连这些单词都不会，你还敢说你学过英语吗？

心情很不美丽的时候

melancholy ['melənkɑːli]
a 忧郁的；郁闷的

depressed [dɪ'prest] a 沮丧的，消沉的
grieved [griːvd] a 伤心的；悲痛的
agony ['ægəni] n 极度痛苦
moody ['muːdi] a 闷闷不乐的
despondent [dɪ'spɑːndənt] a 沮丧的
rueful ['ruːfl] a 可怜的；悲伤的
forlorn [fər'lɔːrn] a 孤独的；凄凉的

克制不住眼泪的时候

wail [weɪl] v 号啕；痛哭

miserable ['mɪzrəbl] a 不幸的；痛苦的
tragic ['trædʒɪk] a 悲剧的
suffering ['sʌfərɪŋ] a 受苦的
fickle ['fɪkl] a 无常的，易变的
frustrated ['frʌstreɪtɪd] a 挫败的；泄气的
dejected [dɪ'dʒektɪd] a 气馁的
sadly ['sædli] ad 悲哀地
poor [pɔːr] a 可怜的，不幸的

需要有人来给予拍拍

consolation [ˌkɑːnsə'leɪʃn]
n 安慰；慰藉

reassuring [ˌriːə'ʃʊrɪŋ]
a 安慰的；可靠的
solace ['sɑːləs] n 安慰；慰藉
relieved [rɪ'liːvd] a 放心的；宽慰的
secure [sə'kjʊr] a 安心的
reliable [rɪ'laɪəbl] a 可信赖的；可靠的

用英语聊天，原来这么简单 / 老外每天说的英语，其实就是这几句。

Sammy: Why? Why didn't he love me anymore?
Zack: Get it up, Sammy. Forget about him.

萨米：为什么？为什么他不再爱我了？　扎克：振作起来，萨米。忘掉他吧。

Situation 1　难过的时候

Tony was heartbroken after his fiancée left him.
托尼在未婚妻离他而去后感到心碎。

I can't hold back my tears when I heard about that heartbreaking news.
听到那个悲痛的消息后我的眼泪一直止不住。

He was so disappointed because his parents didn't join his graduation ceremony.
他因父母亲没有参加他的毕业典礼而感到失望。

I saw sorrow in her eyes. There must be something that happened to ❶ her.
我从她的眼神中看见忧伤。她一定发生了什么事。

Grammar-1
"happen to" 有 "发生在……之上" 的意思，其后若接人称代词时，需以宾格为主。

heartbroken [ˈhɑːrtbrəʊkən] a 悲伤的

disappointed [ˌdɪsəˈpɔɪntɪd] a 失望的；沮丧的

ceremony [ˈserəməʊni] n 仪式；典礼　　sorrow [ˈsɑːrəʊ] n 忧伤

Situation 2　孤单寂寞

Lisa feels so lonely because her parents are both ❷ out for work.
丽莎觉得很寂寞，因为她的父母亲都出门工作了。

Grammar-2
"both（两者的）" 当形容词时，放在冠词、指示代词、所有格之前。

喜怒哀乐爱恶欲

Chapter **14**

 271

She became homesick right after moving out from home.
她搬离家后马上开始想家了。

I suffered from severe homesickness during my freshman year in college.
我上大学的第一年有很严重的思乡病。

Betty felt empty when all ❸ her roommates went home for Christmas.
贝蒂在所有室友都回家过圣诞节后感到空虚。

lonely ['ləunli] a 孤独的；寂寞的
homesick ['həumsɪk] a 想家的
move out phr 搬出
empty ['empti] a 空洞的；无意义的

Grammar-3
"all" 当形容词修饰可数名词复数和不可数名词时，表示"所有的；一切的"。

Situation 3 后悔的时候

I regretted ❹ what I have done. I shouldn't have stolen your watch.
我对我做过的事感到后悔。我不应该偷你的手表。

I didn't make it home in time and I lost the last chance to see my dear granny.
我来不及赶回家，导致我丧失了和亲爱的奶奶见面的最后机会。

stolen ['stəulən] v 偷窃（此为steal的过去分词。）

Grammar-4
"regret（懊悔 遗憾）" 作及物动词，可以接名词、名词从句、不定词或代词。

Situation 4 产生不信任感

We are skeptical about her solution to this problem.
我们对于她解决问题的方法感到怀疑。

I doubt that she claimed herself a supermodel. I can't tell anything special from her.
我怀疑她说她是超模的事。从她身上我看不出什么特别的。

skeptical ['skeptɪkl] a 怀疑的；多疑的

solution [sə'luːʃn] n 解决（办法）
problem ['prɑːbləm] n 问题

Situation 5 安慰你的朋友

Calm down! You are not able to ❺ make the best decision when you are annoyed.
冷静下来！你无法在恼怒的时候做出最好的决定。

Listening to music could help me release negative emotions.
听音乐可以帮助我释放负面情绪。

Grammar-5
"be able to" 后接原形动词，通常以人为主语，有时也以物为主语。

Unit 2 天空蓝蓝的

"be good at" 有 "擅长……" 的意思，后面可以接名词或 Ving。

Gary is good at ❺ comforting others; his friends all turn to him for help when feeling down.
盖瑞擅长安慰别人；他朋友感到失落的时候都会寻求他的帮助。

You should have some chocolate. It can make you feel better.
你该吃点巧克力，它会让你觉得好一点。

calm down phr 镇定下来　　decision [dɪˈsɪʒn] n 决定；判断

annoyed [əˈnɔɪd] a 恼怒的　　release [rɪˈliːs] v 释放；解放

negative [ˈnegətɪv] a 消极的；反面的　　turn to phr 求助于……

 老外不会教你的小秘密

★ 不为五斗米折腰是骨气，但是整天游手好闲在家不做事甚至是在外惹是生非，那就不太好了！为了劝诱朋友回归正轨，我们可以说：
  ✦ *Stop goofing around.* 不要游手好闲。
  ✦ *Don't fool around.* 不要混了。
  ✦ *Why do you want to be a goof off? Do something.*
    你为何要做个懒人呢？做些事情吧！
其中，最后一个句子的 "*goof off*" 可以当成动词短语，也可以作为名词短语使用。

 不怕你学不会

1. Jeffery is good _____ comforting people. Every time I feel sad, I will go to his place.

2. There must be something that happened _____ her. Otherwise, she won't cry so sadly.

答案：1. at 2. to

Chapter 14

Unit 3 午后雷阵雨 Thunderstorms

原来老外这样记单词 / 老外从小到大学习单词的方法，就是看到什么就学什么！

furious [ˈfjʊrɪəs]
a 猛烈的；喧闹的

quarrel [ˈkwɔːrəl]
n 争吵；不和

incense [ˈɪnsens]
v 激怒

jittery [ˈdʒɪtəri]
a 紧张不安的

其他衍生单词：

sulky [ˈsʌlki] a 生气的
rage [reɪdʒ] n （一阵）狂怒 v 发怒
resent [rɪˈzent] v 愤慨；怨恨

temperamental [ˌtemprəˈmentl] a 易怒的
uptight [ʌpˈtaɪt] a 易怒的；烦躁的
angry [ˈæŋgri] a 生气的

老外最常用的单词 / 连这些单词都不会,你还敢说你学过英语吗?

某根筋开始在作怪

impatient [ɪmˈpeɪʃnt] a 不耐烦的

irrational [ɪˈræʃənl] a 不合理的
arbitrary [ˈɑːrbətreri] a 反复无常的,武断的
ruffled [ˈrʌfld] v 烦恼;生气
upset [ʌpˈset] v 使心烦意乱
bother [ˈbɑːðər] v 使恼怒
interruption [ˌɪntəˈrʌpʃn] n 打扰,干扰

尴尬到说不出话来

blush [blʌʃ]
v (因害羞／尴尬等而)脸红

guilty [ˈɡɪlti] a 内疚的;有过失的
self-conscious [ˌself ˈkɑːnʃəs] a 自觉的,怕难为情的
bashful [ˈbæʃfl] a 羞怯的
humiliate [hjuːˈmɪlieɪt] v 羞辱;使丢脸
embarrassed [ɪmˈbærəst] a 尴尬的
shameful [ˈʃeɪmfl] a 丢脸的;可耻的

已经快要疯了

strained [streɪnd] a 紧张的;勉强的

ecstatic [ɪkˈstætɪk] a 狂喜的
fluster [ˈflʌstər] v 慌乱
jumpy [ˈdʒʌmpi] a 神经质的
neurotically [nʊˈrɑːtɪkli] ad 神经质地
insane [ɪnˈseɪn] a 疯狂的
mania [ˈmeɪniə] n 疯狂

喜怒哀乐爱恶欲

Chapter **14**

用英语聊天，原来这么简单 / 老外每天说的英语，其实就是这几句。

Andy! I told you not to put the toys in your mouth! Why don't you listen to me? Bad boy!

妈妈：安迪！我叫你别把玩具放到嘴里！你怎么都不听呢？坏孩子！

Situation 1
化解尴尬

I got into the wrong room in the hotel. How embarrassing!
我在旅馆里走错房间。真尴尬！

My child cried loudly on the train. It really made me embarrassed.
我的小孩在火车上哭得很大声，这让我很尴尬。

How can you litter in public places? Shame on you!
你怎么可以在公共场合乱丢垃圾？真丢脸！

I was acting awkward on the stage because there were too many people.
我在台上表现得很笨拙，因为台下实在太多人了。

I was discomfited by my little sister's unreasonable demands.
我对小妹的无理要求感到为难。

- embarrassing [ɪmˈbærəsɪŋ] a 使人尴尬的
- litter [ˈlɪtər] v 乱丢（杂物）
- public [ˈpʌblɪk] a 公共的；公用的
- shame [ʃeɪm] n 羞辱；耻辱
- discomfit [dɪsˈkʌmfɪt] v 使为难
- unreasonable [ʌnˈriːznəbl] a 不讲理的
- demand [dɪˈmænd] n 要求

Situation 2
心情不好的时候

I am in a bad mood ❶. Leave me alone!
我现在心情不好。不要管我！

Stop touching my things without my permission, or I will tell the teacher.
不要再乱碰我东西了，要不然我会告诉老师。

Fay feels uncomfortable when strangers touch her shoulder.
当有人拍她肩膀的时候，费依觉得不舒服。

The heavy rain drives me crazy. I hate rainy days.
倾盆大雨使我抓狂。我讨厌下雨天。

The boss got sick of Sally's excuses for being late, so he decided ❷ to fire her.
老板已经受不了莎莉迟到的借口，所以他决定辞退她。

Grammar-1
"be in a bad mood" 即"心情不好"的意思，与其相反的短语为"be in a good mood"。

Grammar-2
"decide（决定）"当及物动词，后面可以接不定式或从句。

alone [əˈloʊn] a 单独的；独自的

uncomfortable [ʌnˈkʌmftəbl] a 不舒服的

stranger [ˈstreɪndʒər] n 陌生人　　shoulder [ˈʃoʊldər] n 肩膀

heavy rain phr （倾盆）大雨　　hate [heɪt] v 憎恨；不喜欢

get sick of phr 对……厌恶　　excuse [ɪkˈskjuːs] n 理由；借口

fire [ˈfaɪər] v 【口】解雇；开除

Situation 3
生气的时候

Dad was so furious ❸ that he slapped my brother in the face.
父亲十分生气，所以他扇了哥哥一巴掌。

Frank was mad at her for being late for the important meeting.
法兰克对于她在重要会议上迟到感到生气。

Chef Ramsay seems always pissed off on television.
拉姆齐主厨在电视上总是看起来很生气。

My mother shouted at me outside because I got a bad grade on the exam.
我妈妈在外面对我大声咆哮，因为我考得很差。

Anger can fasten a person's heartbeat and raise a person's body temperature.
愤怒使人心跳加快，体温升高。

Grammar-3
"furious"当形容词时，有"狂怒的"之意，用法相当于"raging"或"mad"等词汇。

slap [slæp] v 扇……耳光

face [feɪs] n 脸；面容 同 countenance ['kaʊntənəns] n 面容；脸色

mad [mæd] a 恼火的

anger ['æŋɡər] n 生气   heartbeat ['hɑːrtbiːt] n 心跳

temperature ['temprətʃər] n 体温

老外不会教你的小秘密

★ 在这物价上涨、薪水却不上涨的时代，有些人为了多赚一些费用而加班，但往往在这样的情况下，压力和工作量会逼得人喘不过气，有时候甚至会发狂、生气。为了表达这样的情绪，我们可以说：

✦ *The workload made me go cuckoo yesterday.*
　昨天的工作量快令我抓狂了。

其中的"*go cuckoo*"还可以替换成"*go banana*"或"*go crazy*"的说法，很可爱吧！

另外，生气还可以用"*piss off*"跟"*tick off*"来表达，例如：

✦ *I'm really pissed off when Richard stood me up again!*
　理查德再次放我鸽子，真是气死我了。

下次，发生令你忍无可忍的事情时，不妨试试这几句！

★ 有时候声音也能够表现出喜、怒、哀、乐等情绪；如在喧闹的场合，需要他人安静时，最常听到的"*Shh...*（嘘）"之外，如果对噪声感到厌烦时，我们可以说"*Hush!*（嘘，别吵！）"；当声音真的吵到令你受不了且有些生气的时候，我们可以说"*Shush...*（嘘，安静！）"，要表达最后一个词时，声音要凶、表情要狰狞一点！

Unit 4 复杂的心情天气图
So complicated

原来老外这样记单词 / 老外从小到大学习单词的方法，就是看到什么就学什么！

jaded [ˈdʒeɪdɪd]
a 厌倦的

listless [ˈlɪstləs]
a 无精打采的；倦怠的

boring [ˈbɔːrɪŋ]
a 令人感到无聊的

burned-out [ˈbɜrndˈaʊt]
a 疲倦不堪的

其他衍生单词：

worn-out [ˌwɔːn ˈaʊt] a 筋疲力尽的
tucker [ˈtʌkər] v 使疲倦；使衰弱
stale [steɪl] a 疲倦的；厌倦的

irksome [ˈɜːrksəm] a 令人厌烦的
humdrum [ˈhʌmdrʌm] a 无聊的；单调的
lazy [ˈleɪzi] a 懒散的

老外最常用的单词
连这些单词都不会,你还敢说你学过英语吗?

不再让你担惊受怕 ★★

startle ['stɑːrtl] v 惊吓

dumbfound [dʌmˈfaʊnd] v 使人惊愕失声
flabbergast [ˈflæbəˌɡɑːst] v 使大吃一惊
dread [dred] v 惧怕;担心
panic [ˈpænɪk] v 使恐慌
apprehensive [ˌæprɪˈhensɪv] a 忧虑的;恐惧的
disoriented [dɪsˈɔːrɪenteɪtɪd] a 使迷惘
anguish [ˈæŋɡwɪʃ] n 苦恼

来看看你是哪种人 ★★

curious [ˈkjʊrɪəs] a 好奇的

crave [kreɪv] v 渴望;恳求
anticipation [ænˌtɪsɪˈpeɪʃn] n 期望;预料
eager [ˈiːɡər] a 渴望的;急切的
emotional [ɪˈməʊʃənl] a 感情(上)的
high-strung [ˈhaɪˈstrʌŋ] a 十分敏感的
complex [kəmˈpleks] a 难懂的;复杂的
insensitive [ɪnˈsensətɪv] a 感觉迟钝的
hot property phr 身价高的人;抢手货

有时候别只顾着看自己 ★★

bloated [ˈbləʊtɪd] a 傲慢的;膨胀的

pretentious [prɪˈtenʃəs] a 自负的;做作的
stuck-up [ˈstʌkˈʌp] a 高傲的
conceited [kənˈsiːtɪd] a 自负的;自夸的
id [ɪd] n 【心】自我
ego [ˈiːɡəʊ] n 自我意识
superego [ˌsuːpərˈiːɡəʊ] n 超我

用英语聊天，原来这么简单

老外每天说的英语，其实就是这几句。

珍妮：把闹钟关掉，我还很想睡。　　奈尔：我也是，昨晚实在太累了。

Situation 1
很累的时候，可以说这几句告诉其他人

- I was so ❶ sleepy that I fell asleep on the bus and missed my stop.
  我太想睡觉，所以在公交车上睡着了，而且还坐过站。

- Larry was exhausted after working for forty hours. He fell asleep as soon as ❷ he lay down in bed.
  莱瑞在工作40小时后感到筋疲力尽。他一躺在床上就睡着了。

sleepy ['sli:pi] a 想睡的　　fall asleep phr 睡着

miss [mɪs] v 错过　　exhausted [ɪg'zɔ:stɪd] a 筋疲力尽的

lay down phr 躺下来

Grammar-1
"so（这样）"为副词，用以表达方式、方法、情况、程度等意义。

Grammar-2
"as soon as"当连词用，表示"一……就、刚……就"。

Situation 2
担心某件事

- Paul is afraid of making mistakes. Therefore, he is very careful in doing everything.
  保罗害怕犯错。因此他做任何事情时都非常小心。

- Don't worry about me. I will take care of ❸ myself.
  不用担心我。我会照顾好自己的。

afraid [ə'freɪd] a 害怕的　　mistake [mɪ'steɪk] n 错误；过失

careful ['keəfl] a 仔细的；小心的　　worry about phr 担心……；焦虑……

Grammar-3
"take care of"后面一般会接某人，用以表示"照顾"的意思。

Situation 3
紧张的心情

That child was nervous about having so many people around her.
那个小孩因为有许多人在她身边感到紧张。

Students were overwhelmed by the sudden earthquake.
学生们对突如其来的地震感到不知所措。

I am anxious before the job interview.
我在面试前感到焦虑。

nervous ['nɜ:rvəs] a 紧张不安的   sudden ['sʌdn] a 突然的；意外的

anxious ['æŋkʃəs] a 焦虑的

Situation 4
被吓到时

The little girl was frightened by a shepherd dog. She didn't stop crying until ❺ her mother came.
小女孩被一只牧羊犬吓到，直到母亲来了才停止哭泣。

Grammar-4
"not... until" 意思为"直到……才"。

The lady lost consciousness when she heard ❻ the bad news.
那位女士在听到坏消息后便失去了意识。

Grammar-5
句子中的"hear"为感官动词，用以表示"听见"。

Linda was almost scared to death when she entered the haunted house.
琳达进入鬼屋的时候几乎快被吓死了。

Everyone was shocked by his abnormal behavior.
每个人都对他的异常举动感到震惊。

shepherd dog phr 牧羊犬

consciousness ['kɑ:nʃəsnəs] n （个人或群体的）意识

almost ['ɔ:lməust] ad 几乎；差不多   enter ['entər] v 进入

haunted ['hɔ:ntɪd] a 闹鬼的   shocked [ʃɒkt] a 震惊的

abnormal [æb'nɔ:rml] a 不正常的   behavior [bɪ'heɪvɪər] n 行为；举止

Situation 5
表达一些情绪

Maggie is very curious about what ❻ is inside the box.
玛吉很好奇盒子里到底放了什么。

Grammar-6
"what"可以当关系代词引导名词从句，相当于"the + 名词 + that"或"all that"；其中"that"为关系代词。

Helen yearns to visit the Milky Way someday.
海伦渴望有一天能造访银河。

She has compassion for the orphans in the orphanage.
她怜悯孤儿院里的孤儿。

Unit 4 复杂的心情天气图

Grammar-7
句子中的"when"表示"当"。

Grammar-8
"at ease"表示"舒适；无拘束"，可以当主词语的语或修饰语，还可表示"轻松的"。

Grammar-9
"own"为代词，表示"自己的东西"，并可以构成介词短语"of one's own（自己的）"及"on one's own（独自）"。

Jenny felt disgusted **when** she saw a fly in her spaghetti.
珍妮看到意大利面里的苍蝇时感到恶心。

Cathy bought many designer handbags in order to satisfy her vanity.
凯西为了满足虚荣心而买了很多名牌手提包。

Lily is a happy-go-lucky person. She is **at ease** everywhere.
莉莉是一个随遇而安的人。她在任何地方都很自在。

She got a sense of achievement after finishing the whole essay on her **own**.
她在独立完成论文后很有成就感。

Sophia is very brave. She faces the challenges fearlessly.
索菲亚非常勇敢。她大胆地面对挑战。

- inside [ˌɪn'saɪd] a 里面的
- yearn [jɜːrn] v 渴望；向往
- Milky Way phr 银河
- compassion [kəm'pæʃn] n 怜悯；同情
- orphan [ˈɔːrfn] n 孤儿
- orphanage [ˈɔːrfənɪdʒ] n 孤儿院
- disgust [dɪsˈɡʌst] v 使作呕
- fly [flaɪ] n 苍蝇
- satisfy [ˈsætɪsfaɪ] v 满足（需要／欲望等）
- vanity [ˈvænəti] n 虚荣（心）
- happy-go-lucky a 随遇而安的
- achievement [əˈtʃiːvmənt] n 成就
- whole [hoʊl] a 全部的
- brave [breɪv] a 勇敢的
- challenge [ˈtʃælɪndʒ] n 挑战
- fearlessly [ˈfɪrləsli] a 无畏地

不怕你学不会

1. Mary is curious about the thing that is in the bag.
   = Mary is curious about _____ is in the bag.

2. She _____ stop crying until her mother agrees to buy toys for her.

3. Jane won the robot competition _____ her own.

答案：1. what / all that 2. won't 3. on

看看老外怎么学
请将右边选项对应到左边的空格中，一起来连连看吧！

1. Break a _____ !
   （祝你好运！）

2. I have _____ .
   （受够了。）

3. I've got the _____ .
   （我很郁闷。）

4. I have a _____ .
   （今天心情很糟糕。）

5. I'm grinning _____ .
   （我笑得合不拢嘴了。）

6. You _____ me off.
   （真是气死我了。）

7. You really drive me _____ .
   （你真的气死我了。）

8. We had a _____ .
   （我玩得太开心了。）

9. I am _____ .
   （太棒了。）

10. _____ yourself together.
    （振作起来吧！）

a. from ear to ear
b. crazy
c. enough
d. piss
e. blown away
f. leg
g. bad hair day
h. Pull
i. blues
j. ball

答案：1.→f　2.→c　3.→i　4.→g　5.→a　6.→d　7.→b　8.→j　9.→e　10.→h

Chapter 15

我看见了……
I can tell...

Unit 1	Unit 2	Unit 3	Unit 4
星座真好玩	东方主义	别再相信没有根据的说法了	科学也无法解释

Unit 1 星座真好玩
Star signs

原来老外这样记单词 / 老外从小到大学习单词的方法，就是看到什么就学什么！

orbit [ˈɔːrbɪt]
n （天体等的）运行轨道

universe [ˈjuːnɪvɜːrs]
n 宇宙；全世界

ecliptic [ɪˈklɪptɪk]
n 黄道

sunspot [ˈsʌnspɑːt]
n 太阳黑子

其他衍生单词：

solar [ˈsəʊlər] a 太阳的
galaxy [ˈɡæləksi] n 银河
nebula [ˈnebjələ] n 星云

comet [ˈkɑːmət] n 彗星
meteoroid [ˈmiːtɪərˌɔɪd] n 陨石；流星
black hole phr 黑洞

Unit 1 星座真好玩

老外最常用的单词
连这些单词都不会，你还敢说你学过英语吗？

一闪一闪亮晶晶

constellation [ˌkɑːnstəˈleɪʃn]
n 星座

Aries [ˈeriːz] n 白羊座
Leo [ˈliːəʊ] n 狮子座
Virgo [ˈvɜːrɡəʊ] n 处女座
Libra [ˈliːbrə] n 天秤座
Sagittarius [ˌsædʒɪˈteriəs] n 射手座
Aquarius [əˈkweriəs] n 水瓶座

挂在天空放光明

astrologer [əˈstrɑːlədʒər] n 占星师

wane [weɪn] n （月）亏；（月）缺
wax [wæks] n （月亮）渐圆；渐满
telescope [ˈtelɪskəʊp] n 望远镜
planetarium [ˌplænɪˈteriəm] n 天文馆
planet [ˈplænɪt] n 行星
satellite [ˈsætəlaɪt] n 卫星
comet [ˈkɑːmət] n 彗星
meteoric [ˌmiːtiˈɔːrɪk] a 流星的

星座神话的奥秘

centaur [ˈsentɔːr]
n 半人半马的怪物

blood brother phr 亲兄弟
blood sister phr 亲姐妹
blue blood phr 贵族阶级；贵族血统
flesh and blood phr 亲人
compatible [kəmˈpætəbl]
a 适合的；能共处的
incompatible [ˌɪnkəmˈpætəbl]
a 不适合的；不相配的

我看见了⋯⋯

Chapter
15

用英语聊天，原来这么简单
老外每天说的英语，其实就是这几句。

I love to read the mythologies of zodiac signs.

Yeah, they're all very interesting.

Kim

Allison

金：我很爱看星座的神话故事。　艾莉森：是啊，它们都非常有趣。

Situation 1
你喜欢星座吗？

It is believed that ❶ star signs could indicate people's personalities.
一般人相信，星座能显露人们的个性。

You can find out ❷ what your star sign is according to ❸ your birthday.
你可以根据你的生日找出你的星座。

Jeff usually reads his horoscope in the magazine to see his overall condition of the whole month.
杰夫通常从杂志上阅读星座运势来看他整个月的整体运势。

Topics on star signs and blood types are very popular among ❹ many TV programs.
星座和血型的话题在许多电视节目中都很受欢迎。

Grammar-1
"It is believed that + S + V" 为名词从句，用以表达客观报道或陈述的句型用法，此为被动语态；也可以将其改为主动，即为 "People believe that + S + V" 的句型。

Grammar-2
"find out"，即 "找出；查明" 的意思，同义词为 "discover（发现；找到）"。

Grammar-3
"according to" 的意思为 "根据；按照"，同义短语有 "in accordance with" 和 "on the basis of"。

Grammar-4
"among" 为介词，用以表示由两个以上事物组成的范围，后面通常会接上名词复数或表示复数的集合名词。

sign [saɪn] n 宫（十二宫）；符号

indicate [ˈɪndɪkeɪt] v 指示；表明；显露 同 demonstrate [ˈdemənstreɪt] v 证明；表露

personality [ˌpɜːrsəˈnæləti] n 人格；品格；个性

star sign phr 星座 同 signs of the zodiac phr 星座

horoscope [ˈhɔːrəskoʊp] n 占星术

overall [ˌoʊvərˈɔːl] ad 大体上；总的来说

Unit 1 星座真好玩

condition [kənˈdɪʃn] n. 条件；情况

topic [ˈtɑːpɪk] n. 题目；话题；论题

blood type phr. 血型

Situation 2
你了解星座吗？

We can read Greek mythologies to get more ideas about star signs.
我们可以阅读希腊神话来多了解星座。

I love getting along with ⑤ Pisces people because they are easy-going and kind.
我喜欢和双鱼座的人相处，因为他们都很善良仁慈。

Western astrology divides twelve star signs into four elements: air, water, earth and fire.
西方占星术把十二星座分成四个象：风象、水象、土象和火象。

Gemini women are stereotyped to be talkative and indecisive.
双子座女性的固定印象是健谈且优柔寡断。

Her Moon sign is Cancer, which shows she is sometimes sensitive and emotional.
她的月亮星座是巨蟹座，表示她有时候会较敏感和情绪化。

Rita is difficult to please. Perhaps ⑥ that is because our star signs don't match.
丽塔好难取悦，或许是因为我们两个的星座不和。

Jack is hard-working and has confidence in what he does. I guess he may be a Capricorn.
杰克工作勤奋且对自己做的事情十分有信心。我猜他可能是摩羯座。

It is said that Gemini is not right for ⑦ Taurus because Gemini is changeable but Taurus is not very adapted to changes.
据说双子座和金牛座不合，因为双子座是善变的，然而金牛座对于变化不是很适应。

In my opinion, Scorpio distinguishes ⑧ likes from dislikes clearly.
在我的观点里，天蝎座爱憎分明。

Greek [ɡriːk] a. 希腊的；希腊语的

mythology [mɪˈθɑːlədʒi] n. （总称）神话

Pisces [ˈpaɪsiːz] n. 双鱼座

easy-going a. 随和的

Grammar-5
"get along with" 有 "和……相处；和……相处融洽" 的意思，后面接表示人的名词或代词。

Grammar-6
"perhaps" 当副词时，有 "或许；大概" 之意，用法相当于 "maybe" 一词；当名词时，则有 "假设；猜想" 的意思。

Grammar-7
"A is not right for B" 的意思为 "A 和 B 不配"，反义的短语为 "A is right for B"。

Grammar-8
"distinguish" 当动词时，有 "区别；辨认出" 之意，通常和介词 "from" 一起使用，相当于 "discriminate"。

Chapter **15**

- astrology [əˈstrɑːlədʒi] n. 占星术
- divide [dɪˈvaɪd] v. 划分；分开
- element [ˈelɪmənt] n. 要素；元素
- Gemini [ˈdʒemɪnaɪ] n. 双子座
- stereotype [ˈsterɪətaɪp] n. 刻板印象
- sensitive [ˈsensətɪv] a. 敏感的 (反) insensitive [ɪnˈsensətɪv] a. 感觉迟钝的
- emotional [ɪˈməʊʃnəl] a. 情绪的；感情的
- please [pliːz] v. 讨好
- match [mætʃ] v. 和……相配；和……相称
- hard-working [ˌhɑːrd ˈwɜːrkɪŋ] a. 努力工作的
- confidence [ˈkɑːnfɪdəns] n. 自信；信心
- Taurus [ˈtɔːrəs] n. 金牛座
- changeable [ˈtʃeɪndʒəbl] a. 变化多端的
- adapt [əˈdæpt] v. 适应；改编；改造
- Scorpio [ˈskɔːrpiəʊ] n. 天蝎座

 老外不会教你的小秘密

★ 不管是东方的十二生肖或是西方的十二星座，对于每个星座或生肖都会有优缺点两面的评价。现在，我们来学学"缺点"的说法，例如"*What's the disadvantage of Taurus?*（金牛座的缺点是什么呢？）"就可以清楚地表达；当然，我们还可以运用"*the flip side to...*"的短语，本身具有"不好的一面；缺点是……"的意思；因此，我们还可以将上面的例句改为"*What's the flip side to Taurus?*（金牛座不好的一面是什么呢？）"来呈现。

 不怕你学不会

1. Scorpio distinguishes likes from dislikes clearly.
   = Scorpio _____ likes from dislikes clearly.
   = Scorpio _____ likes _____ dislikes clearly.

2. I love getting along _____ Pisces people because they are easy-going and kind.

3. Judy is not _____ for Tiffany because Judy is Gemini and Tiffany is Taurus.

答案：1. discriminate, tell, from 2. with 3. right

Unit 2 东方主义
The mysterious East

原来老外这样记单词 / 老外从小到大学习单词的方法，就是看到什么就学什么！

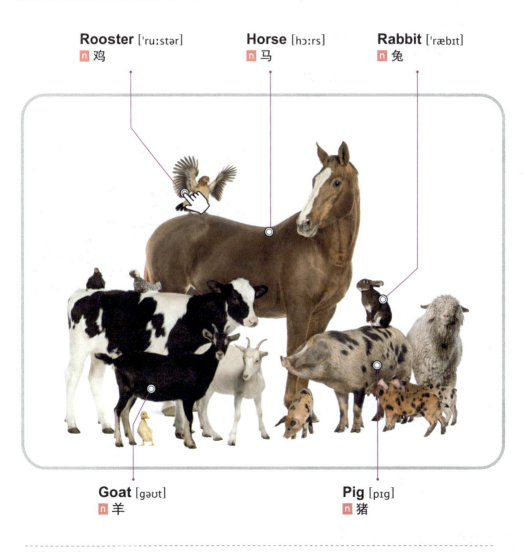

Rooster [ˈruːstər] n 鸡
Horse [hɔːrs] n 马
Rabbit [ˈræbɪt] n 兔
Goat [ɡəʊt] n 羊
Pig [pɪɡ] n 猪

其他衍生单词：

celestial stems phr 天干　　**symbol** [ˈsɪmbl] n 象征　　**earthly branches** phr 地支
zodiac [ˈzəʊdɪæk] n 黄道　　**represent** [ˌreprɪˈzent] v 代表　　**birth year** phr 本命年

老外最常用的单词 / 连这些单词都不会，你还敢说你学过英语吗？

手中藏着好多奥秘

palmist ['pɑːmɪst] n 手相师

fate [feɪt] n 命运；结局
fortune ['fɔːrtʃən] n 好运；财富；命运
destiny ['destəni] n 命运；天命
doom [duːm] n 厄运；毁灭 v 注定；判决
heart line phr 感情线
head line phr 智慧线
lifeline ['laɪflaɪn] n 生命线

教你向老外介绍生肖

gemstone ['dʒemstəʊn]
n 生肖幸运石

Rat [ræt] n 鼠
Ox [ɑːks] n 牛
Tiger ['taɪɡər] n 虎
Dragon ['dræɡən] n 龙
Snake [sneɪk] n 蛇
Monkey ['mʌŋki] n 猴
Dog [dɔɡ] n 狗

东方神秘文化

pagoda [pə'ɡəʊdə]
n （东方寺院的）塔

reincarnation [ˌriːɪnkɑːr'neɪʃn]
n 轮回；转世
transmigration [ˌtrænzmaɪ'ɡreɪʃn]
n 轮回；移居
fatalism ['feɪtəlɪzəm] n 宿命论
practitioner [præk'tɪʃənər] n 风水师
past life phr 前世
current life phr 今生

Unit 2 东方主义

用英语聊天，原来这么简单 老外每天说的英语，其实就是这几句。

雅各布：我们应该根据风水改变一下家具的摆设。 丽塔：我同意。

Situation 1
你知道生肖吗？

Like Western star signs, Chinese has twelve Chinese zodiac animals.
如同西方的十二星座，中国有十二生肖。

My Chinese zodiac is the Rooster. What is yours?
我的生肖属鸡，那你呢？

Western ['westərn] a 西方的   zodiac ['zəudɪæk] n 黄道带

Situation 2
东方习俗

There are ❶ many taboos during the ghost month of the lunar calendar.
在农历的鬼月中有许多禁忌。

> **Grammar-1**
> "There are..." 具有 "有；存在着" 的意思，其后接复数的可数名词。

In Chinese customs, **sweeping** ❷ the floor is not allowed on Chinese New Year's Day because good luck may be swept away.
在中国习俗中，大年初一不能扫地，因为好运可能会被扫走。

> **Grammar-2**
> "sweep" 为动词，有 "打扫；清除" 之意，用法相当于 "calm" 或 "relieve" 等词汇。

Firecrackers **are used to** ❸ scare Year Monster away on Chinese New Year's Eve.
鞭炮是除夕时用来吓走年兽的。

> **Grammar-3**
> 句中提到 "sth. be used to" 的意思为 "某物被用来……"，此为被动语态。

Chapter **15**

293

Grammar-4
"decision" 有"决定；决心"的意思，为名词。

Some people would go to temples to cast lots whenever they cannot make a decision ❹.
有些人在无法做某些决定时会去庙里抽签。

Four is taken as ❺ a bad number by Chinese. As a result, ❻ they would avoid buying on the fourth floor or doorplates with number four.
4被中国人视为一个不吉利的数字，因此他们会避免买公寓的4楼或者有4的门牌号码。

Grammar-5
"be taken as"的意思为"被视为……"，和其用法相当的短语为"be seen as"。

Grammar-6
"as a result"一般用于句中，以逗号与句子分开，表示它前面是后面的原因。

My grandfather always tells me not to ❼ point at the moon. Otherwise, my ears would be cut off by the moon.
爷爷常常告诉我不要指月亮。否则，耳朵会被月亮切掉。

Grammar-7
"tell sb. not to..."为"告诫某人不要……"的意思，后面接动词原形。

Psychics play an important role in tribes because they are in charge of ❽ communicating with ancestors.
灵媒在部落中扮演重要的角色，因为他们负责和祖先沟通。

Grammar-8
"in charge of"表示主动意义，可以当成修饰语和主语补语，当主语补语时，主语一般是人。

Peony is the symbol of wealth in Chinese culture while ❾ crows are considered to be unlucky.
在中国文化中，牡丹象征富贵；然而乌鸦则被视为霉运。

Grammar-9
"while"为连词，有"然而"之意，与其用法相当的词汇"however（可是；不过）"和"yet（可是；却）"，但"however"和"yet"为副词。

taboo [təˈbuː] n 禁忌；忌讳

custom [ˈkʌstəm] n （社会或团体的）习俗

allow [əˈlau] v 允许；准许 ≡ permit [pərˈmɪt] v 允许；许可

scare [sker] v 惊吓；使恐惧

whenever [wenˈevər] ad 无论什么时候

avoid [əˈvɔɪd] v 避免；躲开   floor [flɔːr] n （楼房的）层

doorplate [ˈdɔːˌpleɪt] n 门牌   point [pɔɪnt] v 指；把……指向

cut off phr 切除；切断   psychic [ˈsaɪkɪk] n 灵媒；巫师

tribe [traɪb] n 部落；族种   peony [ˈpiːəni] n 牡丹

wealth [welθ] n 财富   crow [krəu] n 乌鸦

Situation 3
你相信算命吗？

I have gotten fascinated with palmistry recently. I keep ❿ reading others' palms without stopping.
最近我对于手相学非常着迷。我不停地看别人的手掌。

Grammar-10
"keep doing sth."具有"持续做某事"的意思，要特别注意的是"keep"后面连接的动词要以Ving来呈现。

Physiognomy is used to predict people's fortune, such as wealth, luck, and so on.
面相学可以预言人的运气，如财富、幸运等。

Moles on the ears show that this person is more likely to be filial.
耳朵有痣表示这个人可能比较孝顺。

My sister is obsessed with the study of names . She firmly believes that a name could affect a person throughout her life.
我妹妹对姓名学十分着迷，她深信名字可以影响一个人的一生。

- palmistry ['pɑːmɪstri] n 手相学
- recently ['riːsntli] ad 最近；近来
- palm [pɑːm] n 手掌；手心
- Physiognomy [ˌfɪziˈɑːnəmi] n 面相学
- predict [prɪˈdɪkt] v 预言；预料
- mole [məʊl] n 痣
- be likely to phr 有（做……）的可能
- filial [ˈfɪlɪəl] a 孝顺的
- affect [əˈfekt] v 影响；对……发生作用

 老外不会教你的小秘密

★ 请求算命师算命时，我们可以说 "*Tell me my fortune, please.*（请帮我算命。）"；每当算命师看完手相 *(palm reading)* 之后，看他眉头深锁，我们便会焦躁地询问 "*What does the future hold for me?*（我未来的命运会如何？）"，若是答案不尽如人意或顺心，我们只能说 "*It's my fate.*（这就是我的命。）"了！

★ 遇到江湖术士胡乱解说自己一生的命运，想要表达愤愤不平的心情，可以运用下列的句子：
  - ✦ *He / She is full of it.* 他 / 她是胡说八道的。
  - ✦ *He's / She's a liar.* 他 / 她是个大骗子。
  - ✦ *It's nonsense.* 胡扯！

Unit 3 别再相信没有根据的说法了
Superstitious

原来老外这样记单词 / 老外从小到大学习单词的方法，就是看到什么就学什么！

Adam n 亚当

Eden ['i:dn] n 伊甸园

forbidden fruit phr 禁果；非法的欢愉

Eve n 夏娃

其他衍生单词：

deity ['deɪəti] n 神；女神

guardian deity phr 守护神

老外最常用的单词 / 连这些单词都不会，你还敢说你学过英语吗？

西方神秘法术 ★★★

crystal ball phr 水晶球

cartomancy [ˈkɑːtəˌmænsɪ] n 纸牌卜卦
divination [ˌdɪvɪˈneɪʃn] n 占卜；预测
spell [spel] n 咒语；魔力 v 拼写
wizard [ˈwɪzərd] n 巫师
sorcerer [ˈsɔːrsərər] n 巫师；魔术师
Tarot [ˈtærəʊ] n 塔罗纸牌
divine [dɪˈvaɪn] v 占卜

一些和神秘相关的词 ★★★

ark [ɑːrk] n 方舟；平底船

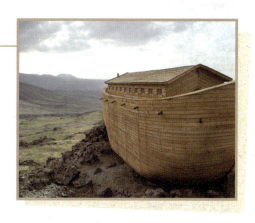

Armageddon [ˌɑːrməˈgedn] n 世界末日
Noah [ˈnəʊə] n 诺亚
Moses [ˈməʊzɪz] n 摩西；领导者
priest [priːst] n 祭司；牧师
sanctuary [ˈsæŋktʃʊeri] n 圣殿；教堂；寺院

地方宗教信仰 ★★★

sacrificial offering n 祭品

hag [hæg] n 女巫
cult [kʌlt] n 膜拜；（总称）迷信者
aborigine [ˌæbəˈrɪdʒəni] n 土著
pyramid [ˈpɪrəmɪd] n 金字塔
shrine [ʃraɪn] n 神社
temple [ˈtempl] n 寺庙

用英语聊天，原来这么简单 / 老外每天说的英语，其实就是这几句。

No! My laptop just died! What should we do now?

I guess all we can do is pray now.

Gini　Weiber

金妮：不！我的电脑死机了！我们现在该怎么办？　韦伯：我想我们只能祈祷了。

Situation 1
坚定的信仰

Maria doesn't **believe in** ❶ any Gods. She is an atheist.
玛莉亚不相信任何神，她是一个无神论者。

Sometimes religion could **soothe** ❷ people's restless spirits.
宗教有时能抚平人们不安的心灵。

Christians have to pray before meals **to thank** ❸ God for giving them food.
基督教徒在餐前都要祷告来感谢上帝赐予他们食物。

Grammar-1
"believe in"有"相信"的意思，同义的短语为"trust in"和"have confidence in"。

Grammar-2
"soothe"当动词时，具有"抚慰；安慰"的意思，相当于"calm"和"relieve"等词汇。

Grammar-3
"to + V"具有"为了"的意思，同义短语为"with a view to"或"with an eye to"，但要注意的是这两个短语的 to 都为介词，所以其后所接的动词需以 Ving 来呈现。

atheist [ˈeɪθiɪst] n 无神论者 反 theist [ˈθiːɪst] n 有神论者；一神论者

religion [rɪˈlɪdʒən] n 宗教

Christian [ˈkrɪstʃən] n 基督教徒　　pray [preɪ] v 祈求；请求

Situation 2
想来点好运吗？

Americans knock on wood in order to ❹ ask for good luck.
美国人会敲木头来祈求好运。

Throw a coin into the wishing well and make a wish ❺.
把一枚硬币投到许愿池里，然后许个愿。

knock on phr 敲；打
throw [θroʊ] v 把……投进
wishing well phr 许愿池

Grammar-4
"in order to" 有"为了……"的意思，与其相似的短语为"so as to"，两者之后的动词皆以原形为主。

Grammar-5
用以表示"许愿"的短语为"make a wish"。

Situation 3
迷信真可怕！

Westem has its special superstitions.
西方都有它特殊的迷信。

A black cat is considered bad luck in American culture.
黑猫在美国文化中被视为不吉利。

Don't be so superstitious about horoscopes; there is no rule without ❻ an exception.
不要对星座过于迷信，规则都有例外。

superstition [ˌsuːpərˈstɪʃn] n 迷信；盲目崇拜
consider [kənˈsɪdər] v 考虑；把……视为
luck [lʌk] n 运气；好运
culture [ˈkʌltʃər] n 文化
superstitious [ˌsuːpərˈstɪʃəs] a 迷信的
rule [ruːl] n 规则；条例
exception [ɪkˈsepʃn] n 例外

Grammar-6
"without" 有"没有；假如没有"的意思，为介词，引导假设句，用以表示条件，相当于"if there...not"或"no..."。

Situation 4
人生有命富贵在天

My lucky color is orange and green this year in accordance with this fortune-telling ❼ book.
根据这本算命书说的，我今年的幸运色是橘色和绿色。

I often turn to Tarot cards for help as I encounter ❽ confusion.
我遇到困惑的时候通常寻求塔罗牌的帮忙。

The fortune-teller told me that ❾ I am going to be very lucky next year.
算命师告诉我明年我将会非常幸运。

Prophets have the ability to foresee what is going to take place ❿ in the future.
预言家具有预见未来会发生什么事情的能力。

Grammar-7
"fortune-telling" 当名词时，意思为"算命"；当形容词时，则有"算命的"之意；当动词时，有"把……列为禁忌"的意思。

Grammar-8
"encounter" 当动词时，有"遭遇；碰见"之意，用法相当于"meet"或"face"等词汇。

Grammar-9
"that" 当从属连接词时，用以引导"名词从句"；当宾语时，that 可以省略。

Grammar-10
"take place" 当不及物动词，没有被动语态，在 place 前面没有冠词，一般以事物为主语，既可以表示盛大的运动的发生，也可以表示会议的举行或化学与物理变化的发生，这些事件一般是经过事先安排的。

In fairy tales, witches usually use crystal balls to see what is going to happen.
童话故事中，女巫通常都会用水晶球来看接下来发生的事情。

Grammar-11
句中的 "conceive that" 为短语用法，即 "认为……" 的意思。

Henry **conceives that** ❶ diligence can change his predestination.
亨利认为勤奋能够改变他的宿命。

lucky ['lʌki] a 幸运的；好运的

accordance [ə'kɔːrdns] n 一致；和谐

confusion [kən'fjuːʒn] n 混乱；困惑

fortune-teller ['fɔːrtʃən,telɚ] n 算命师   prophet ['prɑːfɪt] n 预言家

foresee [fɔːr'siː] v 预见；预知 同 foretell [fɔːr'tel] v 预言；预示

in the future phr 将来；在未来   fairy tale phr 童话；神话故事

diligence ['dɪlɪdʒəns] n 勤奋；勤勉

change [tʃeɪndʒ] v 更改；交换

predestination [ˌpriːdestɪ'neɪʃn] n 宿命

 老外不会教你的小秘密

★ "*Do you believe in superstitions?*（你迷信吗？）"。西方人有 "*If a black cat walks towards you, it brings bad luck.*（如果有只黑猫朝你走过来，它就会带来厄运。）" 的说法；走在人行道上，如果看到梯子便要绕路，因为 "*It's bad luck.*（倒霉。）" 之事会发生在你身上；如果向人炫耀自己从不会失败或是生病的时候，便要赶紧 "*Knock on wood three times.*（敲木头三下。）" 这样才会避免失败或生病！

Unit 4 科学也无法解释
Unknown

 原来老外这样记单词 / 老外从小到大学习单词的方法，就是看到什么就学什么！

skeleton [ˈskelɪtn]
n 骷髅

Frankenstein
n 科学怪人

monster [ˈmɑːnstər]
n 怪物；妖怪

eyeball [ˈaɪbɔːl]
n 眼珠

witch [wɪtʃ]
n 女巫，巫婆

其他衍生单词：

homicide [ˈhɑːmɪsaɪd] n 杀人犯　　**zombie** [ˈzɑːmbi] n 僵尸　　**spirit** [ˈspɪrɪt] n 幽灵

cannibalistic [ˌkænɪbəˈlɪstɪk] a 食人肉的　　**ghost** [ɡəʊst] n 鬼魂

老外最常用的单词 连这些单词都不会，你还敢说你学过英语吗？

神秘难解的事件

UFO
abbr 不明飞行物 (=unidentified flying object)
phenomenon [fə'nɑːmɪnən] n 现象
telepathy [tə'lepəθi] n 心电感应
prophecy ['prɑːfəsi] n 预言
alien ['eɪlɪən] n 外星人
occult [ə'kʌlt] a 难以理解的，奥秘的
out-of-body experience
phr 灵魂出窍的经验
ESP
abbr 第六感 (=extrasensory perception)

别让好运气溜走

dreamcatcher n 捕梦网

wishbone ['wɪʃbəʊn]
n （鸟禽胸部的）叉骨；许愿骨
clover ['kləʊvər] n 苜蓿；幸运草
coincident [kəʊ'ɪnsɪdənt]
a 巧合的；一致的
serendipitous [ˌserən'dɪpətəs]
a 侥幸得到的
omen ['əʊmən] n 预兆；兆头
lucky dog phr 幸运儿

进入你的内心

hypnotherapy [ˌhɪpnəʊ'θerəpi]
n 催眠疗法

subconsciousness [ˌsʌb'kɒnʃəsnɪs]
n 潜意识
personality [ˌpɜːrsə'næləti] n 人格；性格
complex [kəm'pleks] n 情节 a 复杂的
instinct ['ɪnstɪŋkt] n 本能
hysterical [hɪ'sterɪkl] a 歇斯底里的
brainwash ['breɪnwɔːʃ]
v 对（人）实行洗脑
mental disorder phr 精神错乱

用英语聊天，原来这么简单
老外每天说的英语，其实就是这几句。

Unit 4 科学也无法解释

凯特：这实在太酷了！　艾迪：该换我了！　梅根：然后下一个是我！

Situation 1
你爱看星星吗?

It is predicted that ❶ there is going to be a meteor shower on the night of Chinese Valentine's Day.
预计七夕情人节的夜晚会有流星雨。

Do you want to watch the meteor shower tonight with me?
今晚愿意陪我去看流星雨吗？

Summer Triangle **consists of** ❷ Vega, Altair and Deneb.
夏季大三角由织女星、牛郎星和天津四星所组成。

I love to stargaze. Stars are so mysterious to me.
我很喜欢观星，星星对我来说很神秘。

People usually use the Big Dipper to find the North Star.
人们通常利用北斗七星来寻找北极星。

Ursa Major's story was romantic but **horrible** ❸.
大熊星座的故事既浪漫又可怕。

Grammar-1
句中的"It is predicted that..."意思为"预计"，后面引导名词从句。

Grammar-2
"consist of"有"由……组成"的意思，通常以整体为主语，构成整体的各个部分为介词的宾语，其中的动词不及物，只能用主动语态，不用被动语态。

Grammar-3
"horrible"当形容词时，意思为"可怕的"，用法相当于"fearful"或"horrific"等词汇。

我看见了……

Chapter **15**

Both Amy and Tim like to stargaze, so they usually go to the observatory together.
艾米和蒂姆喜欢观星，所以他们常常一起去天文台。

Many people believe that wishing upon shooting stars could help what they wish ⓐ come true.
许多人相信对着流星许愿，愿望就可以成真。

Grammar-4
此句的"what sb. V"为名词从句的用法，即"某人所做的……"的意思。

I will bring the insect repellent for tonight's stargazing.
晚上观星时我会带着防蚊液去。

meteor shower [phr] 流星雨　　Vega [ˈviːgə] [n] 织女星

Altair [ælˈtaɪr] [n] 牛郎星　　Deneb [ˈdenˌeb] [n] 天津四星

stargaze [ˈstɑːˌgeɪz] [v] 观星　　Big Dipper [phr] 北斗七星

North Star [phr] 北极星　　Ursa Major [phr] 大熊星座

observatory [əbˈzɜːrvətɔːri] [n] 天文台；观测所

shooting star [phr] 流星

come true [phr] 实现 ⓢ carry out [phr] 完成；实行

Situation 2
神秘学问

Oneiromancy can explain the meanings of your dreams.
解梦学可以解释梦的意义。

Many people do psychological tests to understand their physical and mental conditions.
许多人做心理测验来了解他们的身心状况。

My major in college is psychology. I had learnt a lot about people's minds during the four years.
我大学主修心理学。这4年内我了解了很多人的心理。

Oneiromancy [oʊˈnaɪrəˌmænsi] [n] 解梦；圆梦

explain [ɪkˈspleɪn] [v] 解释；说明

psychological [ˌsaɪkəˈlɑːdʒɪkl] [a] 心理的；精神的

physical [ˈfɪzɪkl] [a] 生理的　　mental [ˈmentl] [a] 心理的

Unit 4 科学也无法解释

 老外不会教你的小秘密

★ 在你的朋友圈里，有没有人热衷于星相学或是面相学呢？像是 "Annie is into divination.（安妮热衷于占卜。）" 的句子里，我们可以将 "be into ＋ N / Ving" 的短语替换成 "be addicted to" 或是 "be absorbed in" 等用法。

不怕你学不会

1. It is predicted _____ there is going to be an eclipse tomorrow night.

2. Many people believe that wishing upon shooting stars could really help _____ they wish come true.

3. Winter triangle _____ of Procyon(南河三), Betelgeuse(参宿四) and Sirius(天狼星).

4. The story of Orion is sad and a little horrible.
   = The story of Orion is sad and a little _____ .

答案：1. that 2. what 3. consists 4. fearful / horrific

看看老外怎么学 这些图片对你来说有没有很熟悉呢？一起来填填看吧！

Aquarius	Taurus	Sagittarius	Leo
Virgo	Pisces	Cancer	Libra
Scorpio	Gemini	Capricorn	Aries

答案： 1. Aries 白羊座 2. Leo 狮子座 3. Sagittarius 射手座
4. Taurus 金牛座 5. Virgo 处女座 6. Capricorn 摩羯座
7. Gemini 双子座 8. Libra 天秤座 9. Aquarius 水瓶座
10. Cancer 巨蟹座 11. Scorpio 天蝎座 12. Pisces 双鱼座

版权专有　侵权必究

图书在版编目（CIP）数据

全图解用老外的方法学英语 / 林雨薇著.—北京：北京理工大学出版社，2019.6
ISBN 978-7-5682-7206-3

Ⅰ.①全… Ⅱ.①林… Ⅲ.①英语—学习方法—图解 Ⅳ.①H319.3-64

中国版本图书馆CIP数据核字（2019）第131321号

北京市版权局著作权合同登记号图字：01-2017-2397
简体中文版由我识出版社有限公司授权出版发行
全图解用老外的方法学英文，林雨薇著，2015年，初版
ISBN：9789865785833

出版发行 / 北京理工大学出版社有限责任公司	
社　　址 / 北京市海淀区中关村南大街5号	
邮　　编 / 100081	
电　　话 / （010）68914775（总编室）	
（010）82562903（教材售后服务热线）	
（010）68948351（其他图书服务热线）	
网　　址 / http://www.bitpress.com.cn	
经　　销 / 全国各地新华书店	
印　　刷 / 天津久佳雅创印刷有限公司	
开　　本 / 710毫米×1000毫米　1/16	
印　　张 / 20	责任编辑 / 龙　微
字　　数 / 391千字	文案编辑 / 龙　微
版　　次 / 2019年6月第1版　2019年6月第1次印刷	责任校对 / 周瑞红
定　　价 / 80.00元	责任印制 / 李志强

图书出现印装质量问题，请拨打售后服务热线，本社负责调换